Mobilities Design

Contemporary society is marked and defined by the ways in which mobile goods, bodies, vehicles, objects and data are organized, moved and staged. Against the background of the 'mobilities turn', this book articulates a new and emerging research field, namely that of 'mobilities design'. It revolves around the following research question: *How are design decisions and interventions staging mobilities?* It builds upon the 'Staging Mobilities' model (Jensen 2013) in an exploratory inquiry into the problems and potentials of the design of mobilities. The exchange value between mobilities and design research is twofold. To mobilities research, this means getting closer to the 'material', and to engage in the creative, exploratory and experimental approaches of the design world which offer new potential for innovative research. Design research, on the other hand, might enter into a fruitful relationship with mobilities research, offering relational and mobile design thinking and a valuable basis for design reflections around the ubiquitous structures, spaces and systems of mobilities.

Ole B. Jensen is Professor of Urban Theory at the Department of Architecture, Design and Media Technology, Aalborg University, Denmark. He has a BA in Political Science, an MA in Sociology, a PhD in Planning and a Dr. Techn. in Mobilities. He is the co-founder and a board member at the Centre for Mobilities and Urban Studies (C-MUS), Aalborg University, as well as co-founder and co-ordinator of the Mobilities Design Group (MDG) at C-MUS. Ole B. Jensen's main research interests are within Urban Mobilities, Urban Networked Technologies and Mobilities Design. He is the co-author with Tim Richardson of *Making European Space*: *Mobility, Power and Territorial Identity* (Routledge, 2004), and the author of *Staging Mobilities* (Routledge, 2013) and *Designing Mobilities* (Aalborg University Press, 2014). He is also the editor of the four-volume anthology *Mobilities* (Routledge, 2015).

Ditte Bendix Lanng is Assistant Professor in Urban Design at the Department of Architecture, Design and Media Technology, Aalborg University, Denmark. She is an urban designer (Cand. polyt. Urban Design) with practical experience in architecture and city planning. She has a PhD in the area of mobilities design. Her research interests are in urban design and mobilities – a combination of fields that she approaches through cross-disciplinary theory, design experiments, ethnography and as a collective enterprise with planning and architectural practice. She is co-founder and co-coordinator of the Mobilities Design Group (MDG) at the Centre for Mobilities and Urban Studies (C-MUS).

Changing Mobilities

Series editors: Monika Büscher, Peter Adey

This series explores the transformations of society, politics and everyday experiences wrought by changing mobilities and the power of mobilities research to inform constructive responses to these transformations. As a new, mobile century is taking shape, international scholars explore the motivations, experiences, insecurities, implications and limitations of mobile living, and the opportunities and challenges for design in the broadest sense, from policy to urban planning, new media and technology design. With world citizens expected to travel 105 billion kilometres per year in 2050, it is critical to ensure that mobilities research and design inform each other.

Elite Mobilities
Edited by Thomas Birtchnell and Javier Caletrío

Family Mobility
Catherine Doherty, Wendy Patton and Paul Shield

Mobility and Locative Media
Adriana de Souza e Silva and Mimi Sheller

Cargomobilities
Moving materials in a global age
Edited by Thomas Birtchnell, Satya Savitzky and John Urry

Italian Mobilities
Edited by Ruth Ben-Ghiat and Stephanie Malia Hom

Mobilities Design
Urban designs for mobile situations
Ole B. Jensen and Ditte Bendix Lanng

Forthcoming

Dialogues on Mobile Communication
Edited by Adriana de Souza e Silva

Changing Mobilities
Monika Büscher

Mobilities Design

Urban designs for mobile situations

Ole B. Jensen and
Ditte Bendix Lanng

LONDON AND NEW YORK

First published 2017
by Routledge
2 Park Square, Milton Park, Abingdon, Oxon OX14 4RN

and by Routledge
711 Third Avenue, New York, NY 10017

Routledge is an imprint of the Taylor & Francis Group, an informa business

British Library Cataloguing-in-Publication Data
A catalogue record for this book is available from the British Library.

Library of Congress Cataloging in Publication Data
Names: Jensen, Ole B., author. | Lanng, Ditte Bendix, author.
Title: Mobilities design : urban designs for mobile situations /
by Ole B. Jensen & Ditte Bendix Lanng.
Description: Abingdon, Oxon ; New York, NY : Routledge, 2016.
Identifiers: LCCN 2016007720 | ISBN 9781138852983 (hardback) |
ISBN 9781315723099 (ebook)
Subjects: LCSH: City planning. | Pedestrian areas. | Urban transportation–
Social aspects. | Spatial behavior. | Human geography.
Classification: LCC HT166 .J446 2016 | DDC 307.1/216–dc23
LC record available at http://lccn.loc.gov/2016007720

ISBN: 978-1-138-85298-3 (hbk)
ISBN: 978-1-315-72309-9 (ebk)

Typeset in Times New Roman
by Wearset Ltd, Boldon, Tyne and Wear

Contents

Figures

Foreword

We do it everyday: walk, drive, bike through mundane landscapes of someone else's design and intentionality. The built environment and our habitual movements within it are a mundane and very ordinary life background for all of us. At the same time, however, we want to invite you to embark on a journey through this familiar territory, after which we hope to have defamiliarized and denaturalized these mundane infrastrutural landscapes for you. The key interest of this book is to render these ordinary sites and mundane practices differently and full of potentials – for new experiences, different activities, alternative practices and forms of interaction. We see the redescription of the familiar leading to the unfamiliar and new insights as the most important contribution of this research to society. The field of mobilities, design and everyday life is the venue for our contributions to that trajectory. The aim of this book is to see how an urban design agenda and a mobilities-research framework may intersect through the new and emerging field of 'mobilities design', to which this book is a key contribution. It is a reflection of many years of research into mobilities, as well as the fact that the authors represent the two rather disparate fields of urban design and sociology. However, we have the firm intention of neglecting this distance of thought and practice and of joining forces in an argument for connecting mobilities theory and urban design.

We wish to acknowledge a number of significant institutions, networks and people, who in different ways have all helped shape this book. Internationally, all the good people from the *Cosmobilities* network, the *Pan-American Mobilities Network*, and the *Centre for Mobilities Research* (CeMoRe) have been involved in discussions over the years that have shaped ideas within this book. The *Department of Architecture and Media Technology* (AD:MT) at Aalborg University, and the *Section for Urban Design* have been perfect hosting environments for this cross-disciplinary endeavour. The same goes for the *Centre for Mobilities and Urban Studies* (C-MUS), which has served as the perfect institutional venue for academic deliberation, but also for setting up stages upon which we have explored the notion of mobilities design. The *Mobilities Design Group* (MDG) is one such substage under C-MUS that has worked as our intellectual playground. We wish to thank everyone from AD:MT, the Urban Design Section, C-MUS and MDG for stimulating conversations and explorations. Also, the *Media Architecture and Design PhD Lab* (MAD Lab) has been a space of exploration for this work. The

Master in Urban Design and the Master in Mobilities and Urban Studies programmes, both hosted at the Architecture and Design Study Board, have also been important institutional frames for this work. We wish to thank students within these programmes for playing along and exploring the 'more than A to B' and the many 'What if …?' sessions that we invited you to. Many of the ideas you will find in this book were discussed by and tested on the students from these two curricula. A final institution in need of thanks is the *Centre for Strategic Urban Research* (CSB), which graciously supported this work financially to enable the development of the visuals and diagrams in this book.

We also wish to acknowledge particular individuals. Thanks to Hans Bruun Olesen and Jeppe Krogstrup Jensen for drawings and graphic work. Thanks to Claus Lassen and Simon Wind for being 'critical friends' for reading and commenting on the manuscript. At Routledge, we wish to thank the 'Changing Mobilities' Series Editors Monika Büscher and Peter Adey for taking on this book, which looks nothing like the rest of the series. Also thanks to Gerhard Boomgaarden and Alyson Claffey for editorial support.

During our work on this book, we discovered quite a bit of interest in our ideas from practitioners of planning and design. As a result, we are running workshops with municipalities, as well as giving presentations to engineering and architectural companies. We have been instrumental in formalizing a collaboration agreement between C-MUS and Aalborg Municipality which pivots on the notion of mobilities design. This arrangement informs our mutual institutions about any project of interest within the emerging field of mobilities design and joins forces in practical collaboration and research projects between the university and the municipality. These create opportunities for engaging theory with practice and will be an area of further work for us in the future. As such, we stand on the edge of the next phase, which is bringing mobilities design into direct and collaborative contact with practitioners.

The empirical cases are based on the PhD thesis by Ditte Bendix Lanng (Lanng 2015) but have been significantly reworked for this publication. The case studies would not have been possible without the openness and generosity of the travellers who took part in the research. A second-semester MSc Urban Design student workshop held on a few occasions at Aalborg University, most recently in the spring of 2015, and a workshop at the conference 'Trafikdage' at Aalborg University in August 2013 have significantly contributed to the development of Chapter 7. The authors wish to thank all participants.

On a more personal note, Ole B. Jensen wishes to dedicate this book to the loving memory of his parents who made him the person and scholar he is today.

Ditte Bendix Lanng wishes to express gratitude to her family for encouragement and support. The little ones, in particular, motivate an engagement into insightful urban design for the future, at which this book aims.

Ole B. Jensen and Ditte Bendix Lanng
Aalborg
February 2016

1 Introduction to mobilities design

Mobile situations and inconspicuous materialities

Imagine a rainy autumn afternoon. You are walking along the pathway on your route to do some grocery shopping. In a few more steps you will enter a tunnel, providing a passage under a big road. As you move through the tunnel, you get a moment of shelter from the rain. A few kids enter from the opposite direction, stopping to shout some words, which resonate in the enveloping concrete space. You notice some new, bright graffiti on the concrete wall, and quickly – without deliberation – you stroke your hand across it. As you exit the tunnel, you encounter the rain and grey skies again. You make a turn to the left and must put some effort into getting across a muddy puddle on the side of the path before you move slightly upwards. You now have a view of a parking lot. Not that many cars are there, and you stroll directly onto the asphalt surface. A few larger puddles have collected here and there, and as you walk around one, you notice a trace of oil in it. In one of the others, a toddler is jumping up and down, laughing loudly. You run into an acquaintance along the way and stop between a parked car and the shopping-cart shed to greet him and chat. A bit farther on, you reach the supermarket. After your shopping, you need to go to the pharmacy. It is located on the other side of the road, only a few hundred metres away. You make your way with your grocery bags to the verge of the road. It is slippery now; only small tufts of grass keep the ground from getting too muddy. Some cars drive by, and you move back a little to avoid getting splashed. Shortly after, you seize the chance to take some quick steps across the first two lanes and you reach the central reserve. Again a few cars drive by. This time you cannot avoid your clothes getting splashed. There's a pause in the flow of cars and you continue across the road.

Along this imaginary journey, you have been engaged with various ordinary materialities of mobilities: a pathway, a concrete tunnel, a muddy reserve, an asphalt parking lot, a wide road, etc. In diverse ways, these materialities have enabled and put constraints on your journey. They have been performative in co-orchestrating your experience and practice of mobility. But these materialities have not acted in isolation. Rather, they have worked in situational effects, with multiple visible and invisible material and immaterial bodies: the rain, your (wet) shoes, your grocery bags, cars and many other things. Not least, as you moved through these physical environments, many other people have been on other journeys, creating myriads of small interactive situations. The many small interactions with other people and with materialities are marked by routine and the mundane habitual practice that you are hardly conscious of . A few may, however, have been marked by their breaks in routine. As you travel, you are 'doing mobilities' as a set of embodied performances that reaches from walking on various pavements to measuring your quickest route and negotiating your crossing of a big road.

This book is about Mobilities Design. Obviously, the mobile situations of everyday mobilities, like the imaginary ones above, are marked and defined by decisions taken elsewhere: in planning departments, architectural offices and city governments. Design contributes to 'staging mobilities from above'. But a large number of decisions and choices are also made by you, 'staged from below', either in a non-reflexive, routine manner or in deliberate and conscious accord with your values and perception of Self (for example, sustainable transport-mode choices or the way you choose to walk past people or the negotiation of a seat on the bus). Mundane mobile situations are taking place in physical environments, often as social interactions and always as embodied performances. This 'situational approach' to mobilities is presented theoretically and empirically elsewhere (Jensen 2013, 2014). In this book, we wish to zoom in on the material dimension of mobile situations by exploring the physical sites and artefacts of mobilities. We will not omit the social and the embodied dimensions (which are the two other elements in the situational analytical framework) but we will centre attention on the 'doings' of designed materialities, as these provide the physical environments for mobilities to be played out. We shall in particular look into the urban design field, which contributes by shaping mundane mobile materialities, and we will explore how the fascinating nexus between materialities and bodies on the move pan out in specific designs. En route, we shall visit again the inconspicuous and ordinary material sites of the imaginary journey above. These belong to some of the ubiquitous material realities of our mobile, everyday lives. By connecting the situational understanding of mobilities as they are practised and experienced with urban design, we 'learn to see' such ordinary mundane 'non-places' (Augé 1995) as materialities ripe with mobilities design issues significant to our well-being, social life, safety, equal rights and the future of cities and mobilities. In short, the sites we will visit epitomize both important design potentials and design problems. We hope you are ready for the journey, which most likely will take you to familiar territories but hopefully in fairly unfamiliar and rewarding ways.

The structure of this introductory chapter is the following: after the imaginary journey and the opening motivation above, we walk you through the background for our articulation of the field of mobilities design. Hereafter, we shall make a formal and brief introduction to the 'mobilities turn' as the research field within which we locate our work. Next, we devote a section to identifying the relevant dimensions of the design field we propose to engage. In this initial voicing of mobilities design, we are predominantly looking towards urban design. After the urban design identification and discussion, we explore a wider set of issues related to the ways in which designers more broadly contemplate, act and innovate – what we term 'designerly ways of thinking', which we appreciate as a nerve to mobilities design. Following this exploration, we present the three selected 'matters of concern' for this endeavour into mobilities design: atmospheres, environmental sustainability and inequality. We shall motivate their relevance and presence within this work and we shall qualify their relationships to three empirical cases that we also present in an overview format. The chapter ends with an outline of the general structure of the full book.

Background

Contemporary societies are marked and defined by the ways mobile goods, bodies, vehicles, objects and data are organized, moved and 'staged'. Against the background of the 'mobilities turn' (Cresswell 2006; Urry 2007), this book articulates a new and emerging research field, namely that of 'mobilities design'. It revolves around the following research question: *How are design decisions and interventions staging mobilities – or how are they preventing particular mobilities?* It builds upon the Staging Mobilities model, referred to above (Jensen 2013) and in theoretical and empirical research into the nexus of mobilities and design (Jensen 2013; Lanng 2015), in an exploratory inquiry into the problems and potentials of the design of mobilities. The exchange value between mobilities and design research is twofold. For mobilities research, this means getting closer to the 'material' and engaging in the creative, exploratory and experimental approaches of the design world, which offer potential for innovative research. Design research, on the other hand, might enter into a fruitful relationship with mobilities research, offering a 'mobilized' design thinking and a valuable basis for an approach, which can recognize mobility, contingency and relationality in the design of structures, spaces and systems of mobilities. The aim of and motivation behind writing this book is, in other words, to explore the design-dimension of the mobile practices in the everyday life of billions of people. (The cases and examples explored here are, however, predominantly from our Western experience and need further exploration into the global multiplicities of multicultural experiences in order to be fully justified.) We see a need for transgressing the disciplinary and regulatory silos that offer us either academic analysis and theory building or planning solutions based on the worldviews of discrete professions. We shall illustrate this by engaging the design and architecture of the spaces of everyday life from the point of the new 'mobilities turn'. By doing so, we connect two important domains that until now have had too little interaction. We are thus motivated to write this book by the desire to advance how design may learn from mobilities research and, conversely, how mobilities research may learn from design. There are many design professions that may have relevance and pose various relevant questions. In very general terms these include: how industry shapes artefacts and vehicles; how service design shapes information interfaces; how building architecture shapes the houses hosting mobilities; how interaction design creates the system interfaces; how software design shapes the apps that facilitate urban navigation, etc. Such numerous design disciplines are of relevance to a fully fledged understanding of the importance of design to mobilities. Here, however, we shall mainly refer to urban design as the design field in question (and we shall return to our understanding and definition of this below). This is because we wish to focus on the spaces 'between the buildings', where much quotidian mobile life takes place, and because the research underlying this book originates from an academic urban design research environment.

From mobilities turn towards mobilities design

Before we can discuss the field of mobilities design, we need to explain the key ideas behind the 'mobilities turn'. We shall do this rather in brief since there is no shortage of fine review texts and overviews (for example, Adey *et al.* 2014; Cresswell 2010; Cresswell and Merriman 2011; Keeling 2008; Shaw and Hesse 2010; Sheller 2011; Sheller and Urry 2006; Vannini 2010). The main concern is movement. As the field has expanded into various disciplines, the movement of people, goods, vehicles, information, data, images, ideas and much more has entered the agenda. As well as many others, we consider Urry's landmark text (2000) to be one of the central launching pads of the new 'mobilities turn'. Needless to say, no single person constitutes a completely new field of research and many other scholars will be referenced in this short overview (see Jensen 2015: 1–18 for a more detailed discussion of the history of the 'turn', its focus areas, disciplines and not least 'intellectual infrastructures').

Urry's key point was a critique of a static and 'mobility blind' approach to social sciences in general. 'Society as a thing' rather than society as a 'set of relations' was the intellectual backdrop of this academic revolt. Certainly one may find different indications of this understanding before: for example, Simmel's work (1998) is identified as predominantly important in this respect (see Urry 2007; Jensen 2015). However, the ambitions of building grand theories of an 'a-spatial' and 'mobility blind' nature (Urry 2007) was in many ways the order of the day within mainstream social science (geography being a clear exception). Besides arguing against such a 'sedentary' understanding of the social in times of globalization (ibid.), the mobilities turn also took as its underpinning rationale that all the myriads of different movements we are embedded in have more than their mere physical effects of displacement, aggregation and movement. Thus the one-liner credo of the mobilities turn: *Mobilities is more than A to B!* The repercussions of these complex mobilities in different directions such as social networks, capital formation, politics, planning and environment are important enough on their own, but the 'more than A to B' claim goes deeper. In our research, we have traced how the 'more than' effects of mobilities deeply touch the way we inhabit the material world, the way we interact socially and the way we think of ourselves in the midst of all this. The credit of the mobilities turn is thus to have rendered well-known and self-evident practices, systems and structures open to new understanding and interpretations. The mobilities turn has, with its eclectic approach, combined many strands of thinking, from post-structuralist thinking on Actor-Network Theory (ANT) to Science and Technology Studies (see Sheller 2011 for a discussion of the wide array of theoretical inspirations for the mobilities turn).

So instead of speaking of transport as the displacement of things, people and goods, the mobilities turn articulates the wider-reaching term 'mobilities', generating a non-sedentary research agenda for exploring the fact that sociality is defined by flows and movement (or obstruction). This, however, does not imply that transportation scholars are unaware of the insights in mobilities research. In fact, mobilities research opens up this exploration even more towards a cross-disciplinary endeavour. Here we will reference two of the major voices in the field, Urry and Cresswell. We rely on Jensen's previous work for a rough map of the key concerns (Jensen 2015: 1–18). According to Urry, a new and mobility-oriented social science should (2000: 18–19):

- Develop a sociology focusing upon movement, mobility and contingent ordering
- Examine the effects of corporeal, imagined and virtual mobilities of people
- Consider things as 'social facts'
- Embody the analysis by including the sensuous constitutions of humans and objects
- Investigate the uneven and diverse reach of networks and flows
- Examine temporal regimes and modes of dwelling and travelling
- Describe the bases of people's sense of dwelling and their dependencies upon various mobilities
- Comprehend the changing nature of citizenship, rights and duties
- Illuminate the increased mediatization of social life and their 'imagined communities'
- Investigate the changing powers and determinations of state powers
- Explain changes within states' regulating mobilities
- Interpret chaotic, unintended and non-linear social consequences of mobilities
- Explore whether there is an emergent global and autopoietic system.

On a more profound and yet basic level, Cresswell proposes that a mobilities-research agenda should foreground the following six key questions (Cresswell 2010: 22–6):

- Why does a person or thing move?
- How fast does a person or thing move?
- In what rhythm does a person or thing move?
- What route does a person or thing take?
- How does it feel to be moved/be moving?
- When and how does a person or thing stop?

This is a rather shorthanded approach for the sake of the overview. Since we will dive deeper into the theoretical arguments and approaches later, this should give the reader a sense for now of what the mobilities turn means and how it is an important backdrop to this book.

From the overview of key ideas within the mobilities turn, we now move to our main issue: the interface between mobilities and design. The new and emerging research field of mobilities design pulls threads from both mobilities and design research in addressing the persistent issues of shaping spaces, structures and systems of mobilities in our contemporary world. It is no novel insight that integrative and cross-disciplinary thinking is needed to deal with societal challenges related to mobilities. Lynes wrote a brief paper, titled 'Mobility and Design', in the Harvard University design journal in 1965 connecting these two issues, albeit in an early discussion of the matter. Likewise, Buchanan raised the issue in the his seminal 1963 British report 'Traffic in Towns': he noticed that one of the challenges in achieving good planning and design solutions seemed to lie in the separation of 'traffic' from 'architecture' (Buchanan 1964: 67). In a rather bold proposition, he put forward the notion of 'traffic architecture' to remedy this problem. As history has proved, the problem of separating traffic from architecture is still around. However, we believe there was a lot of truth and insight to this. In a similar vein, and with contemporary urbanism and mobilities as the context, we propose that one of the ways we may move towards more insightful and innovative proposals and solutions for the challenges facing contemporary cities is to embark on a trajectory of thinking that combines mobilities with design. The promise of an emerging field of mobilities design is explored in detail later. One note of clarification is important though. Just as the mobilities turn has rendered the notion of transport too narrow, so has the particular situational and pragmatic focus on everyday life mobilities provided an impetus to move from architecture to 'design'. As we ask the key question *how are design decisions and interventions staging mobilities?* we immediately move towards a wider understanding of the material conditions underpinning mobilities. Hence the move towards 'design'. For example, it is relevant to not only discuss buildings and public pathways but also algorithms of traffic-light intervals, apps guiding people through the means of a new digital layer of information, the user-technology interface of all sorts of contemporary infrastructural systems, and so on. Therefore, rather than looking at architecture proper (which does have the attention of mobilities design), we open up the perspective utilizing the notion of mobilities design to understand the choices and decisions taken 'elsewhere' which shape the situational context (see Figure 1.1). We are, in other words, broadly interested in design decisions and interventions that shape situational practices of mobilities, but we also base this investigation on the city and its public spaces and infrastructural landscapes – hence the foregrounding of urban design.

We are not alone in arguing for the wider scope of design. In an interview for the design journal *Domus*, McGuirk discusses with the dean of Harvard's Graduate School of Design, Moshen Mostafavi, a wider design understanding

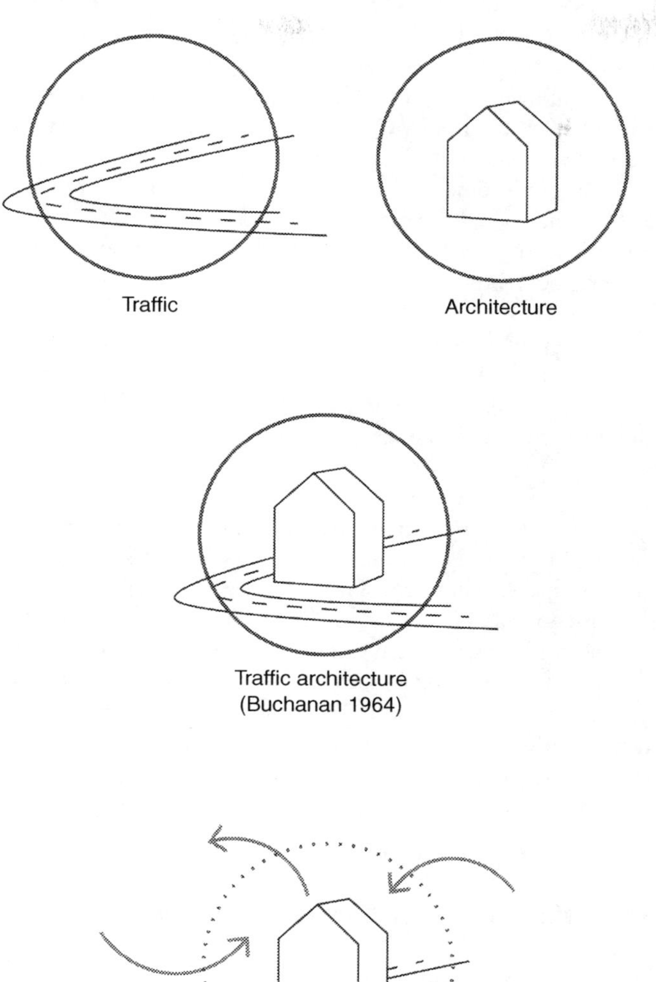

Figure 1.1 Mobilities design diagrammatized (illustration: Ditte Bendix Lanng).

versus a more narrow architecture conception. McGuirk finds that the concept of design has become more 'elastic' over the last decade, so that it is no longer considered a sub-discipline of architecture but rather a wide field, ranging from products to systemic design. He states that 'design has developed a more ambitious discourse than architecture, an almost expansionist rhetoric in terms of the things that design believes it can tackle' (McGuirk 2015). Mostafavi agrees in retaining such a principal concept of design and suggests that architecture could be better able to 'incorporate some of the attributes of design by becoming more proactive in societal issues' (ibid.). The distinctiveness of the design and architecture disciplines may be maintained, though, to benefit cross-disciplinary practices from their different expertise fields:

> Architecture can become very formal and hermetic, and I want to emphasize the values of those formal qualities but also engage in this bigger project that design, as you say, has had more success at because of its ability to connect to governance and to politics, and to design thinking.
>
> (Ibid.)

Aligned with this inclusive understanding of design, situational mobilities design targets a wide interest in the design of many structures, systems and spaces, for example, from public spaces and large infrastructure systems towards small-scale situational interactions and interfaces with machines, artefacts and technologies. These are related to various design fields that can significantly influence how mobile situations are 'staged from above' (Jensen 2013). In the words of Votolato, 'beyond moving us from A to B, every vehicle in which people travel provides an interface with the natural, physical world' (2007: 9). As a conceptual lens, mobilities design explores precisely the manifold interfaces between mobile subjects and the material world staged by design decisions and interventions.

Mobilities in situ – the nexus of mobilities practices and design

With the point of departure being in a situational perspective on everyday life mobilities and their materialization, mobilities design addresses a gap in research on an issue of increasing concern and societal importance. Jensen has described the idea of focusing on the actual situation (or 'mobilities in situ') in detail (2013). In accordance with the pragmatist position of Dewey, the focus is on what he termed the 'situational primary experience' (Gimmler 2012: 53). The practices unfolded in their mundane material contexts are precisely where lived experience meets design interventions and decisions. This connects well with Goffman's (1959) dramaturgical perspective on the social. Much inspired by the latter, Jensen has argued that situational mobilities are 'staged from above' through design, regulation and systems, as well as being 'staged from below' by social agents presenting themselves in social interaction. In order to create an operational tool for situational-mobility analysis, the Staging Mobilities framework works within three analytical spheres in any given mobile situation (see Figure 1.2). First, a mobile situation must be understood as taking place within a material site. Second, practised mobility is a social affair rendering 'traffic' a complex social interaction, where the normativity and cultures of mobile subjects are situationally calibrated with mobile others in the flux of everyday mobile situations. Third, the framework gives particular attention to the fact that we are 'doing mobilities'; in other words, mobilities are embodied performances. This means that physical as well as cognitive capacities together with our multiple sensorial registers (haptic, auditory, visual, kinaesthetic, olfactory, etc.) are mediating the mobile situation.

Consider this brief illustration: a person driving to work will leave her home, walk to the car and move through material environments shaped by planning, architecture, design and much more. Between home and her parking spot and then in morning traffic, multiple 'mobile others' will be present and our

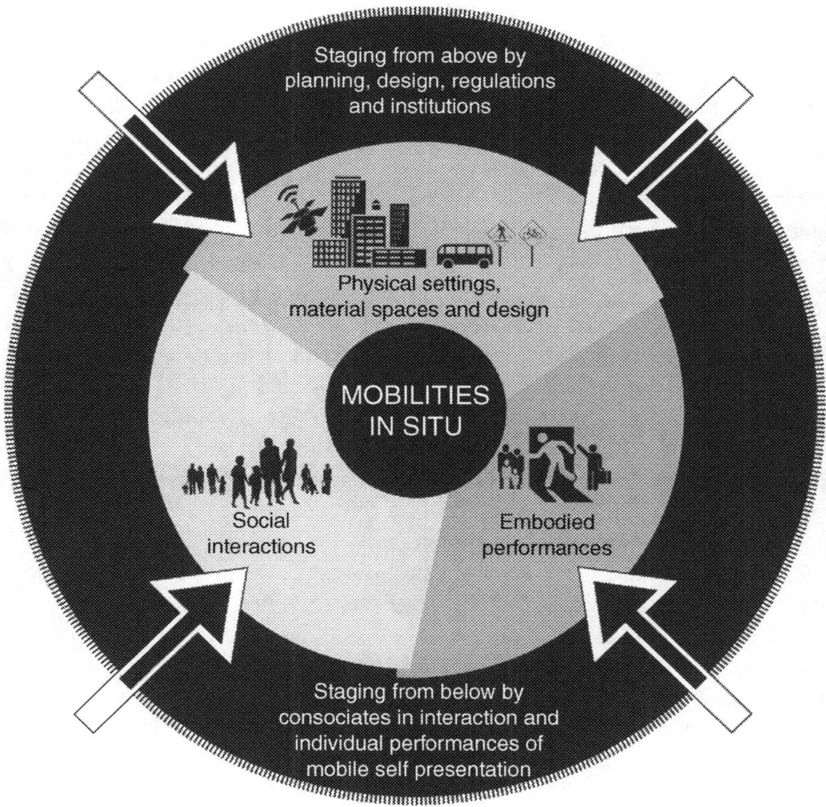

Figure 1.2 The Staging Mobilities model (published in Jensen 2013).

imaginary main character will have to 'negotiate in motion' on a number of occasions (from leaving the car park and turning out onto the busy street, to embarking on a lift ride eight floors up to the office). Alongside the multimodal and mundane travel, our character's bodily capacities and sensations have been instrumental in how the morning ride has been practically performed, sensed and experienced. The staging of such a series of mobile situations spans the decisions and interventions made in planning, design, regulations and institutions (or staging from above) and the multiple situational effects of choices, affects, mood, rationalities and strategies for making everyday life mobilities a habitual practice (from below). The dramaturgical metaphor of staging thus lends itself as an analytical tool that renders the multiple material interfaces between mobile subjects, infrastructures, sites, technologies and systems visible as pragmatic effects of the question *what makes these mobile situations possible?*

The Staging Mobilities framework is applied empirically to a number of cases with a particular sensibility to design issues (Jensen 2014). It is furthermore articulated within a stream of thought termed 'Critical Mobilities Thinking' (Jensen 2013). This refers to a double research strategy that remains critical towards various disciplines' automatic interpretations of, for example, train stations, motorways and parking lots as unconspicuous 'non-places'. The perspective of Critical Mobilities Thinking provokes these moral geographies by simply exploring actual situational practices and how people make sense of these. This particular research strategy may render under-used potentials in sites and systems a clear effect, as we start 'seeing opportunities' in the mundane mobilities sites, when we are not morally bound up in prefigured judgements that prohibit us from appreciating action possibilities. In other words, the notion of Critical Mobilities Thinking carries the possibility for social analysts to see potentials in the mundane situations. Obviously, we are not free from normative investments, and this research is driven by social values that we shall return to identify in the three empirical chapters. However, we do claim to rid the preconceptions of mobility being 'cost' alone and the sites of mobilities as 'non-places' only. Further, there is another dimension to Critical Mobilities Thinking that lies closer to the mainstream understanding of 'critical' research. This is a sensitivity and awareness to when systems break down, when failure and accidents are important features of infrastructures, when environmental degradation and 'externalities' threaten the life conditions of communities, and when mobilities are being staged with social exclusion and inequality as effects. These elements are, to put it simply, the 'dark sides' of mobilities design, which must focus on the problems created for people, communities, natures and ecologies. Put together, we may argue that Critical Mobilities Thinking is concerned with both 'problems' and 'potentials'. This connects well to our ambition of formulating a research agenda that focuses on design decisions and interventions and allows us to consider the pragmatic and practical consequences. By establishing a research field of mobilities design on a background of Critical Mobilities Thinking, we aim for a productive synergy between the strongholds of the diverse fields.

Urban design – yes, but what kind?

When we refer to urban design, we need to explicate our understanding of this field, since it is a label that covers a wide and often-contradictory territory. The term itself is a result of the Harvard Graduate of Design conference organized in 1956 (Krieger 2009). In those early days, there was some leverage and horizontality to the definition, embracing the planning processes, the architectural dimension and citizens' experiences in the public spaces of the city. For people more deeply interested in the genealogy of urban design, we refer to other sources. (For a general discussion of urban design, consult Carmona *et al.* 2010; Madanipour 2003; Lang 2005; Shane 2005; or see Jensen 2013: 46–64 and 175–93 for a specific discussion of the urban design/mobilities research nexus.) Generally, we are inspired by and sympathetic to the urban design strands of thinking which advocate bottom-up approaches to urban design, where the mundane and ordinary citizen experiences are the pivotal point of departure, as opposed to top-down, abstract blueprint plans or comprehensive package-design solutions and commercial products offering turnkey-urbanism solutions. We navigate from landmarks given by positions, such as Everyday Urbanism (Chase *et al.* 1999; Harris and Berke 1997), Landscape Urbanism (Corner 1999a; Waldheim 2006), and the strands of urban design working on public space design (Gehl 2010; Jacobs 1961; Hajer and Reijndorp 2001; Lynch 1981; Whyte 1988). In common therein is a concern for the city's public spaces and the citizens' inhabitations and progressive appropriations hereof.

In the context of this work, we shall understand urban design as a practical endeavour of intervention that addresses situated problems from (mainly) urban realities by means of architectural design. As such, the scope of urban design is primarily to evoke potentials, to create something new. In such processes, the discipline of urban design is entangled with many other disciplines (Krieger 2009). A pragmatic interdisciplinarity thus characterizes urban design, assembling concepts and frames of thought from elsewhere, when found to be useful in handling specific design problems (which, like mobile situations, do not stick to disciplinary boundaries). Urban design deals with aspects of both social and natural sciences, including users' needs and wishes, transportation and civil engineering, water and waste management, zoning and public policy, and other areas (see Krieger 2009). It works to shape urban environments for the many, including the multiple, diverging values and interests of authorities, private developers and users (see Madanipour 2006, on the ambiguous roles of urban design in relation to these groups), as well as technical measures to produce, build and maintain spaces. Creating urban design in practice, then, requires a sensibility and acceptance of multiple sources of input. It means being 'a synthesizing generalist' (Krieger 2009: xvi), engaging in 'true interdisciplinary endeavours' (ibid.: xii). In such an interdisciplinary field, urban design is a morphing and diverse effort, with the common pursuit of finding ways for spatially accommodating an ever-changing urban condition. In this complex and fluid discipline, the core knowledge, the field of operation and the boundaries of urban design are continuously discussed. Moudon (1992), for example, discusses a wide, integrated field of what urban designers 'should' know, describing an open list of nine areas of concentration that encompass research of relevance to urban design. Some of these are urban-history studies, environment-behaviour studies and material-culture studies. Following these characteristics, it is arguably not easy to fix a frame around the interdisciplinary field of urban design. There is no simple, widespread definition of the term as such, and it might be regarded 'less a technical discipline than a frame of mind shared by those of several disciplinary foundations committed to cities and to improving urban ways of life' (Krieger 2009: vii; see also Andrade *et al.* 2012). Urban design can be regarded as an adaptive and mutating discipline, in which the designer is always on the lookout for potential and new concrete tools with which to navigate and intervene in contemporary (urban) conditions, thus, in some instances at least, employing an explorative and experimental attitude.

In their paper 'Toward an Urban Design Manifesto', scholars and urban designers Jacobs and Appleyard outline a critique of the world's functionalist urban environments and suggest a set of goals for urban design. Among the points of critique was a continuous 'centrifugal fragmentation' (i.e. sprawl), resulting in vast low-density monocultural urban areas. Another point was loss of public life, 'massive transportation systems [...] segregated for single travel modes [...] that make people feel irrelevant' (1987: 114) and a 'rootless professionalism' in which urban designers design for places without knowing the people who inhabit them: 'There is too little inquiry, too much proposing' (ibid.: 115). The authors formulate explicit goals for urban design, including 'liveability', 'identity and control', 'access to opportunity, imagination and joy', 'authenticity and meaning', 'community and public life', 'urban self-reliance' and 'an environment for all'. Their manifesto is indicative of the attempts of urban design to formulate normative, spatial-material responses to the contemporary urban condition. Nowadays, the urban condition is marked by intense cycles of boom and bust, deepened socio-spatial segregation and the privatization or decline of public space (Madanipour 2006). In this condition, and similar to the manifesto referred to above, an important urban design goal continues to be to overcoming fragmentation and segregation by promoting 'accessible and inclusive environments for many, rather than exclusive places for a few' (ibid.: 186). In such processes, public space is one of the core interests of a 'socially concerned' urban design enterprise, which seeks to safeguard values and interests related to 'campaigning for making connections, articulating the common ground, and arguing for a socially integrative and environmentally responsible urban form' (ibid.: 188). The continuous focus on public space can be perceived as a response to a gap between '[p]ublic organisations' that, in the 1970s and 80s, 'focused on particular functional tasks, while private developers and designers focused on particular sites, showing no interest in urban space, which was everyone's space and no-one's' (ibid.). In a similar vein, Krieger and Saunders (2009: xvii) dedicate their recent urban design anthology to 'avoiding satellites of population revolving around nothing and to helping shape the kinds of environments that an urban species deserves and can love'.

Some well-known advocates for public space design with careful attention to the human scale are found in the works of American journalist and urbanist Whyte (1988) and Danish architect Gehl (1971), both of whom have done studies on how people use urban squares and plazas. Whyte's study methods include cautious observations on where and how people tend to gather, take a rest or enjoy people watching. One of his unpretentious conclusions, for the densely populated urban squares of New York, is that a decisive factor for the thriving of public life in such squares is the number of comfortable options for sitting down; these options may – or may not – have been specifically designated for sitting. Gehl is equally occupied with providing some pointers for us to understand the relationship between the physical environment of public spaces and the amount and type of activities that are likely to occur there. Public space design continues to proliferate in urban design. It includes careful attention to inner-city urban squares, to repurposed industrial sites and to streets that are recognized as a remarkable part of the public urban realm. One of the central concerns of urban design is the discouragement of public street life in the wake of the modern city, and the reimagination of the street as a thriving public space (see, for example, Jacobs, 1961, 1993). Not least, there is in urban design noticeable attention being paid to in-between spaces, peripheral conditions and infrastructures as public spaces. In their 'search for new public domains', Hajer and Reijndorp, for example, call for the (urban) design field to focus more on connections and in-between spaces, in order to create places of human interaction that relink the dissected zones of modern planning:

> [W]e must focus much more on the design of the transitions, the crossings, the connections and the in-between spaces than in the past. It is here that we can imagine public domain experiences (confrontation with otherness, a change in perspective, an exchange).
>
> (2001: 129)

A similar conclusion is reached in the Dutch-led study 'Mobility: A Room with A View' (Houben and Calabrese 2003). Acknowledging that urban design cannot solve the weighty social issues of the city, urban planning professor Loukaitou-Sideris (2012) nevertheless insists that the discipline at least employ spatial strategies of embedding that seek to interrelate places and buildings, targeting the inclusive rather than the exclusive, the overlapping rather than the segregating, the interlinkages rather than disconnected landscapes. This is a conception of a public urban landscape that extends the space between buildings, 'gluing' together the city (Krieger 2009). The associations – relationships, edges, transitions and connections – between diverse elements and zones of such landscapes are of great importance here (Loukaitou-Sideris 2012).

Within the current urban conditions, to which urban design must relate, there remain the still-important challenges related to the functionalist city and the rise of automobility. This left 'the exterior to the motor car, which tore the urban fabric apart, where buildings stood as unrelated objects in vast, floating open spaces' so that there is a clear idea of 'a need to establish connections between these fragments, and weave the urban fabric together again' (Madanipour 2006: 190). As pointed out above, several contemporary 'urbanisms' or design movements can be identified, which respond to such needs in highly varying ways (see Kelbaugh 2007; Loukaitou-Sideris 2012). These include New Urbanism, a formal (mainly American) movement concerned with re-establishing the classic urban virtues of a mixed-use, compact and walkable city. Everyday Urbanism, an informal, citizen-controlled stream, is concerned with facilitating ordinary life through improved mundane places, such as parking lots and sidewalks. Post-Urbanism is an avant-garde stream of bold and experimental urban works by, for example, Koolhaas and Hadid, in line with academic post-structuralist thoughts on the global world. Green Urbanism promotes a greener and more energy-efficient vision of cities. Finally, Landscape Urbanism advocates a processual and relational approach and an interweaving of the natural and the urban in site design. Loukaitou-Sideris (2012) stresses that none of these movements have had a profound impact 'on the ground', and that many of the urban problems mentioned earlier (sprawl, fragmentation, placelessness, loss of public life) persist and even grow. Market-driven urbanism remains the strongest stream, and often the outcome is sterile or mildly greener versions of conventional developments (ibid.: 486). In this field, Sorkin has proclaimed the 'end of urban design' (2009: 155), as urban design has not been able to respond to the current urban condition in satisfactory ways. Loukaitou-Sideris argues that instead of lamenting Sorkin's proclamation, urban design should seek to expand its scope and impact. In her delineation of a set of goals for urban design, she calls for it to be much more than an aesthetic exercise, and to instead draw on and respond to the economic, cultural, technological and environmental situations within which it exists and must work. Aligned with the intentions of this study, she argues that urban designers should not simply aim at bringing 'buzz' and spectacle to the cities in its work with 'grand civic settings', such as public squares, main boulevards, central parks and civic centres. It should also include spaces that exist in spite of urban design and not because of it: the 'ordinary and residual spaces of everyday life' such as streets, sidewalks, bus stops, transit terminals and parking lots. Too little urban design effort has been put into 'making the modest and ordinary landscapes more comfortable, liveable or humane' (Loukaitou-Sideris 2012: 476). Similarly, urban-planning professor Bertolini defines the current challenges of urban design as being about designing places we need and want in concordance with the infrastructural networks of 'intrinsically mobile nature of contemporary urban societies' (2006: 19). Expanding her description of the aim, Loukaitou-Sideris argues that urban design should be much more dedicated to embedded, contextualizing strategies, demanding that urban design 'be a collaborative endeavour that draws from different disciplines and gets its "clues" from the patterns of life' (2012: 482). These sources suggest that, if urban design is to have strength as a relevant frame of mind for approaching contemporary design problems, it must recognize its embeddedness within wider assemblages, including hybrid sociotechnical dimensions. This is key to our development of mobilities design in this book, as we gather a focused field of design considerations concerned with rational ordering of flow and with public space, politics, sustainability and embodiment.

This kind of integrated thinking can also be traced in the Landscape Urbanistic movement, which casts the contemporary metropolis as an urban landscape, regarded not in scenic terms but as strategic fields (Corner 1999a; Stoll and Lloyd 2010; Waldheim 2006). Time, space, relations and agency are key terms that suggest an understanding of spaces as dynamic, ever-changing fields constituted by multiple practices, experiences, logics, imageries and so on. Many mundane mobilities sites have an accepted place in Landscape Urbanism's focus on in-between, marginal and peripheral conditions, which have traditionally been neglected by planners and architects in the top-down and inside-out approach of the modernist city (Marot 1999: 47). A main aim of Landscape Urbanistic interventions is to stage 'the conditions necessary for ensuring the participation and engagement of people in [such] new public spaces' (ibid.: 49), with some sources pointing directly to the issue of embodied mobility, as, for example, Descombes does in his 'haptic, kinaesthetic approach to design' (1999: 80). Pointing to relational and dynamic thinking about ill-defined spaces in order to surpass landscape as a 'sort of a palliative to modern urbanization' (Marot 1999: 47), Landscape Urbanism's approach thus holds promise for mobilities design. In particular, architect and scholar Allen proposes a field of 'infrastructural urbanism' (1999, 2010). Allen finds mobility systems and structures to be obviously in need of the specificity of design expertise; a mindset is required that exceeds the performance of infrastructures to minimum engineering standards. Such infrastructural design should be 'capable of triggering complex and unpredictable urban effects in excess of its designed capacity' (Allen 2010: 38–9). He draws on Landscape Urbanism and his own practice (Stan Allen Architects) to articulate three working strategies for infrastructural urbanism: 'connectivity', 'architectural specificity/programmatic indeterminacy' and 'anticipatory design'. With connectivity, he points to the fact that '[c]onnection is infrastructure's primary mode of operation. Infrastructures work to move goods, people, energy and information around, establishing pathways and nodes that make connectivity possible' (ibid.: 39). Yet, he questions the conventional linear systems of infrastructure, working on principles of movement and minimization of conflict. He proposes searching for potential connections not through lines but through surface conditions, through expansive landscapes that can be warped and folded, working with surface connectivity in continuous matrices 'differentiated locally as movement, building, infrastructure, or open space' (ibid.: 40). With architectural specificity/programmatic indeterminacy, Allen points to using landscape as a means to rethink the relation between programme (activity) and site; the open field holds the promise that anything can happen – both formal events such as festivals, demonstrations and concerts, and informal, unstaged events (from above, that is). However, the field has to invite events, and infrastructure is a capacity for doing so:

> [I]nfrastructure creates concentrations of density that in turn trigger concentrations of activity. Program can never be scripted per se; the necessary freedom of the urban realm depends not on top-down determinations but on bottom-up, collective formations. The limits of design need to be strategically reworked to leverage architecture's potential to specify movement, create attractors and loosely steer program. The field is never neutral, and it is infrastructure that creates difference and the possibility for a vital life in time, organized collectively by the multitude of possible inhabitants.
>
> (Ibid.: 41)

With anticipatory design, Allen calls our attention to the designer's responsibility specifically to initiate the conditions for activities and relations. However, such initial conditions should not close in on specific messages; rather, '[t]he design of infrastructure is [...] open and anticipatory' (ibid.: 43). He acknowledges this openness as the reason for infrastructure's operation as public space: 'It represents the movement and exchange of information, without specifying the content of information or the range of movement' (ibid.). Though we should not dismiss the fact that control of connections is a huge component of designing infrastructural systems (through means of separation, switches and checkpoints), Allen finds that 'we know there is always something slightly out of control when infrastructures proliferate' (ibid.).

In sum, the field of urban design lends itself vividly to our articulation of mobilities design, as it is concerned with designing the actual physical environments of mobilities and, furthermore, as it has a body of practical, methodological and conceptual work to utilize. As this section has demonstrated, we find it important to consider the complexity of urban infrastructures. Therefore, in the chapters that follow, the engagement with urban design will be developed with notions of 'assemblage' (Farías and Bender 2010) and 'actor-networks' (Latour 2005a; Latour and Yaneva 2008; Yaneva 2009a) in order to better grasp the relational interdependencies of materialities, bodies, regulatory frameworks, design codes, etc. As architect Easterling argues in her book *Extrastatecraft*, 'The object of design is not a single form but an apparatus for shaping many forms. A vessel of dissensus rather than consensus' (2014: 239).

Designerly ways of thinking

The notion of mobilities design means not only that we are looking at design but also that we are engaging with 'designerly ways of thinking'. Here is a clear reference to Lawson who speaks of 'designerly ways of knowing' (2004: 3). With the focus on the less formalized 'thinking' rather than 'knowing', we wish to broaden to a discussion about 'ways of thinking' in order to approach the types of reflections and creative processes that designers are associated with. As the basic frame of understanding is the situational understanding of real, everyday life mobilities and, moreover, we pose the question of which designs actually afford those particular mobilities, we are touching upon multiple design decisions and interventions across a number of technologies, artefacts, built environments and sites. Here we see affiliations with the stream of thought termed 'pragmatism'. We find that some of the basic insights from American pragmatists such as Peirce, Dewey, and James should be reinvigorated (Dewey 1916, 1931, 1986; James 1884, 1899; Peirce 1994). In particular, we find the focus on the actual outcomes of design decisions and interventions is associated with this line of thought. Furthermore, the thinkers within pragmatism applied 'thought experiments' to a large extent, just as asking 'What if . . .?' questions are a key feature of designerly ways of thinking. We stretch the analytical imagination and embark on envisioning potentials not yet materializing, as we start applying this pragmatic question in a systematic manner. There is a utopian undercurrent to this work that relates to a rich stream of scenarios and experiments on mobility and the city, which push our imagination and discussions about visions for the future (Jensen and Freudendal-Pedersen 2012). As a research field, then, mobilities design aims to capitalize on an ongoing reflective oscillation between theory and practice that places 'making' as a central approach. In other words, 'not as an object for theoretical processing or verification, but as an investigative, creative and compositional practice that may be put at interplay with several theoretical frameworks, specific concepts and experimenting activity' (Dyrssen 2011: 227). In this, process '[a]nalysis is accomplished through action, by staging, provoking or changing the situation' (ibid.). As Dyrssen argues, handling such a process demands 'a developed sense of intuitive accuracy' of the 'researcher-artist-designer' to navigate and identify strategic points in the open system of the 'research assemblage' (ibid.: 228). She finds that such skills are key to any research practice. In particular, the researcher-artist-designer should be trained to linger 'in the complex and "fuzzy" state of exploration and uncertainty but at the same time make a situation respond and drive discovery forward as strongly as possible' (ibid.: 229). Mobilities design is therefore not a strategy of rational problem-solving but points at design as a research practice which, in a problem field of uncertainty, aims to open up a pathway for the future of the associations of materialities and mobilities rather than defining a set target (see also Ingold 2014).

Within social science, the very practice of doing experiments seems to have been forgotten, or at least downplayed (exceptions may be so-called action research approaches). Setting up experiments in various senses is a well-established method within design (reaching from architecture to product design to urban design). These include the testing out of the ways people engage with particular artefacts or designed spaces, and the mere idea that the built environment is a form of shared 1:1 laboratory in which ideas are tested, and accordingly adjusted, rejected or renewed in the next designs. They also include the profound processes of making open models in the design process. Such models are far more than media for spatial and formal experimentation, but rather sites where ideas and design meet and are constrained by technology, engineering, site conditions, client expectations and finance (Yaneva 2005). A model is 'a conduit for entrapping and "achieving", reassembling and reconciling bits of reality in a whole' (ibid.: 530). As a typical, designerly engagement with the public, mobilities design and experiments therein carry a participatory potential (see Erlhoff *et al.* 2008 for an elaboration of the notion of 'public design'). This resonates with ideas of design as a sort of 'public conversation' that other authors have raised (Ingold 2014: 244; Lawson 2004: 84). Thrift is vocal in arguing for reinvigorating experiments in social science as a part of a shift towards non-representational thinking (2008: 12), as we will elaborate on later. We see the research displayed in this book as having quite strong affiliations with key dimensions of precisely non-representational thinking (Anderson and Harrison 2010; Thrift 2008; Vannini 2012).

We want to turn to yet another intersection point with the designerly ways of thinking that mobilities design should profit from. A key concept connected to the materiality of spaces and artefacts is the notion of 'affordance' (see also Jensen *et al.* 2016). The concept has not been widely used within design and has mainly had its presence within social science and psychology. Coined by Gibson as a discussion of what the environment 'offers the animal, what it provides or furnishes, either for good or ill' (2015: 119), this seems to us to be a handle to bridge the design realm with an analytical interest in what shapes the action-spaces for human mobilities. He argues that affordances concern all the 'action possibilities' (1977: 67) latent in environments. Such a span of possibilities for action is a relational phenomenon where the animal may or may not make use of the potentials offered by the environment (ibid.). His notion of affordance has been critically reworked by Heft, arguing for a more 'action-based approach' (2010) and underlining an insight that most designers would know very well, namely that the physical environment may offer possibilities to humans but never in a uniform process, but rather as a dynamic interaction with spaces and artefacts. Moreover, such a situational and action-oriented understanding lends itself with particular sensitivity to mobilities studies, since we are facing mobile situations where the perception of an environment's potential for this or that may have to be figured out on the fly, so to speak. The mobile subject is enrolled into a complex setting of material spaces and artefacts and other consociates, trying to 'make sense on the move' (Jensen 2013). As Rob Shields argues in his discussion of affordance:

> For pavement, you can walk on it; you can sit on it; you can drive on it… […] You have to actualize it as this or that. What will it be? It is your choice at any given time. So, in the actualization, people play essential roles. But one should not underestimate the materials: their hardness, their softness, their ability to maintain a shape. All this makes the material a player in a way that is significant, causative, but not causal.
>
> (Farías 2010d: 297)

We find the notion of affordance a good fit with the notion of design and pragmatism. Designerly ways of thinking also allow for another set of design literature. We see potentials in ideas such as 'speculative and critical design' as articulated by, for example, Dunne and Raby (2015), who argue that 'Critical Design uses speculative design proposals to challenge narrow assumptions, preconceptions and givens about the role products play in everyday life. It is more of an attitude than anything else, a position rather than a method'.

Another relevant branch of literature connects to research done in relation to practice theory and the design of everyday life artefacts (Molotch 2005; Pink and Mackley 2014; Shove *et al.* 2007, 2012) as well as to the literature of design as 'environmental affordance' (Degen *et al.* 2010: 60) and 'enacting the social' (Yaneva 2009a: 282). As a more general research field, the book *Design Research*, edited by Bærenholdt *et al.*, also testifies to a renewed interest into design research. They argue here:

> Uncertainty, unpredictability, impossible emergence and the lived everyday creativity of collectives makes the world fluid. This fluidity must be matched by sensitive, responsive, and 'fluid' practices of researching and designing. It requires processes of researching and designing that enable people to participate responsibly and creatively in the making of researchers, makeshift users and designers as well as the making of wished-for change.
>
> (2010: 12)

A more general-research design agenda such as this has close affiliations to the one we want to present, with a more specific focus on mobilities. In particular, we are inspired by the idea that the fluidity of the everyday life world should be matched by research strategies sensitive to such dynamics. A common denominator for these approaches is a focus on the mundane and everyday life that has the denaturalization of the ordinary as a key concern. Many mobilities structures, spaces and artefacts are precisely mundane, invisible sites where under-utilized potential for change may lie in the very way we comprehend them. The potential of mobilities design thus resides in offering alternative views and new gestations of mundane sites, artefacts and infrastructures of mobilities.

Matters of concern: tunnel atmospheres, sustainable parking lots, road-crossing inequalities

From this outline of the framework and the streams of work underlying mobilities design, we want to briefly introduce the empirical content of this book. During the last few years, as part of a PhD study, a number of design explorations in a suburb of the Danish city of Aalborg have been developed. The study has advanced the linkages between urban design, mobilities research, Actor-Network Theory and non-representational research (Lanng 2015); the empirical cases of Chapters 5, 6 and 7 are all related to this study. The physical area of concern will be presented in detail in Chapter 4, but for now it should be mentioned that the suburb of Aalborg East carries the hallmark of modernist-heyday city planning, with traffic segregation between cars, bicycles and pedestrians as a main principle. The district accommodates dedicated housing areas set aside from industrial zones, a low-building density and a high percentage of open landscape, such as green lawns. In some respects, it is a layout in accordance with the modernist town-planning principles of the CIAM (International Congress of Modern Architecture) doctrine and inspired by Swedish SCAFT (City Building, Chalmers, Working Group for Traffic Safety) traffic-planning principles (Hagson 2000). The study developed around three archetypical mobilities sites within this vernacular landscape: a tunnel, a parking lot, and an informal road crossing (see Figure 1.3). Each of these typologies will be explored fully in the three empirical analyses, so we shall not present them in any detail here. Rather, we shall explain how these three design typologies connect to three underlying themes or matters of concern. As we progress through the book, we will demonstrate how the tunnel, the parking lot and the road crossing in Aalborg East each epitomize key themes of site-specific, as well as more generally relevant, mobilities design.

The three sites will be examined with regard to atmosphere, environmental sustainability and inequalities. We have identified these themes as vital pointers for an analysis and discussion of how mobile situations are staged by design decisions and interventions. The choice of the three themes of atmosphere, sustainability and inequality are precise illustrations of a combination of theoretical exploration and practical design interest. Our research interest in the social and material context of mobilities and how these connect to the potential of future generations, to experience both flourishing and the regular conditions of everyday life practices, has led us to these themes. The three sites are ordinary and inconspicuous indeed. In fact, so much so that a senior colleague of ours kindly suggested to us that this was 'too thin' to be serious material for a PhD study, let alone a further-research exploration. We aim to contribute to making visible some of the invisible, yet significant, potentials and problems of these sites, and thus prove this opinion incorrect.

The first mobilities design typology we shall explore is the tunnel. In the suburban district, most of the larger roads are underpassed by concrete tunnels established for the traffic separation of 'soft' modes such as pedestrians, cyclists and recreational runners. A universal design solution is chosen for the tunnels so that all the tunnels, built around the early- to mid-1970s, are made of grey concrete; their dimensions differ slightly, going up to around 5 metres wide and 3 metres high. The tunnel space is usually separated with dedicated lanes for faster traffic (cycles and mopeds) and marked sidewalks for pedestrians. They are artificially lit and often the canvas for the neighbourhood's aspiring graffiti artists. In short, they embed the generic mobility landscape of 'non-places' where monofunctional, standardized and – to some travellers – alienating artefacts are supposedly necessary evils of safe and efficient traffic organization. Some might be provoked by any attempt to render such design artefacts livable or even worthy of attention. But we will show, through a detailed exploration of one particular tunnel, how this is a site of interaction which works as a landmark and meeting space alongside local, everyday travels of the neighbourhood. The analysis will thus demonstrate how kids and young people in particular inhabit and

Figure 1.3 A tunnel, a parking lot, an informal road crossing – three mobilities design study sites (photos: Ditte Bendix Lanng).

appropriate the tunnel in manners that require a much more fine-grained vocabulary than simply 'alienating non-place'. With a situational outset, and through go-alongs (Büscher *et al.* 2011b), interviews, observations and design experiments, the chapter on the tunnel will exemplify situated, personal and affective inhabitations of a tunnel and will point to the atmospheric resonance of this mobilities site. The tunnel is not merely a functional, neutral background upon which mobilities are performed. It is a strongly laden, affective space where multisensorial and emotional relations to the tunnel materialities matter to the mobile experience and use of the place. In one situation, for example, the tunnel is a joyful sensorial fabric for embodied experiences; in another it is animated by a feeling of anxiety. Certainly, the tunnel works as a functional transport artefact, its design scripts shuffles travellers through space at this particular point in the area. However, travellers also show non-conformity to the design's implicit guidelines for mobile behaviour. They are channelled through the tunnel and dispersed on the other side, but they also contest the sterile rigidity of the tunnel's functionalist traffic design with their affective engagement with it. The concept of atmosphere supports an argument for challenging a primarily technical-only design agenda for sites of mobilities. It also challenges the privileging of vision in much design and advocates re-embodying people's relationships with these sites, of which many are perceived as sterile or gloomy. In the chapter, we propose a multisensorial sensibility in mobilities design. This means conceptualizing mobilities sites as part of a sensory urban fabric. The chapter opens the operation of mobilities design towards a range of considerations beyond the more instrumental, quantitative facts of bodily movement. It aims at the less representational affective experiences inherent in performing embodied journeys. We suggest cultivating insight and foresight into concrete, atmospheric mobile situations. This is done in order to articulate mobilities design in terms of the ways in which it is part of staging affective embodied mobile ways of life. Our suggestion pays profound attention to lives lived on the move and to the powerful effects of atmospheres. This means that our association of mobilities design with atmospheres should not be mistaken for a decorative-design approach. It is about the weighty agency of materialities: what mobilities sites *do* and what they could do in our mobile ways of life (see Chapter 3). In this way, we highlight the significant performative effect of atmospherically laden materialities on daily life mobilities. Materialities of mobilities should be regarded in their entanglement with hybrid sociotechnical networks, which reach across multiple realms. Our inclusion of atmopshere as a persistent issue in mobilities design aims to do just that.

The second mobilities design typology we explore in the empirical section is the parking lot. Through the study, we came to see the one particular parking lot that was analysed as an important local plaza, travelled through by a significant variety of people on an everyday basis. It is a traditional, asphalt-surface parking lot, serving a local grocery store. However, it is also a 'place' where people meet, mingle and interact. Yet, any surface parking lot epitomizes a series of serious environmental concerns. First, it does not stand alone. The parking lot is an omnipresent urban typology, and the environmental problems should be seen in the light of the global ubiquity of surface parking. In 2009, there were 600 million passenger cars in the world, and the number is growing. Cars are immobile 95 per cent of the time, and in the US alone there are 500 million surface parking spaces (Ben-Joseph 2012). Parking spaces cover a lot of space, and they are intricately linked to the car-centric city and therefore are important parts of the automobility system that tends to foster unsustainable car-dependency. In that chapter, we tease out some of the important environmental problems of parking lots that can reasonably be addressed by mobilities design. The path that we will follow is a designerly outlook for potentials, beginning with the optimistic note that parking lots can be more than just too-large areas of underperforming asphalt. These can be multiprogrammed, well-connected, green, sophisticatedly engineered and landscaped urban spaces; they can be Critical Points of Contacts (Jensen and Morelli 2011) along journeys, connecting urban and mobilities networks, and encouraging experiences and meetings. With a mobilities design approach, sustainable parking-lot design is an integrative effort of balancing the utilitarian demand for efficient surface parking with strategic and concrete considerations for the environment, and thus the low-carbon mobile situations and patterns of life that the parking lot should support. Situational mobilities design offers a certain approach to sustainable urbanism and mobilities, which takes its outset in concrete situations where materialities and lived mobile lives come together. This approach highlights problems and potentials for more sustainable user choices, embedded in the materialities, which we will discuss in relation to connectivity, barriers and the coercion or promotion of various modes of mobilities. We follow Latour's insight into the 'radically careful, or carefully radical' promise of design (2008; see Chapter 2 of this book), and our account implies the modesty and attention to details which are some of the key traits for this promise, which does not directly offer itself to grand systems and challenges. In the chapter, we tease out some of the small material changes that could be made to the parking lot to accommodate steps on the way to a more sustainable future. Such materialities may be able to co-evolve and co-adapt with multiple other entities, to add up to form a tipping point for a sustainable trajectory (see Urry 2007).

The last typology explored is the road crossing. We have examined a particular stretch of road which is supposed to cater to fast-driving cars, but which proves to be a widely used, informal pedestrian crossing.

This piece of road is the site of a conflictual co-existence of the directional flow of car traffic and of the cross-directional flow of vulnerable pedestrians and bicyclists. The ordinary, informal road crossing is manifest of the dilemma that the design staging of convenient mobilities for some produces immobilities for others. The physical environment of the road, its width, uniformity and sparse signage show very little indication to car drivers that this is a place where vulnerable travellers might cross, and the crossing travellers face a huge barrier to their local mobilities as they must move close to the cars without much safe space or timing. Thus, and in accordance with mobilities design speculations on alternatives and potentials, this place epitomizes concrete questions of equality and mobilities design priorities. Across the world, each street crossing, road dimensioning and traffic-light code carry a load of choices, normativity and priority between user groups. This is an obvious effect of the fact that multiple user groups often need to share the same space. The zero-sum game of infrastructure provision is, however, not a simple matter of deducing values into design. Choices are made. This is the situation in Aalborg East, where the segregation of mobility modes was inscribed into the design doctrine of functionalist urban planning, with a vision of creating a highly efficient and seamless 'traffic machine'. Speed and connections across distances, most often by car, were seen as a promise of progress, involving ideological associations of mobility with universalism and freedom (see Adey 2010; Cresswell 2006). However – and this is not just confined to the case of the road crossing – mobilities design is not neutral. As Adey argues, mobilities cannot be treated in depoliticized and universal ways; it is a deception that we can have free and equal mobility (Adey 2010). In any mobilities design intervention, issues of inequality, power and politics are embedded. In the chapter, we will discuss this and its significance. We point to some of the important dimensions of the knotty issue of mobilities, politics and design, including questioning the democratizing force of new design developments, as well as issues of inequalities related to gender, bodily capacities (impairment) and ethnicity. The staging of mobile situations by design encompasses possibilities for many ways of 'engineering relationships among people' (Winner 1980: 124), and this, we argue, pushes us to seek critical insight into the politics of mobilities design. The chapter then demonstrates that mobilities artefacts, mundane and indiscernible perhaps, may encompass serious political purposes or repercussions, in and beyond their immediate use.

Structure of the book

This introductory chapter has laid out a map of where mobilities research meets design in articulating mobilities design. The key positions and state of the art of mobilities research and urban design, respectively, have been introduced; we have elaborated upon designerly ways of thinking as a key attitude that flows through the book, and we have suggested and framed its three themes of atmospheres, environmental sustainability and inequalities. In Chapter 2, we explore the new material turn towards design in more detail. It discusses mobilities design as pointing to a material pragmatism. En route, it deliberates ethics, normativity and involvement in design, non-representational approaches and their significance to mobilities design, as well as drawing up mobilities design's linkages with pragmatism and experimentalism. In Chapter 3, we move on to conceptualizing materialities per se. With the basis in pragmatism, non-representational research and Actor-Network Theory, the chapter argues for mobilizing artefacts in order to comprehend them as relational materialities enmeshed in networked cultural, political and social formations. The chapter explores what artefacts *do* in the midst of ongoing mobilities, mundane and unnoticed as they may be. Chapter 4 is the last of the theoretically and methodically framing chapters of the book. In it we discuss methods of mobilities design, which can capture its socio-material hybridity, its dynamics and its designerly disposition towards intervention and change. We will introduce the specific suburban area and the particular methods of the empirical studies of the following chapters. These include methodological sensitivities to analysing what artefacts do, as well as speculating upon what they *could* do. Chapter 5 is the first empirical chapter, on tunnel atmospheres; we invite the reader to learn about actual mobile situations, some of which transgress first-hand assumptions of what a tunnel does. We elaborate on the power of atmosphere on mobilities design, circulating between entities of these situations, and we bring forth design imaginations on alternative potentials for the tunnel's design. In Chapter 6, we continue the empirical journey, considering sustainability and mobilities design. As in the previous chapter, we open with a tangible mobile situation, this time in a parking lot, and we move on to unfold how serious environmental problems epitomize this surface parking-lot design. On an optimistic, designerly note we experiment with visions for an alternative future for the parking lot, teasing out some of the carefully radical changes that could be done to embark on a journey towards a more sustainable future. Chapter 7 is about mobilities design and politics and focuses on inequalities, which occur when vulnerable pedestrians must cross a regional road. This mobile situation represents the dilemma in which mobilities for some may produce immobilities for others. A neglect of actual users' needs and mobile lives in infrastructure design can be traced in this and points to how materialities of mobilities are inherently political, beyond their immediate use. The final chapter gathers the key points of the book together in a framework for the new field of mobilities design. This is a field with several interweaving trajectories: a new material turn within the academic field of mobilities research, a design approach and focus, and – possibly – a fresh set of practices and materialities of mobilities. This new territory holds promises for both analysis and intervention.

2 A new material turn in mobilities research

Introduction

Despite its cross-disciplinary identity, the mobilities turn has not capitalized sufficiently on the potential in exploring issues of material design and physical form. This chapter proposes that mobilities research draw on experimental and creative styles of knowing from the design disciplines, in a concrete, critical and potential-oriented engagement with the material world. In Chapter 1 we considered designerly ways of thinking which create the experimental, potential-seeking approaches and evocative attitudes we wish to harness in mobilities design. The analytical disciplines of mobilities research might benefit from such approaches and attitudes, in not only identifying problems but also potentials; this would contribute to resolving larger-scale challenges related to mobilities and societies, such as climate change, demographic shifts and resource scarcity. The goal of this chapter is to pin down the underlying assumptions and streams of thoughts that influence the way we ultimately articulate the emerging research field of mobilities design.

Pragmatism is one such stream of thought that we see as an important underpinning of mobilities design. Academics within as diverse fields as geography and philosophy seem to share our understanding of pragmatism as an important source of inspiration (albeit not the only one). From the perspective of geography, Bridge (2008) argues convincingly that pragmatism lends itself, as an analytical framework, to understanding human practices and communication as multisensorial, embodied and not necessarily embedded into language. The extra-linguistic properties of human sense-making and communication have precisely to do with the embodied 'micro-politics of social life' that the classic pragmatists, as well as Goffman, were so alert to (ibid.: 1574). And from the perspective of philosophy, Gimmler (2005, 2008, 2012) identifies a shift from a contemplative to an experiential understanding of knowledge and knowledge production as a key dimension of pragmatism. Furthermore, she illustrates that pragmatism focuses on the situational, experimental, relational, interventionist, anti-representational, material, multi-sensiorial and embodied dimensions of human practice, and that empirical phenomena such as mobilities and mobile technologies lend themselves well to the focus of pragmatic investigations.

Furthermore, we find that the modest attitude of pragmatism resonates with the way we like to think of our research endeavour, and Bacon expresses it elegantly thus:

> Pragmatism reminds us of the ways in which our practices contain errors and injusticies, and draw upon those practices in order to offer re-descriptions with a view to making our lives and our world richer and freer.
>
> (2012: 201)

The structure of the chapter is the following: after this introduction, we turn to questions of design, ethics, normativity and public involvement in section two. Section three is then dedicated to a discussion of what is termed 'non-representational' approaches, artefacts and new materialities. After discussing these contemporary approaches, we draw a line back to classic thinkers within pragmatism and their interest in experimentalism. We end the chapter by setting out a rough outline of the research agenda of mobilities design: it is one that we wish to discuss provisionally under the heading of 'material pragmatism' as an indication of the new material turn that mobilities design will articulate and institute.

Design, ethics, normativity and public involvement

In a lecture for the Design History Society in 2008, Latour argued that the notion of 'design' carries a more modest connotation than key words from modernism, such as 'construction' and 'building'. Rather, design signals a modest interest in detail, a sense of skilfulness, and craftsmanship (2008: 3). Further, he argues, as we start thinking of artefacts in terms of design, we start seeing them less as 'objects' and more as 'things'. This means that the embedded and networked character of the item in question connects to its realm of practice and use (thing) and not as an isolated, detached entity (object). This move counters the separation of objects from thoughts, materialities from ideas. The idea of design is also always a question of redesign since there is always a history of givens in pre-existence to whatever we need to design. Put differently, 'to design is never to create ex nihilo' (ibid.: 5). Among the number of advantages Latour highlights in his talk, the final one is perhaps the most interesting. Accordingly, the utilization of the concept of design involves an ethical dimension related to the question of 'good design' versus 'bad design'. Rather than referring to some abstract or ideational realm, the fact that we are engaging with acts of design renders some mysterious creator a mere fiction and leads to a more confrontational position, in which any design could (or should) be held accountable in normative terms. In other words, moral questions of the effects of design decisions and interventions are unavoidable and thus, potentially, lead to deliberations about social and political consequences. The 'revolutionary potential' that Latour identifies within design has not to do with grand political schemes and ideologies, but precisely the opposite: modesty, care, precautions, skills, crafts, meanings, attention to details, careful conservations, redesign, artificiality and ever-shifting transitory fashions. The task (and promise) of design is, then, in Latour's words, 'to be radically careful, or carefully radical' (2008: 7). His vision, which we share in the pragmatic agenda for mobilities design, is thus to balance the radical ambitions with the subtle and emphatic engagements. The pragmatic agenda of mobilities design leads less to grand and abstract theories and more to real problem-solving. The project 'Design like you give a damn' (Architecture for Humanity 2006) is one such illustration of how design deals with the very concrete and specific social and environmental challenges and need, rather than some abstract principle (see Guy 2013: 148–9 for this argument).

This connects well to the previously mentioned idea of Critical Mobilities Thinking and how that always incorporated discussions of both problems and potentials. But it also connects to the pragmatic stream of thought that we see as part of the intellectual undercurrent to mobilities design. This is because, rather than referring to abstract ideologies or universal principles, the focus on (mobilities) design takes us to the pragmatic question *what makes this situation possible?* and, further, *what are the actual consequences of this design decision or design intervention?* As argued by Ingold, 'designing environments for life' should involve a 'conversation' (in broad terms) between designers, users and the wider public (2014: 245). Coming back to Latour, this means that the normative dimension inherent in design offers a 'good handle' to extend the question of design to politics (2008: 6). We will take this a step further at the end of this book, when we argue for a 'politics of design' and suggest how to use the new field of mobilities design to move beyond material and aesthetic manifestations of design decisions and interventions into the normative realms of social, ethical and environmental consequences of design. This will also lead us to discuss the nature of the public deliberation or 'conversation', as Ingold terms it, and will connect to the discussion of collaborative design. It is, however, important to point out from the beginning that even though we realize the importance of collective processes, institutionalized conversations and deliberations, our specific design interventions and experiments represent only the first phase of a process. In this, we propose to move from 'learning to see' the potentials rendered invisible by habitual practices (for example, the routinized practices in everyday mobility) towards the second phase of 'invitation to act'. We readily acknowledge that this distinction may seem a bit mechanical and that we might seemingly want to separate knowing from doing. This is by no means our intention, and we believe that the two are immanently connected. But we also realize that we need some sort of system and 'heuristic handle' on these initial attempts to articulate a new field. Therefore, we ask the reader's indulgence in accepting this simple distinction as a tool that will facilitate this new work. Too much pre-conditioning and theorizing may lead to sophisticated writings but too little practical and empirical work. The first step in 'learning to see' is dependent on opening up the material sensitivity towards understanding how things are more than objects with fixed properties. Or in the words of Ingold:

> Though we might be inclined to say that a stone bathed in moisture is more 'stony' than one bathed in dry air, we should probably acknowledge that the appearances are just different. It is the same if we pick up the stone and feel it, or knock it against something else to make a noise. The dry stone feels and sounds differently from the wet one. What we can conclude, however, is that since the substance of the stone must be bathed in a medium of some kind, there is no way in which its stoniness can be understood apart from the ways it is caught up in the interchanges across its surface, between medium and substance [...]. Stoniness, then, is not in the stone's 'nature', in its materiality. Nor is it merely in the mind of the observer or practitioner. Rather, it emerges through the stone's involvement in its total surroundings – including you, the observer – and from the manifold ways in which it is engaged in the currents of the lifeworld.
>
> (Ingold 2011: 32)

Based on earlier work on situational mobilities, we highlighted the complex relationship between materials and bodies as they move. This suggests a notion of 'mobility affordance' as a way to understand the relation between the moving body and its material environment (Jensen 2013: 120). This resonates with Degen *et al.*'s work on 'environmental affordance' (2010: 60) and Yaneva's proposal to consider design as a way of 'enacting the social':

> Design [is] a way of producing additional attachments that make a variety of actors congregate, forming different groupings and assembling social diversity. Tracing networks with wood, steel, polished surfaces and blinking signals, bip-bing doors and blinking elevator buttons, design connects us differently, linking disparate heterogeneous elements and effects, thus entering a game of producing, adjusting and enacting the social.
>
> (2009a: 282)

The discussion about the ethical dimensions, as well as the repercussions of public engagement through processes of co-design, is much more comprehensive than what we may cover in depth here. We have clarified our standpoint and shown some of the roads ahead, but for now we will wrap up this discussion with a reference to Ingold's 'Design Manifesto' (2014: 244):

- Environments are inherently variable; therefore design should enhance the flexibility of inhabitants to respond to these variations with foresight and imagination.
- The impulse of life is to keep on going. Design unfolds within constantly transforming life conditions, and should open up pathways for creative improvisation.
- There is always a tension between hopes and dreams for the future and the material constraints of the present; therefore design should invite people from all walks of life to join a conversation around this tension.

We are sympathetic to this open, creative and co-involving approach to design and find the call for a joint 'conversation' among people from all walks of life appealing. However, as with the double-phased strategy above, there might be a need for some more professional shaping of the agenda. For all the sympathetic inclusion, there might be quite a lot of people who will not see the hidden potentials of everyday life infrastructures and who need attention-shaping before they may actively engage in transformative and co-creative practices. This, as a matter of fact, is the ethical claim laid down on designers and planners, as well as on academics. On a more substantive note, we are leaning towards normative statements on the values behind urban design and planning, as articulated by Friedmann (2002) and his notion of 'human flourishing', for example, and Sandercock (2003) with her multicultural sensitivity and democratic involvement of all social classes. These may sound abstract but, as we revisit them in the discussion chapter after the empirical case studies, they shall become much more tangible.

The mobilities design research programme we propose here will both seek to redescribe the well-known in novel ways and will invite action with a collective sense of change. We are aiming to illustrate the connection between the mobilities turn theories and the design world, thus pointing to the hidden potentials in a didactic move we term 'learning to see'. We are shedding light on the premise through theoretical work and design experiments. This requires a short disclaimer as we readily should reject words such as 'seeing' and 'light' if these are understood as truthful uncovering of essences; this is by no means the case. What we propose are different ways of seeing as an option and a move within the attempt to rethink the routinized and habitual environments of everyday life mobility. It is also important to notice that learning to see is a process we undergo ourselves and is not something to be forced upon others. Anyone engaging with mobilities design has the potential to learn to see the well-known in surprising ways. This has been an important stimulus for this research. Through creative explorations of the 'What if ...?' questions, we have explored many novel ways of seeing what we thought we knew well in advance (from tunnels to parking lots to road crossings). The second phase of co-design and collective involvement that we term 'invitation to act' is what we work with, through design workshops and seminars. In this first phase, we need to connect theories and arguments carefully to design thinking and practices. We work to establish a vocabulary, a language and a set of experimental practices that we conceive as a precondition to further public engagement. This is part of the 'politics of visibility' argued for elsewhere (see Jensen 2013, as well as the concluding chapter of this book). In the second phase of invitation to act, the politics of visibility should be connected to 'making things public' (to use the title of Latour and Weibel's exhibition project of 2005).

In a sobering paper, Kimbell (2011) argues that we should be careful not to privilege the designer as the omnipotent agent in design and, furthermore, that the very notion of 'design thinking' may in fact contribute to keeping the dualism between thinking and acting alive. Also she takes a critical stand on the corporate application of 'design thinking' as creative and innovative expressions of the new creative capitalism. In the corporate discourse of design thinking, the designer is firmly depoliticized and abstracted into the closed, creative circuits of corporate organization and management. Finally, she urges us to be careful not to ignore the diversity of designers and the plurality of practices therein. Having said that, she argues for an understanding of design and designers as situated and practised, as connected to embodied routines and mundane, but highly differentiated heterogeneous practices. In a follow-up paper, Kimbell (2012) draws more explicitly on anthropological insights, as well as on material and networked understandings of the importance of objects and artefacts, in constituting design practices. This is indeed a perspective on design that resonates well with our pragmatic understandings of mobilities design. We must conceive of design and designerly thinking as connected to messy, mundane and heterogeneous practices that are situated, embodied and shot through with all sorts of normative agendas. These are neither fully rational, nor fully artistic and creative, but as professional practice, often destabilized by pressures of powers, technologies and resources.

As we aim to learn to see new things in mundane and ordinary sites staging everyday life mobility, we are also acknowledging the multiplicity of meanings and understandings that such sites potentially carry. Our go-along interviews and field studies have been instrumental in our rethinking about what mundane sites of mobility may offer in hybrid embedded ways, beyond being sites of transport. Through the empirical material, this multiplicity of sites (herein the differentiated meanings held by users) will be used to problematize the homogeneity of well-established traffic-planning categories. Bicyclists, pedestrians, car drivers and bus-riders are rich groups of subject positions (see Jain 2009; Merriman 2004; Middleton 2010 for mobilities research that unfolds some of the embodied situational intricacies inherent in passengering, driving, and walking) that may have a specific mode of transport in common for each group but may also in fact have more in common across categorical lines of demarcation. Here, we touch upon the critical potential of mobilities design, with its sensitivity to embodied practices and actual situations as an antidote to a universal categorization, which tends to lie at the heart of much rational, top-down city and transport planning and design.

Non-representational approaches, artefacts and new materialities

'Non-representational' approaches within social science is one of the major inspirational sources for mobilities design. The reason we find the non-representational approaches attractive is that these new positions and streams of thought reach across and reconcile dichotomies of modernist thinking (body/mind, society/individual, culture/nature, etc.). We view attempts to offer fruitful correspondences applicable to our interest in actual, dynamic situations and in the heterogeneous elements affording them. In particular, we shall lean on three sources: Thrift's *Non-representational Theory: Space. Politics. Affect.* (2008), Anderson and Harrison's *Taking-Place: Non-representational Theories and Geographies* (2010) and Vannini's *Non-representational Methodologies: Re-envisioning Research* (2015). Elsewhere Jensen has summarized these positions and, for the sake of simplicity, we offer this list as a framing of the position (Jensen 2016, own translation):

1 Non-representational Theory (NRT) approaches work on the fluid and process-oriented dimensions of everyday life practices. In other words, they throw light on the often non-articulated and non-verbalized parts of sociality, as well as the dynamic and non-static qualities of the mundane which, according to NRT, should have much more credit in social research.
2 NRT is anti-biographical and pre-individual in the sense that it dismisses the imagined self-contained subject articulated through a coherent life narrative. In the NRT perspective, the pre-discursive and affect-oriented is given a prominent place, rendering the linguistic and conscious a less important place in its map of the world.
3 NRT puts focus on practices, actions and performances. It moves away from an imaginary connection to underlying 'explanations' and 'structures' by directing its attention to specific situations. Attention is given to embodied practices, rather than conscious explanations and verbalizations (which are often seen as ex-post rationalizations).
4 NRT expresses a 'relational materialism' (with a reference to Actor-Network-Theory). This leads to an understanding of objects and humans relationally connected in 'hybrid assemblages', where the human subject cannot be positioned as privileged. Furthermore, materiality is understood very concretely and not in any abstract sense (Ingold moves this distinction even further by advocating a shift from the 'material' towards 'materials' (Ingold 2011)).
5 NRT has an experimental foundation and this is often articulated through a direct, collaborative approach, with using arts and artists as means of transgressing traditional social science.
6 NRT puts emphasis on the body and its multisensorial embedding in the world. As a consequence, affect and emotion are considered as relevant as reason and rationality.
7 NRT sees it as its duty also to explore the ludic, lively and vital part of human existence. Furthermore, the position deliberately seeks radical and 'wild ideas'. Creativity, abduction and methodological experimentation are central. In this context, abduction is connected to the creative leaps of mind in search for new solutions and thought experimentations.
8 NRT is situational and event-oriented, which is considered to be non-deterministic and principally open-ended so that a pre-event deduction of their outcome is considered impossible (in other words, they are contingent). Due to such a principal indetermination, NRT also sees

open-ended and emergent situations as containing the seeds for alternative futures. Anti-reduction and emergence are key perspectives.

9 NRT privileges the study of relations (and here we see a link to Simmel's (1998) understanding of 'society' as associational). The relations are emerging within complex networks, non-hierarchical systems and assemblages, including humans, artefacts and localities.

10 NRT privileges the background and speaks against moral geographies which elevate certain spaces as important typologies, at the same time as it renders a number of materialities unimportant, soulless and as non-places (for example transit spaces, shopping malls, parking spaces, etc.).

There are internal heterogeneities in non-representational research, and speaking of a homogeneous position is inaccurate. Therefore, we aimed to draw out key features of non-representational thinking in order to see how these might connect with mobilities theories in general, and with ideas of mobilities design in particular. Clearly, we consider the latter to be the case by far. Other streams of thought, like 'alien phenomenology' (Bogost 2012) and 'Object-Oriented-Ontology' (Harman 2011), are also voicing new ways of seeing the material world. These are not synonymous with NRT but are a further testament to the move away from representation and the attempt to rethink the human subject in the midst of objects, artefacts and materialities. There is much critique and debate related to these positions as well; see, for instance, Ingold's critique of object-oriented ontology for being a static and 'dead' world with no dynamic properties (2015: 16). Here we have deliberately presented an eclectic survey of the key propositions within NRT that synchronize with mobilities design. Furthermore, the research in NRT and other recent positions also correspond with key elements in classic pragmatism, convincingly illustrated by Jones (2008), to which we now turn.

Pragmatism and experimentalism

We will address one last stream of thought in this chapter, the now-classic, American pragmatist thinking. We primarily see the thoughts of James, Dewey and Peirce as laying out some of the foundation to the design-oriented way of thinking that we are interested in. A number of features seem to run across the situational-mobilities perspective, the designerly ways of thinking and the non-representative streams of thought, and they connect to key ideas within pragmatism. First, the very nomenclature of 'pragmatism' suggests a clear connection to practice and situations. *Pragma* means 'behaviour' and thus suggests that it is in the specific and concrete everyday life situations that our key attention needs to be directed. Second, the pragmatist position of thought often entertains the 'What if ...?' question. Here we see an obvious connection between a situational-mobility understanding and the designerly creative seeking-out of potential outcomes of design decisions and interventions. So, as well as asking the key pragmatic question *what affords this mobile situation?* and thereby focusing on the actual consequences of actions and decisions, we also pose the more open-ended and creative question of 'What if …?' as a variant of the informed guess, abductive reasoning and the thought experiment. The third touchstone between designerly thinking and pragmatism is the focus on experiments, often full-scale (or what we term '1 : 1'). By this we mean the approach to construct and intervene on a direct 1 : 1 scale in the world (either by actually building 'stuff' or by creating mock-ups). This is precisely the approach followed in the empirical cases we shall explore later in this book. A fourth connection is the sensitivity to the body and the multisensorial qualities of our engagement with material spaces and technological artefacts. Growing out of this concern is the critique of rationalism and the inclusion of affects and emotions, as equally important ways of orienting ourselves in the world. Finally, we want to point to the understanding of materials. Here we follow Ingold in arguing that we are not thinking about an abstract materiality, but concrete and physical spaces and things, where the choice of material surface, for instance, makes all the difference to the mobile situations afforded. (An example is the difference between cycling on gravel, asphalt or cobblestone.)

The term 'pragmatism' was coined by Peirce with reference to its Greek root *pragma* (Kilpinen 2008). So the fundamental idea was both to articulate a philosophical position with focus on the pratical outcome of any given idea, rather than on some element of abstract vision. Moreover, the behavioural focus of pragmatism also means that it is a 'philosophy of action' (ibid.: 1). We cannot go into the genealogies of pragmatism in much depth (see Bacon 2012; Misak 2013; Richardson 2010; Talisse and Aikin 2011; Thayer 1982). But from its inception in the latter part of the nineteenth century in New England, one of the foundational building blocks was to be know as the 'pragmatic maxim' voiced by Peirce. It might have been put more elegantly and is perhaps unnecessarily twisted in its language but it stands as the foundation indeed:

> Consider what effects, which might conceivably have practical bearings, we concieve the object of our concepts to have. Then, our conception of these effects is the whole of our conception of the object.
>
> (Bacon 2012: 25)

With this maxim, Peirce wanted to direct the attention to issues that 'really mattered'. Also, the understood, experimental attitude is embedded within this maxim, which basically invites us to be imaginative and creative in our analytical understanding, at the same time as being fully concentrated on the real effects of things and phenomena. Needless to say, as one probes deeper into this simple statement, issues of dispute surface. How does one in fact decide what the 'practical bearings' are? Which methods and what context in terms of time and space are to be included for one to say that the question as been fully answered? Despite these issues (which we do not see as disqualifying or invalidating but rather as necessary elaborations to be made), the 'pragmatic ethos' (Bernstein 1988) and its focus on actual consequences rather than abstract and imaginary dimensions are appealing to a research agenda that is interested in real mobile practices of everyday life. As is clear from the rich literature on pragmatism, there are also different understandings among its key thinkers about what the crux of the matter really is, but many of the founding thinkers share a common interest in looking for the concrete, rather than the abstract, effects of worldly phenomena. James's version of the pragmatic maxim is perhaps more clearly phrased when he states, 'To develop a thought's meaning we need only determine what conduct it is fitted to produce: that conduct is for us its sole significance' (1899: 186) or, sounding more like a slogan, 'There can be no difference which doesn't make a difference' (ibid.: 187). Dewey had statements that could equally be seen as his paricular take on the pragmatic maxim: 'The effective meaning of any philosophical proposition can always be brought down to some particular consequence, in our practical experience ...' (1931: 27). Here the key is, of course, the 'effective meaning' which also may attract critical questions. Dewey further connected the maxim to the field of action when he stated:

> In order to attribute a meaning to concepts, one must be able to apply them to existence. Now it is by means of action that this application is made possible. And the modification of existence which results from this application constitutes the true meaning of concepts.... It is [therefore] not the origin of a concept, it is its application which becomes the criterion of its value: and here we have the whole of pragmatism in embryo.
>
> (Ibid.: 25, 37)

Dewey's point about the action-relation connects to another key feature of pragmatism, that is, that pragmatism assumes a 'process world' or, put differently, it leans on a process ontology according to which the focus is less on 'what is' (ontology) than on 'what happens in the world' (Kilpinen 2008: 4). In Kilpinen's reading, all classic pragmatists are 'process thinkers who agree that reality always undergoes change' (2008: 5; see also Dewey 1986: 110; Healey 2009: 280). According to Richardson, James knew that 'truth is a process, that reality is experience – but all of experience – and that truth and reality are actually verbs' (Richardson 2010: x). This indeed connects to the process-oriented dimension of NRT, and we see such process-thinking as an expression of an ontology of becoming (Amin and Thrift 2002: 30; Ingold 2015: 117). This represents a profound opposition to sedentary understandings of societies and is therefore a vital theoretical and metaphyscial underpinning of moblities design. In relation to this theme, Dewey is very clear-headed:

> Pragmatism thus has a metaphysical implication. The doctrine of the value of consequences leads us to take the future into consideration. And this taking into consideration of the future takes us to the conception of a universe whose evolution is not finished, of a universe which is still, in James' terms 'in the making', 'in the process of becoming', of a universe up to a certain point still plastic.
>
> (1931: 33)

Such a focus carries with it an inherent evolutionary and temporal understanding – or, as Amin and Thrift put it, a focus on 'moments of encounters' (2002: 30). This is a further crossing point to the mobilities turn with its underpinning critique of a sedentary understanding of places and the world (Cresswell 2006) and of the idea of society as 'a thing' (Urry 2000). Furthermore, the process- and temporal oriented understanding, combined with the focus on specific actions, connects directly to the situational focus of the Staging Mobilities framework, as well to the landmark ideas within mobilities design to which this book is a contribution. The ontological position also connects to some of the dimensions of the NRT perspectives just discussed, as traditional epistemology and ontology often are based on the assumption that humans approach the world in order to gain knowledge. In the light of the pragmatist process ontology, we may, however, just as well claim the opposite, namely that 'the world approaches us!' (Kilpinen 2008: 7). The decentring of the human subject, as well as the privileged anthropocentric viewing position, is at stake here, and this resonates with NRT and with the position of Ingold (2011, 2015). In particular, the opening up of the understanding of human-non-human relationship is evident here:

> In a process world, action comes ahead of knowing, in the sense that the subject first has to establish a steady relationship to his or her world, before closer investigations about it and the truthful statements that they possibly yield come onto the agenda. In static ontology the steady relation is assumed as given. In pragmatism, the steady relation is established in the subject's concrete doings.
>
> (Kilpinen 2008: 7)

In our exploration of pragmatism as an important influence on mobilities design, we may consult the discussion that takes place within geography. In a 2008 theme issue of the journal *Geoforum*, a number of papers addressed the question of pragmatism's relation to geography (Wood and Smith 2008). Most of the authors point to the fact that pragmatism does have a positive relation to geography; some take that into the more philosophical and reflective dimensions, whereas others take it directly to the core of geography. Cutchin does the latter and argues that the relational and process-oriented understanding of 'place' that Massey argued for (and which we have argued for as a vital part of the mobilities perspective on place) is a predominantly pragmatic perception (Cutchin 2008: 1565). In particular, Cutchin argues that a Deweyan view of place 'becomes one in which human and natural are continuously in transactive processes together' (ibid.). Here the holistic understanding of 'organism-in-environment-as-a-whole' that Dewey advocated for at the end of his career (ibid.: 1563) is strikingly in accordance with Ingold's holistic perception of the 'world' as an unified meshwork (2011, 2015). From this discussion of geography and pragmatism, we also find Dewey's notion of the 'situation' to resonate with the one we advocate as the foundation of mobilities design. Dewey argued for a 'situated sociality', which was defined at the same time as universal and generic by way of their continuity and contingency, and individual and unique by way of their space-time and qualitative specificity. Human practices are always situated and contextualized, but within underdetermined and open conditions (Cutchin 2008: 1561). This justifies a sharpened awareness to the experimental attitude. Further, the focus on action's real consequences connects to the general critique of the theory/practice distinction (Jensen 2004; Melles 2008a, 2008b) and inserts the issue of knowledge production into a practice understanding:

> There is no such thing as genuine knowledge and fruitful understanding except as the offspring of *doing*.... Men have to *do* something to the things when they wish to find out something; they have to alter conditions.
>
> (Dewey 1916: 275)

Further, the action-attuned understanding of knowledge and knowing connects to our discussion of designerly ways of thinking, upon which Dewey also had some clear opnions:

> The function of intelligence is therefore not that of copying the objects of the environment, but rather taking account of the way in which more effective and more profitable relations with these objects may be established in the future.
>
> (1931: 37)

In his presidential address to the American Philosophy Association in 1988, Richard J. Bernstein identified five themes defining the 'pragmatic ethos': anti-foundationalism as opposition to the idea that knowledge rests upon fixed foundations; fallibilism wherein there is no belief or thesis that is not open to further interpretation and criticism; the social character of the Self and the need to nurture a critical community of inquirers; the awareness and sensitivity to radical contingency and chance as hallmarks of social life; and plurality as a positive awareness of multiple traditions, perspectives and philiosophical orientations (1988: 7–10). The address was given to a collective of philosophical peers in the heyday of postmodern critique and thinking which led Bernstein to argue that:

> Philosophy has been decentered. There is no single paradigm, research program, or orientation that dominates philosophy. The fact is that our situation is pluralistic. But the question becomes how we are to *respond* to this plularism.
>
> (Ibid.: 17)

Not surprisingly, Bernstein leans on pragmatism as an answer to how to respond to the directionless and chaotic situation described, and with its open-minded and non-dogmatic unerpinning, we find this call of relevance even three decades later. Pragmatism may also be described as having the ambition to move beyond the Cartesian dichotomies such as mind/body, fact/value and theory/practice (Healey 2009: 279; Wood and Smith 2008). Pragmatism was heavily criticized by Bertrand Russel within philosophy itself, but also by geographers such as Andrew Sayer and Dick Peet. The problem, they seem to agree, was a relativistic and sloppy position (Barnes 2008: 1542, 1547). Here is one apt response by Latour:

> Those American philosophers [Dewey, James and Peirce] call their tradition pragmatism, meaning by this word not the cheap realism associated with being 'pragmatic', but the costly realism requested by making politics turn toward pragmata – the Greek name for 'Things'. Now that's realism!
>
> (2005b: 38)

Barnes's sympathetic account for what, if anything, geography may find in pragmatism suggests the humble and open-minded trial and error approach as a sobering vista. In particular, he concludes with a rephrasing of the famous Beckett quote that he sees emblematic of the pragmatic ethos: 'Try. Fail. Try harder. Fail better' (Barnes 2008: 1552). A very pertinent and expressive way of capturing the pragmatic ethos indeed! Pragmatism addresses a 'community of inquiry' where the solving of practical problems is seen as a communal and collective effort (Coaffee and Headlam 2008: 1588). This notion, taken from Dewey, touches upon the ideas of co-creation and collaboration that we have suggested for the second phase of mobilities design (the invitation to act). Moreover, the experimental attitude of classic pragmatism is inspirational for mobilities design, as:

> Experimentation, for both Dewey and James, was intimately associated with experience and the articulation of a more tolerant, democratic future which rested upon people being able to bring about change and make a difference in the world.
>
> (Allen 2008: 1620)

The attention to experimentation is seen as a legacy from Darwin by Hepple who argues that the 'founders of pragmatism were children of Darwinism, believing that experiment and experience could lead to social and intellectual progress' (Hepple 2008: 1532). Pragmatism is more of an ethos than a doctrine or a homogeneous school of thought (ibid.: 1531), and the open-minded position that led Russel and others to citicize the position heavily is precisely where we see its virtue. In accord with Dewey, we also see theories as 'tools' (Bacon 2012: 49), and agree with Bernstein's understanding of pragmatism as an 'engaged conversation' rather than a rigorous approach: 'I don't think of pragmatism as a set of doctrines or even as a method … it is an ongoing engaged conversation consisting of distinctive-sometimes competing-voices' (Bernstein 1988: 6). Bernstein might have taken his cue from Dewey here, when he also spoke of the 'pragmatic attitude' rather than a fixed doctrine:

> From a general point of view, the pragmatic attitude consists in looking away from first things, principles, 'categories', supposed necessities; and of looking towards last things, fruits, consequences, fact.
>
> (1931: 31)

This resonates with the way we think of mobilities design research generally, but also with the focus we devote to 'ordinary' things and mundane places. It is in accordance with a critical discussion of the world as deep and complex, and an analytical tendency to hail to the complex, abstract and deep, thus bypassing the insights harvested by understanding that the (social) world is as much about surfaces, signs and 'superficiality' (Dahl 2008). In this work, we have turned to pragmatism and NRT perspectives as two ways to rid the misunderstanding that the social world is comprehensible only through abstract categories and complex theories.

As we identified the importance of the embodied and multisensorial dimensions both within NRT and pragmatism above, we now turn to the notion of 'atmosphere' as a way of exploring this dimension. The invoking of multisensorial ambiances might not be thought of as relevant to public spaces and infrastructures, but only within the realm of art and aesthetics. However, as Böhme argues, the paradigm of the 'stage set' makes us see the staging of atmospheres not just with the realm of aesthetics but rather across vast dimensions and areas of society: 'the staging of politics, of sporting events, of cities, of commodities, of personalities, of ourselves' (Böhme 2013: 6). In accordance with earlier writings inspired by Goffman, the 'staging' of mobile situations is thus a very prevalent image to uphold (Jensen 2013). However, we would argue that it is not just an important analytical and theoretical dimension: the creation, manipulation or manufacturing of ambiances and atmospheres connects to the dimension of pragmatism that highlights the experimental and interventionist approaches. So we learn from the mobilities analysis to set the staging of mobilities at the centre, but also from the design approaches and interventions, which de facto are creating the experienced sites and situations through particular assemblages of technologies, materialities, mobilities and embodiments. The material world and the sites we inhabit are staged and prompted not just by objective material factors (surface material, measurable objects, quantifiable properties) but are equally informed by subjective sensorial engagements with sounds, visions, tactilities and interactions. The notion of 'atmosphere' as an intermediary concept, trying to capture what is between subjects and objects (Böhme 2013; Ingold 2015), may be one way of engaging with this complexity. The pragmatic understanding of experiences, experiments, and interventions through design is also an attempt to approach this complexity. Here the awareness of the importance of understanding the embodiment and multisensorial dimension of human experience was clearly articulated by James who argued that: 'A purely disembodied human emotion is an non-entity ... for us, emotion dissociated from all bodily feeling is inconceivable' (1884: 8). The notion of mobilities design is at this nexus and engages with the designerly ways of thinking as well as with the pragmatic experiences of inhabiting the world through embodiment. Here we see an interesting potential for including urban design, or in the words of Amin and Thrift:

> Policies for urban design could explore not only the joys and dangers associated with intermingling in the city's open spaces, but also how they might be designed as breathing spaces – places where people can remove themselves from the rush and noise, and slow down.
>
> (2002: 153)

Jensen has pointed at the connection between mobilities design and pragmatism elsewhere (Jensen 2014), and we need to continue exploring the philosophical underpinnings of this at a much higher level of detail and qualification. However, for the purpose of contextualizing the design experiments in this book, we hopefully have made our point for now. Thus, we want to end this chapter with a few concluding remarks and summarize the position advocated.

Towards a material pragmatism? Concluding remarks

This chapter proposed a way of thinking and engaging with the nexus of mobilities and design, of which the core perspective is 'material pragmatism'. As the point of departure, we may start by acknowledging that mobilities often take place in what some call 'non-places' and its 'more than' effects are often less visible. So the foregrounding of mundane and often morally stigmatized geographies and locations opens up to some of the insights presented here. Furthermore, the research into design and mobilities reveals a material pragmatism seeking to understand and provide languages for these mundane but important practices and their embedding into systems and sites, whose material properties are felt and sensed as much as they are comprehended and contemplated. To move towards a concept of material pragmatism means to connect the pragmatic and situational question *How are design decisions and interventions staging mobilities?* with another type of inquiry asking *What's the name of my mobility experience, what does it mean and how does it materialize?* To explore the meaning of everyday life mobilities and the importance of design decisions and interventions, across a wide set of professions that shape the situational conditions of billions of people in mundane settings, means to add a new sensitivity to situational, affective embodiments and the inhabited, perceived environment. It means to heighten one's awareness and sensitivity to the material surfaces, the tactile engagements with technologies, the spatial volumes shaped by architectural intervention, the sociotechnical geographies of complex networks, and so on. In seeing a new way of understanding this, we aim to articulate the analytical position of mobilities design, which is based upon a foundation of material pragmatism, connecting mobilities-turn concepts and theories with designerly ways of thinking. More precisely, how do the design field and the position of NRT and pragmatism show relevant overlappings and interfaces? We would argue that they do so within (at least) nine dimensions, which also are the defining features of material pragmatism:

1 Practice and 'pragma' as indicators of a focus on the actions taking place in the world.
2 The situational/*In Situ* awareness.
3 The creative and abductive potential of the *What if…?*
4 The focus on actual consequences.
5 Interest in 1:1 real-world experiments.
6 Focus on the multisensorial dimensions to a mobile inhabitation of the world.
7 Embodiment as the key to understanding mobile practices.
8 A focus on materialities as something concrete and non-abstract.
9 A modest ambition in terms of theories and explanations as something that does not 'represent'.

The list of these nine common grounds between mobilities design, pragmatism and NRT could be elaborated on extensively. However, we want to single out the third common ground for a little closer inspection. Posing, pondering and practising the *What if…?* question is one of the most important inquiries in mobilities design. This line of reflection evokes issues related to abduction, creativity and thought experiments – hallmarks of designerly ways of thinking that informs the emergent field of mobilities design, and a set of ideas deeply rooted within pragmatism. In order to scope the definition and identification of the research agenda of the emerging mobilities design field, we would point to an (open-ended) set of foci for studies: situated practices, doings, acts and interactions, objects, artefacts, systems, technologies, spaces, the intersections between human and non-human, sensed and embodied mobile practices (kinesis). We would see relevant methods and approaches to be these, among others: experimental, creative and performative, situated and empirical and, more generally, any approach that would be foregrounding the material to the textual. As should be clear from the discussion in this chapter, the epistemologies and frames of thinking range in the territory between pragmatism and the more-than-representational/non-representational.

It is from such a materially sensitive understanding and modest conceptualization that we want to scope the argument towards a discussion of how the designed artefacts are making themselves known in the world, so to speak. In the next chapter we will therefore explore the mobilizing of designed artefacts.

3 Mobilizing designed artefacts

Introduction

As argued in Chapter 1, there is a need to better understand the dynamic social, political and cultural entanglements of tangible mobilities sites, as well as to better work with their design potentials beyond affording utilitarian movement. Hannam *et al.* talk about 'moorings' (2006) and Adey calls them 'enablers' (2010): materialities that shape and facilitate our highly mobile lives and societies. The mobilities turn deals with how physical environments are not inert backdrops on which mobilities simply happen but performative material actors that co-orchestrate everyday life worlds. Likewise, urban design and architectural practice and research are associated with such performances, as a substantial part of acknowledging that materialities not only have certain looks, styles, shapes, symbolic meanings or uses but are also active mediators in how we inhabit the world. This counts, not least, for the fragmented, urban infrastructural landscapes, which will be our focus in the following chapters of this book.

In this chapter, we want to draw the attention to the repercussions of the non-representative and pragmatic understanding presented in Chapter 2, we also connect mobilities design to Actor-Network Theory. The situational perspective and the relational-processual understanding of mobile practices lead us to rethink the role of artefacts, materialities and agency. In this chapter therefore, we suggest to 'mobilize' designed artefacts. Our suggestion implies a move from what we could term a static, or 'sedentarist' (Cresswell 2006) thinking about materialities of mobilities, which is influential in, for example, transport planning (Urry 2007), where it has been suggested that design and architecture are too often thought of in sedentarist terms (see Adey 2010; Till 2009; Yaneva 2012). It is our observation that the design of materialities of mobilities tends to be a technical concern of organizing inert matter to facilitate efficient flows. Designed artefacts tend to be confined to fixed solidities, to 'static objects' in Euclidian space (see Latour and Yaneva 2009; Yaneva 2009a, 2012). Sedentarist thinking about mobilities artefacts and sites tends to reduce mobility, fluidity and contingency. Such rough reductions are widespread in architecture and design as a means of imposing 'architectural order' on a messy reality, and architectural scholar and practitioner Jeremy Till has therefore argued that, in architecture, there is a need to overcome the gap between thinkers and practitioners who would have the world be one of reason and order, and the way the world really is 'in all its contingency' (Till 2009: 48). This divide is arguably not confined to architecture or design; rather, it is present in the modern project as such (in all its strived-for order). Yet, indeed, it is observable when architects' drawings present a ruthless editing of contingency, trying 'to manipulate that world into (a semblance) of order' (ibid.: 37). It is important to acknowledge the great need in design to balance complexity and comprehensiveness of lived worlds with clarity and comprehension, simply in order to be able to approach concrete design tasks. A central aim of this book is, therefore, to work towards the articulation of mobilities design as an approach which can recognize mobility, contingency and relationality in design and design research.

Let us illustrate the point with a brief example. If we think about the design potentials of, for example, an ordinary site of mobilities, such as an asphalt parking lot, we are often occupied with its functional place in the 'chain-like' infrastructural system of the car. Infused with a sedentarist mindset, ideas of boundedness, authenticity and representation will have priority (see Cresswell 2004). A search for redesign potentials of that parking lot might then be initiated first by its functional efficiency, then by trying to fix its real meaning, to find the essence of its identity. The overflow of mobilities of that space will probably seem like a threat to such an essence. What are we to make of a space which is utterly mundane, where nobody stays, where the car rules and where asphalt and concrete dominate? We will perhaps denominate it as 'placeless' or as a 'non-place' to point to its perceived lack of authenticity and cultural and social value (Augé 1995; see also Arefi 1999). The following quote from geographer Edward Relph, who addresses the 'mass movement of people' as well as the deficient relationship between many mobilities sites and their surroundings ('the landscape'), makes this point vivid:

> Roads, railways, airports, cutting across or imposed on the landscape rather than developing with it, are not only features of placelessness in their own right, but, by making possible the mass movement of people with all their fashions and habits, have encouraged the spread of placelessness well beyond their immediate impacts.
>
> (Relph 1976: 90)

Though many fragmented mobilities sites exist and many parking lots do indeed appear dismal, we will oppose the notion that movement of people is a threat to the social and cultural value of a place, and that it necessarily devastates a place's identity. Mobilities research has to a great extent shown us that there is more to mobilities than the mere displacement from point A to B; that everyday mobilities are indeed culturally and socially productive in multiple ways, as well as being political, systemic, embodied, (un)sustainable, (in)equal, powerful, etc. Hence, even the most mundane mobilities artefacts, such as the parking-lot asphalt surface, are poorly addressed with the terminology of placelessness.

Accordingly, mobilities design is about more than minimum engineering standards and placelessness. It is about tangible materialities, such as asphalt, concrete and kerbstones; about flow efficiency and safety; but also about embodiment, atmosphere, public space, inequalities, sustainability and much more. However, design is still awaiting to fully embrace mobilities and move away from the inclination of imposing a too-reductive, strived-for order onto the artefacts of its focus. And mobilities is still awaiting to fully embrace design and make the most of the designerly devotion to question and innovate the networked performance of material artefacts. Here, we wish to contribute to conceptualizing solidly designed artefacts in mobile ways, in order to set out on a rewarding path to extending their capacities beyond minimum engineering standards. Designed artefacts of mobilities sites are always networked with people's mobilities and with many other dynamically assembled actors. Even the dullest asphalt surface is at any given time involved in complex human and non-human associations.

In this chapter, we shed light on a networked conception of mobilities design, and we engage with rethinking the role of artefacts, things and 'stuff' in order to lay down the conceptual understanding of the potential inherent in many mundane mobility spaces, for becoming much more in both political and cultural terms. The concluding section points these research-agenda issues towards the empirical investigations to follow in Chapters 5 to 7.

A conceptual move towards networked mobilities design

A main theoretical and methodological stream of mobilities design is to work with materialities of mobilities as networked and active hybrids. A mobilities site or artefact is tied into networks that stretch beyond it; it is by no means an isolated 'island' (Sheller and Urry 2006). This chapter begins with reiterating a few important sources of inspiration across mobilities and design research to clarify the conceptual move from transport thinking to a networked mobilities design conception. We then move on to argue that designed artefacts of mobilities should be researched in the midst of ongoing mobilities; that is, not as autonomous objects but as relational materialities embedded in cultural, political and social formations. The relational materiality concept of Actor-Network Theory proves accommodating in our goal to find a way to a nuanced and dynamic work with solid artefacts (see Fallan 2008); it supports this aim by addressing the active 'agency' of designed artefact in their 'complex entangled ecologies' (Yaneva 2012). Furthermore, we argue that a productive engagement with artefacts of mobilities is to target their performance in specific, situated alliances with people and other actors (artefacts may here both be 'things' and sites as a 'collection of things', such as a train station). Here the notion of 'affordance' (Gibson 1986) pushes us beyond the primacy of a static or symbolic essence of the artefact towards its instrumental 'doings'. It is in these doings that artefacts gain much of their significance. The last section of the chapter address how we 'mobilize' our concrete research of three sites of mobilities, which will be unfolded in the following chapters. We use a situational perspective to unravel designed artefacts in the midst of specific ongoing mobilities, spatial and temporal engagements, as well as providing the outset for design speculations. With this 'mobilization of designed artefacts', we hope to unfold some of the reach across multiple realms and layers of mundane materialities of mobilities.

Mobilities spaces need to meet more than minimum engineering standards. Their design could, for example, revolve around ideas of local commons; they could be approached as daily life environments inhabited by travellers who undertake journeys involving stories, identities, motives to travel, practices, meanings and experiences of participation, belonging, cooperation and involvement in the world. Vannini's non-representational research on ferry mobilities in Western Canada (2012) provides an important inspiration for this way of thinking. Drawing on anthropologist Tim Ingold's extensive reflections on entanglements of life (Ingold 2000, 2007, 2011), Vannini argues for a transformed view of ferry mobilities: from a transport model to meshwork assemblages. He analyses how the ferry routes of Canada's west coast tend to be thought about by decision-makers and the company that runs them. In this thinking, they are:

> Chain-like static geometric assemblages unconcerned with the local meanings of movement. 'Point-to-point connectors' (Ingold 2007: 75) of this kind are completed, fixed objects that neither grow nor develop in harmony with the places they link, and nor are they particularly responsive to local needs. They are assembly-chain-like in nature, based on principles of fragmentation, instrumental orientation and centralized planning.
>
> (2012: 135–6)

Referring to Ingold, Vannini writes about how this is a 'transport model' way of understanding the ferry system; both are critical of this way of thinking and question the model. Vannini's deep, mobile ethnographic inquiries into ferry travelling expand upon this point. They show that, unlike what the transport model suggests, there is indeed an immense weaving of local meanings of movement inherent in the instrumental means of getting from A to B. Vannini, like Ingold, suggests that instead of a transport model, there is, rather, a need for a 'wayfaring model' or a 'meshwork assemblage' that understands and meets the wayfaring ways of life of the people it serves. According to Vannini, such an alternative is possible, with the following characteristics:

> In contrast to an insensitive transport model such as the present one, one inspired by a meshwork assemblage would be unthinkable outside of the stories, identities and motives pulling and pushing people to move. A meshwork assemblage would be and should be respectful of coasters' and islanders' desire to be living in relatively self-sufficient places and still be free to move. Such an assemblage would be built on the basis of a profound understanding of their users' basic needs – rather than from the distant, centralized perspective of an ignorant corporation [the BC Ferries company].
>
> (Ibid.: 155)

Ingold's delicate argument of meshworks and assemblages is central here. It runs through his work of unpacking the 'line' as both a conceptual formulation and a host of mundane objects and doings, beyond its alleged 'single-track logic, of modern analytic thought' (Ingold 2000: 2). In this argument, he foregrounds the idea that:

> people inhabit a world that consists, in the first place, not of things but of lines. After all, what is a thing or indeed a person, if not a tying together of the lines – the paths of growth and movement – of all the many constituents gathered there?
>
> (Ibid.: 5)

He imagines lives themselves to be a 'manifold woven from the countless threads spun by beings of all sorts, both human and non-human, as they find their way through the tangle of relationships in which they are enmeshed' (ibid.: 3). Thus, life is lived along paths, not only in places, and should not be conceptually contained in enclosed entities. The concept of meshwork assemblage brings these ideas to the fore. Meshworks are 'interwoven trails … along which life is lived' (Ingold 2007: 81). Things, too, are web-like gatherings or compositions, i.e. 'assemblages', and the trails or lines of their continuous coming-into-being are foregrounded. Thus, meshworks are not entirely similar to the 'networks' of Actor-Network Theory (Ingold 2011: chapter 7), in that the lines or relations between points are privileged, as opposed to the nodal points or actors in the ANT perspective.

Meshwork assemblage can be understood in correlation with the processual and relational ontology of the city, argued for by Amin and Thrift (2002). This is a conception, they write, in which 'the city is made up of potential and actual entities/associations/togetherness which there is no going beyond to find anything "more real"' (ibid.: 27). It is an 'open' ontology that highlights the process and potential of the 'encounter' when networked entities come together: 'encounter, and the reaction to it, is a formative element in the world' (ibid.: 30). In this ontology, they argue, cities 'cannot be reduced to one. They are truly multiple. They exceed, always exceed' (ibid.). Through this idea, we can think about architectures not only as enduring materialities but also in terms of their variable entanglements. Architectures are what they 'do'; they are not solely inert matter, but embedded in relations and processes. They are part and parcel of the 'web of life', of the 'meshwork of entangled lines of life, growth and movement' (Ingold 2011: 63). As we read Amin and Thrift, the non-hierarchical understanding of lines of connectivity points to a meshwork understanding rather than a network understanding. This may also be said to be in congruence with the notion of 'rhizome', drawn from Deleuze and Guattari (1987/2003).

Coming back to Vannini's research on ferry travelling, he writes about his wished-for transition from the current transport model to a wayfaring-based meshwork assemblage. He writes about a transition to regard ferries as local commons, which are capable of meeting the long-term sustainability needs of islanders and coasters and of contributing to the local economy, instead of being detached in these senses from the places they connect. Vannini further explains his distinction between a transport model and a meshwork assemblage, referencing Ingold:

> 'Transport', Ingold writes, is characterised 'by the dissolution of the intimate bond that, in wayfaring, couples locomotion and perception' (Ingold 2007: 78). 'The transported traveler', he continues, 'becomes a passenger, who does not himself move but is rather moved from place to place'. Such is the organising model behind BCFS: a transport model which presupposes that the value of convenience lies in obliterating the seascapes it crosses – or at best in using them as visual backdrop for tourism promotion and in transforming the communities it links as spaces removed of their insular distinction. In contrast, a wayfaring-based mobility constellation or a meshwork assemblage would (re) center upon inhabiting place; that is, not upon 'taking one's place in a world that has been prepared in advance for the populations that arrive to reside there' (Ingold 2007: 81) but rather upon practices, meanings, and experiences of participation, belonging, cooperation, and involvement of the world's coming into being, without a final destination, through the interweaving of its paths and close-knit textures.
>
> (Vannini 2011: 156)

Vannini's remarks on a transformed view of the ferry mobilities inspire our mobilities design thinking. To think of mobilities spaces as functional only, facilitating instrumental transport from A to B, means – similar to Vannini's point – that their value lies only in determining functionalities and obliterating the distances they cross. When one is looking out for under-used potential, the transport understanding seems too constraining. Granted, we are painting a rather monochrome picture here as, for example, flight operators and highway designers are well aware that there is an experiential component to the trip. However, we are critical of the general tendency to either omit this dimension or to put it at the very bottom of the hierarchy of dimensions connected to mobilities. Rather, we want to engage with how mobilities spaces are composed by and entangled with lines of life, cultural and social formations. By understanding, organizing and designing mobilities from a transport model point of view alone, our capacity to engage with their materialities is highly limited and overlooks important effects, as well as design potentials. Vannini's argument of local commons, produced by entanglements of a richness of lives lived on the move, provides another form of awareness, an inspiration to reconsider design of mobilities spaces in and through their quality as networked dynamic materialities.

In architecture and design research, this specific approach can find some resonance. D'Hooghe, for example, writes about moving the conceptual understanding of infrastructures from technocratic systems to objects, from logics to artefacts, from tubes to spaces. He argues that:

> [I]nfrastructures of mobility are the prime candidates to become a public space, or, better yet, a public form that is true and proper to the exigencies and demands of modern society. Such an approach would privilege infrastructure by imposing on it all the demands that culture and the arts usually reserve for themselves but rarely apply to the technocracy that structures the very society in which they operate.
>
> (2010: 78)

This is in parallel with our earlier ideas for 're-politicizing the armatures' of the city (Jensen 2013). The infrastructural landscapes must be understood as sites of interactions between socially hetereogeneous groups and thus actually a vital part of the public spaces of the city. Instead of thinking about spaces of political voice and articulations as plazas and agoras only (the classical model of urban public spheres), the infrastructures are potentially the new 'mobile agoras' of the city. When 'infrastructure-as-technocratic-system' is localized and objectified, the singularity of transportation as the primary function of the object is downplayed, and we can regard it in plural terms as, for example, 'civic space' (not solely 'zone of speed'), as 'transversal connections' (not solely 'linear') and as 'multiple flows' (not solely one) (D'Hooghe 2010). Indeed, Stoll and Lloyd, editors of *Infrastructure as Architecture* (2010) in which D'Hooghe's essay appears, emphasize that the form and performance of infrastructures need renegotiation. This is not a matter of style, shape, meaning or symbol, they find, but about instrumentality and performance in relation to use.

While this aspiration is convincing to us, and we urge an acute awareness of the user-performance of designed artefacts, we also find it essential to explore the forces which intersect in the hybrid sociotechnical network of a designed-artefact range, from the real to the metaphorical, from the natural to the political (Till 2009). The artefacts of mobilities design are widely entangled with economics, power and politics. Often, as we will demonstrate in Chapters 5 through 7 of this book, large societal issues are indeed persistent when we begin unpacking the networked performance and instrumentality of even small and mundane instances of mobilities design.

Architect Stan Allen has articulated a field of 'Infrastructure Urbanism' (1999, 2010; see also Stoll and Lloyd 2010), from which we can learn much about mobilizing designed artefacts. Allen argues an understanding of architecture as a '*material* practice – as an activity that works in and among the world of things, and not exclusively with meaning and image' (1999: 52). He thus proposes to move away from architecture's representational, static imperative. Allen, who is an important scholar in Landscape Urbanism and Landscape Urbanistic streams of work, redirects 'reifying trends of some architects' into a kind of relational thinking, targeting 'the conditions of production in the public sphere' (Marot 1999: 52). In connection with 'working' (i.e. active) landscapes (Høyer 1999), the processes and relations of spaces, objects, events and people are recognized, sought and unfolded:

> Here, the term landscape no longer refers to prospects of pastoral innocence but rather invokes the functioning matrix of connective tissue that organizes not only objects and spaces but also the dynamic processes and events that move through them. This is landscape as active surface, structuring the conditions for new relationships and interactions among the things it supports.
>
> (Wall 1999: 233)

Consistent with these streams of work, we propose mobilities design to move beyond portraying designed artefacts as autonomous objects. What we need in mobilities design is to explore how the solid designed artefact in fact is a reflection of mobilities, relationality and process (see also Fallan 2008; Law 2004). Apart from the sources referred to above, a valuable point of departure for this move is Actor-Network Theory. In the next section, we consider how ANT can provide us with a useful perspective in mobilities design. In particular, the attention to agency of non-human actors can prove helpful in operationalizing the networked mobilities design.

Agency of artefacts

Fallan argues that ANT can be a rewarding perspective for illuminating the complexity of 'architecture in action'. ANT is relevant to architecture, and to mobilities design, because its insistence on non-human actors unfolds a networked understanding of the artefact as well as the design activity; it shows 'the assertion that it doesn't make sense to consider a technological artefact as autonomous. Not only is its meaning constructed in a sociotechnical network; the artefact itself is constructed in a sociotechnical network' (2008: 87). The action and complexity which Fallen adresses do not only exist in the controversies of, for example, the production and mediation of architecture (see Yaneva 2012) but also in the many commonplace situations and everyday experiences of any designed artefact, as we will return to below.

'Architecture in action' has two overall phases, according to Fallan: planning, design and construction, and use and mediation. In both these phases it is characteristic for architecture to be entangled with a host of concerns and actors, beyond the object and the architect, even though, as Fallan states, there is a tendency to portray architecture as 'an autonomous *objet d'art* and eulogize the architect as *author*' (2008: 91). Indeed, as Latour posits in the following, it is in fact familiar in architecture to speak of the many human and non-human forces which co-create the artefact, though this tends to happen in vague terms:

> Even if some architects see themselves as God, none would be foolish enough to believe they create *ex nihilo*. On the contrary, architects' stories of their own achievements are full of little words to explain how they are 'led to' a solution, 'constrained' by other buildings, 'limited' by other interests, 'guided by the inner logic of the material', 'forced to obey' the necessity of the place, 'influenced' by the choices of their colleagues, 'held up'

> by the state of the art, and so on [...]. If we become attentive to humbler ways of speaking, this agency shifts from the all powerful master to the many 'things', 'agents', 'actants' *with which* they have to share action.
>
> (2003: 30)

Our point is that it is not unknown for architectural thinking to consider the designed artefact as a network – as 'an effect of its relations with other entities' (Law 2002: 93). Actually, it is an integrated part of architecture, and of architectural tradition, to regard not only the symbolic or stylistic characters that physical spaces, buildings, forms and materials can have but also the capacities for performance: experiences and activities which they invite or impede (see Doucet and Cupers 2009; Fallan 2008). It is this devotion to concrete materialities which we claim is productive to mobilities research. And ANT is a highly applicable common ground to build on, when it concerns the performance of architecture in use. It explicitly draws our attention to what designed artefacts *do* in networked relations with other things and people. In other words it concerns the *agency* of the artefact (see Fallan 2008; Yaneva 2009a and 2012). In ANT terms, the agency of designed artefacts is derived from the conceptualization of a radical symmetry of human and non-human entities, recognizing not only humans but also things as active actors in dynamically assembled networks:

> [*A*]*nything* that does modify a state of affairs by making a difference is an actor [...]. Thus, the question to ask about any agent is simply the following: Does it make a difference in the course of some other agent's action or not?
>
> (Latour 2005a: 71)

Though the notion of agency may evoke a certain mysticism, as if designed artefacts were equipped with immaculate intentionality (and instances of that exist in architecture, Fallan 2008), the productive understanding we wish to bring forth here is that artefacts are enacted and made to act in specific alliances with other actors. One way to understand this is to approach the ways in which the agency of humans is coupled with that of non-human objects. Indeed, Urry states that objects appear:

> to be crucially part of how humans effect agency. Agency is to be seen as an accomplishment and this is brought about through various objects, such as desks, papers, computer systems, aircraft seats and so on. This agency is achieved in the forming and reforming of chains or networks of humans and non-humans. The human and the material intersect in various combinations and networks, which in turn vary greatly in their degree of stabilisation over time.
>
> (2000: 78)

In other words, as Bender has argued, ANT has a capacity for connecting humans and non-humans in design and architecture, the solid designed artefact with 'the human life it supports' (2010: 313). Our interest in the agency of designed artefacts, however, must not background the fact that the artefact cannot determine what the human actor can do and experience; as Jacobs and Merriman remind us, 'architecture is one of the many "envelopes" within which human activity proceeds' (2011: 213), thus highlighting the complex, networked and contingent entanglement of the designed artefact. In other words, it is in the assemblages of material spaces, infrastructural technologies and human bodies that the agency of artefacts materializes.

Following these points, mobilities design is a suggestion for studying materialities of mobilities spaces through their networked relations. Though we broaden the object of study from what could be received as a narrow conception of architecture to designed artefacts of mobilities at large, we correspond with the statement: 'to study the stable architectural object (architecture-as-noun) is the effect of various doings (architecture-as-verb)' (ibid.: 212). In the next section, we will move closer to one way of studying these doings. We return to Allen who, in his efforts to address infrastructure as urbanism, moves away from the autonomous artefact as such and directs the concern towards its instrumentality. Instrumentality, he argues, should regain our attention, because it is 'the site of architecture's contact with the complexity of the real' (1999: 52).

The 'politics of stuff' – materialities and the social

There is an important academic debate on the status of objects, artefacts, and 'stuff' that we cannot do justice to here. (For example, see Bogost 2012 for an advocacy for the so-called 'object-oriented-ontology' and Ingold 2015 for a critique thereof.) Elsewhere, we have argued for a new attention to materialities and 'stuff' as a strategy for connecting the agency of artefacts and the potential of mobility spaces and infrastructure. We may start to think about a 'politics of stuff' as a way of verbalizing such a strategy:

> It is precisely the qualitative, pragmatic and situational properties of things and objects rather than some abstract notion of the material that should be our concern. I am thinking of 'stuff' and how it shapes situational mobilities. So I propose that we need a new mobilities analysis of the design and politics of 'stuff', as well as the embodied and interactional dynamics of mobile humans and 'stuff'.
>
> (Jensen 2014: 239)

As Latour argues (2005b), there is a vital link between 'the political' and 'the material' in the sense that the 'atmospheres of democracy' has to do with much more than abstract political principles and ideas. The political is, as in any other practice, connected to the things and materialities that conditions the bringing together of people, ideas and deliberations. Not only should 'things' be treated as elements of practice (Shove *et al.* 2012: 23) but they should also be recognized for the fact that they are enrolled into complex assemblages of practices and spaces. As Latour points to, 'things' are not simply isolated 'objects' but rather artefacts that connect and afford actions in the world (2005b).

This line of thinking invites us to think about, for example, industrial 'products' in terms of verbs rather than nouns (Shove *et al.* 2007: 134). There is, in other words, a strong link to the process-thinking explored in Chapter 2, as well as to the situational focus of analysis. 'Things' and artefacts are brought together with bodies and cultures in mobile situations. As the mundane sites of mobile practices increasingly are areas of interaction and intermingling, they are also potential sites of political voice and articulation. As Hajer and Reijndorp rightly point out, the contemporary city's complex material landscapes contain 'in-between spaces' that may function as 'public domain' (2001). Besides the fact that these sites may be inconspicuous and lacking the symbolic glory of the mainstream political instutitions and assemblages (for example parliament buildings or public plazas), they are the de facto sites of hetereogenous social interaction. The politics of stuff needs to engage with this new reality, which also implicates that we are not looking at one homogeneous public sphere (Habermas 1961) but rather at a set of heterogeneous and diverse publics (Fraser 1990). We can connect this to the situational and pragmatic focus of studying what enables this situation and establish an understanding of how the artefacts, spaces, and materials (or 'stuff') are immanently connected to the horizons of possibility and practices, but also to the social and cultural differentiations taking place beyond the notion of a unified public. This argument resonates well with Clark who argues (with a reference to Dewey's idea that there is no homogeneous 'Public' but rather multiple heterogeneous publics) that design activities have the potential to generate publics (2013: 199). Rather than thinking about abstract people forming an abstract public, pragmatic and situated design analysis should focus on the lived experiences and practices of people.

Seeking out the potientials of a politics of stuff, we have taken some inspiration in the work of Bennett, who aticulates her main philosophical project as: 'to think slowly an idea that runs fast through modern heads: the idea of matter as passive stuff, as raw, brute, or inert' (Bennett 2010: vii). In other words, 'the fixed and the solid' is only fixed and solid in an abstract sense. Even the inert and passive 'stuff' has temporalities and dynamics to them, from the molecular scale up to the global. We take the point from Bennett that 'matter' is far from passive. This, indeed, is in accord with Ingold's call for thinking about materials rather than material, and about 'things' rather than 'objects' (2011). But it also touches upon Latour's attempts to revalorize the importance of non-human actants, technologies, and artefacts (Latour 2005b). But most importantly, the politics of stuff leads us to recognize potentials in spaces and places of less public esteem and to see these as potential political spaces. In the floating agoras of the contemporary city, identities are being shaped and opinions are being formed. In this way, our interest in what enables the mobile situations connects to a much wider philosophical enquiry and critique. On the surface, this is about understanding that 'stuff' is more than a passive substratum to human life. But the understanding reaches deeper into the recognition of matter and stuff as vital parts of human-non-human assemblages or new ecologies of practices. Bennett speaks of 'thing-power' as a way of entering the complex relationship between humans and 'stuff':

> Thing-power gestures towards the strange ability of ordinary, man-made items to exceed their status as objects and manifest traces of independence or aliveness, constituting the outside of our own experiences.
>
> (2010: xvi)

We want to encourge a reinterpretation of 'well-known' mobilities based on a new understanding of things, materialities, and publics which connects well to Gatt and Ingold's idea of an 'education of attention' through design (Gatt and Ingold 2013: 147). Likewise, Walker argues convincingly that the role of speculative design is not to provide 'viable solutions' but rather to probe and challenge our assumptions (2011: 130). This we see as a rather accurate description of the ambition connected to 'learning to see' the mundane world in a new light. Furthermore, if we are to learn to see differently through design, this also means that we may rethink the role between research for design, research into design, and research through design (Simonsen *et al.* 2010: 3). In our current work we are dealing with all three dimensions, and we see the theoretically informed 'new gazes' and the design exercises and explorations in this book as cutting across the research for, in and through design.

Mobility affordances of designed artefacts

While travelling, we sense the world: 'Movement often involves an embodied experience of the material and sociable modes of dwelling-in-motion' (Urry 2007: 11). We encounter designed artefacts of mobilities spaces, structures and systems along our various journeys, composed by different speeds, rhythms, durations, socialities, bodily experiences, etc. The traveller's journeys are mediated in different ways. When, for example, a traveller moves by bike through a tunnel, a mobile hybrid is composed, enabling the passage: a 'traveller-tunnel-bike' hybrid (see ibid.: 78). The mobile situation of travelling through a tunnel can thus be regarded as co-agency, effected by and through the relations between the traveller, the tunnel, the bike and other actors. In this co-agency, designed artefacts have the capacity to facilitate and speed up the circulation of people, or to slow down or stop it. They can enable and disable various types of inhabitation or dwelling-in-motion (Urry 2007).They can, for example, invite passage for (specified types of) travellers, sensorial experiences, meetings and exchanges, the use of certain modes of traffic, etc. or they can (purposely) fail to do so.

In this section we will move closer to an operational take on mobilities design. We will return to the concept of 'affordances', which we introduced in Chapter 1, as this is an important tool of mobilities design. As we have argued elsewhere (Jensen *et al.* 2016), the notion of affordance carries a strong material focus that allows us to bring to the foreground the active role of artefacts in mobile situations. Furthermore, affordance hones our attention to the dynamic physical and affective interplay and the interface between artefacts and their users. And in so doing, the concept of affordance allows us to become attuned to the performativity of materialities of mobilities – what they *offer* and what they *do.* Recalling Allen's point (1999), we thus address mobilities design as a *material practice* which works in the midst of ongoing mobilities. It accompanies the small material-performative details, in order to study the instrumental 'doings' of designed artefacts of mobilities, in relation to daily life mobilities. Hence, as a material practice, mobilities design is 'less concerned with what things look like and more concerned with what they can do' (ibid.: 53).

In the ANT-related focus on the agency of artefacts, it is assumed that designed objects can 'trigger' actions (Latour and Yaneva 2008; Yaneva 2009a). Yaneva highlights Gibson's notion of 'affordance' (1986), paying close attention to 'how design shapes, conditions, facilitates and makes possible everyday life sociality' (Yaneva 2009a: 280). The agency of designed artefacts comes forth in the complex and dynamic mobile situations, in which we can regard the artefact as a 'type of connector' that mediates our being in the world (Yaneva 2009a). Yaneva provides us with an example from her daily staircase climb to the university auditorium:

> The different qualities of the handrail afford particular actions. In its smoothness and warmth, the rail's wooden surface contributes to the easier gripping actions of my hand as I go up. Its wide and inviting surface makes me lean upon it in conversation with colleagues during an on-stair encounter. The narrow stairs make it impossible to ignore others whom I might meet occasionally. The stairs' design triggers spontaneous face-to-face conversations, making us extend the auditorium discussions in other university spaces.... Meeting and chatting on the staircases, I find myself involved in relationships mediated by the particular design of the building, the staircase and the numerous artifacts that facilitate my morning trajectory, making my arrival pleasurable.
>
> (Ibid.: 275)

Here, the mundane architectural artefacts of the staircase work as resources for action and bodily sensorial experience. They invite, oblige and impede practices. Designed artefacts push us through space; they invite us to linger; they embrace us in tiny rooms; they carry our weight. However, their affordances are not determinate prescriptions of behaviour; rather, they are suggestive propensities, which we might or might not actualize as intended (Farías 2010d: 297).

Based upon this, we can see that the notion of affordances allows us to move beyond solely thinking of the physical properties of architectural artefacts and what they might permit or prescribe in an isolated manner, and instead to focus on the assembling of heterogeneous actors that, when brought together in mobile situations, might actualize certain affordances for action and experience. However there has, as Norman rightly argues, been as misunderstanding by some in the direction that affordances was to be seen as the property of a thing or an artefact. This is unhelpful and inaccurate since 'affordance is not a property. An affordance is a relationship' (2013: 11). We agree, and this resonates with our attempt to wed the idea of affordance to an actor-network inspired approach that allows us to conceptualize affordances as effects of socio-material assemblages. This analytical move directs our attention towards the situational specificity of alliances between non-human and human actors. One of the contributions of the later developments of ANT (or post-ANT: see Anderson and Harrison 2010: 15; see also Gad and Jensen 2007; Ingold 2011) is to emphasize such specificity and situatedness of relations in various contingent assemblages. Hence, the affordances of a designed artefact are best understood as a relational quality that comes to life in concrete assemblages with other objects, spaces, people, weather, etc. Ingold explains this agency as 'a hive of activity' (2011: 17) rather than as an abstract potential 'inside closed-up objects' (ibid.: 16). Like Shields, Ingold emphasizes materials as key for the doings of designed artefacts. He encourages the study of qualities of materials: how we sense them, use them and transform them, and also how they change – through wear and tear, for example. Such emphasis on concrete material qualities are indeed in the heart of architectural practical thinking, as confirmed by Fallan: '[M]ateriality and the properties of materials have a very prominent presence in architecture' (2008: 92). A wooden surface, for example, would often be considered for its tactile quality of softness and warmth. It can be used and formed in design to invite us to touch it, to take our shoes off or to sit down. The tree would often be worked with through its play of light and shadow and its leafy smell. The asphalt *is* its smoothness. The enclosed hard-walled space *is* its reverberation. Hence, when we consider what designed artefacts offer to daily life mobilities – if the asphalt enables, disables, encourages, discourages, invites or inclines certain journeys, activities and experiences – the very quality of the materials should not be underestimated.

Affordances of artefacts sets the ongoing lived world in the centre of mobilities design. It forces us to push our study of these materialities beyond their visual, formal and symbolic qualities and towards their doings in hybrid sociotechnical networks.

Conclusion

This chapter has proposed to 'mobilize' the designed artefacts of mobilities sites. This proposal brings forth at least three suggestions. First, a relational and mobile way of thinking about and working with mobilities design is necessary in order to embrace its significance and potential. Designed artefacts should be moved from their isolation as autonomous objets d'art or as utilitarian-only technocratic systems (D'Hooghe 2010) to their entanglement in hybrid sociotechnical networks, which reach across multiple realms. Networks of artefacts extend from the very near to the very far, from the traveller's daily life mobile encounter with an ordinary parking-lot surface to major societal issues of power and sustainability. Second and following this, a 'mobilized' designed artefact is fruitfully researched in the midst of ongoing mobilities, mundane and unnoticed as they may be. Mobilities research has provided us with rich knowledge of manifold aspects of these mobilities. Such knowledge is essential for mobilities design, which addresses the interaction between artefacts and sites and these multiple mobilities. Third, mobilities design begins 'in situ'. Here, in specific situations, people and things interact, forces intersect and central issues of mobilities become concentrated. Mobilities design as a research field thus focuses on the actual situation, the pragmatic question of what affords this situation, as well as the process-oriented approach to materialities, which opens up to a radical re-reading of its potential in re-articulating the politics of stuff. Here we are indeed close to the position of Anderson and Wylie when they argue for a new material sensitivity:

> Textures and densities, liquidities and radiances, thus act as sets of imperatives within and through which movement and sensation are inspired and performed ... materiality, in this reading, is multiple: the term connotes forces and processes that exceed any one state (solid, liquid, gas), and are defined ultimately in terms of movement and processes rather than stasis.
>
> (2009: 326)

Such new sensitivity to artefacts, bodies and movement is inherent in the research design we have established for this work. We have put forward the underpinning theoretical and conceptual framing of this work in Chapters 1 through 3. As should be clear, we have taken on the assignment of connecting the realm of designerly ways of thinking and doing with the realm of mobilities analysis. This may be done in many different ways, but in this particular work we have used the situational approach to mobilities as our main framework. This has a number of repercussions. First, the material dimension becomes very vivid as we explore the nexus of artefacts, movement and people. Second, this has to be done through a relational understanding that reaches from sites and spaces over artefacts and technologies to social interaction and embodied practices. The third important repercussion is that we cannot analyse and comprehend the situational mobilities with the concepts and vocabulary of the mobilities turn alone. We need the language of architecture and design to probe deeper into the materialities of mobilities. The fourth point derived from this is that we are not just analysing and interpreting situational mobilities. A key ambition is to engage and intervene with concrete cases of mobilities design. Thus the double strategy of learning to see/invitation to act.

The next chapter connects the theoretical and conceptual part of the book with the empirical explorations in the chapters that follow; we will describe and discuss the empirical research methods and the site of the empirical investigations and field studies in more detail.

4 Methods in mobilities design

Introduction

The research and practice field of mobilities design calls for methods, which can capture its socio-material hybridity, its dynamics (movement) and its designerly disposition towards intervention and change. In this chapter, we discuss urban mobilities design methods in the light of these requirements. We set out with an outline of what we regard a productive interplay between 'mobile methods' (Büscher *et al.* 2011b; Fincham *et al.* 2010) and (urban) design methods. As we explore this nexus between mobilities and design, we embrace the material dimensions of design (i.e. materials, surfaces, volumes, spaces, and so on) as well as the methods and creative approaches (related to what we have termed 'designerly ways of thinking'; see Chapter 1).

In the mobilities literature, there has been some debate as to what precisely to include under the heading of 'mobile methods' (Büscher *et al.* 2011b). Are the methods applied within mobilities research of a specific nature and unique to this field of study, or rather are we looking at any relevant method that suggests itself as pragmatically useful for the study of mobilities? Here we follow Jensen (2015: 16) and lean on the latter position and argue for a pragmatic identification of what may be useful methods in the exploration of mobile phenomena. We turn to the situational perspective on mobilities studies and zoom in on the dynamic, fluctuating and processual practices of everyday life mobilities. At the same time, we are exploring the field of socio-material hybridity, in which there are important and new insights to be gained when we start to probe deeper into the relations between (embodied) mobilities and material spaces and artefacts. Furthermore, we apply the methods chosen to everyday life situations. The situational perspective is of particular relevance to mobilities and urban design, which Paans and Pasel assert in their hands-on designerly articulation of a 'situational urbanism':

> The term 'situation' defines **a recurring set of relations which connects scales.** It moves away from hierarchical distinctions, and exerts its influence on the block level, the entrance level, the pedestrian level, the balcony level, the street corner level ... Situational Urbanism is the method of connecting

> the potentials and weaknesses of each situation with possibilities that present themselves. We aim to change daily routines and habits by intervening at certain points in the architecture. Precision is key here – each situation should be thoroughly studied and different scenarios should be formulated.
>
> (2014: 138)

In practical terms, our work has employed a methodological pluralism, including ethnographic field studies, qualitative research interviews, film-elicitation, go-along interviews, urban design mappings and document analysis. These have all been chosen not because they are mobile methods but because they are pragmatic tools giving us the opportunity to explore and analyse the empirical cases. Being inspired not only by pragmatism but also by non-representational approaches to social and material phenomena, we have put together a methodological portfolio that aims to research mobilities design with precision at the same time as keeping an open horizon towards the unexpected.

This chapter is structured by six sections. After the introduction, we move on to delineating important methodological attentions in the crossfield between urban design and mobilities, focusing on research into 'mobilized' materialities (see Chapter 3) through situated analysis and design speculations. We then introduce the specific suburban area where our study was carried out; we also motivate the selection and customization of the specific methods of the study. In the fourth and fifth sections, we elaborate and reflect upon the methods used to research what urban artefacts *do* in mobile situations, and what they *could* do in mobile situations. We conclude with mobilities design's orientation towards approaches, mindsets and designerly ways of thinking, in which an openness to the mobile, fluid, processual field is crucial, as is an explorative and playful attitude to experiments as a key identifier.

Methodological attentions – between urban design and mobilities

We agree with Büscher *et al.* in their identification of 'mobile methods' as largely focusing on researching the 'the fleeting, distributed, multiple, non-causal, sensory, emotional and kinaesthetic' (2011a: 1). The mobilities turn generates an emerging methodological landscape, in which researchers seek ways to move with the phenomena of mobilities (as well as immobilites) and to allow themselves and readers to be moved by these studies. In other words, the various methods spur a transformative feel that pushes the student of mobilities towards new explorations and experimentation.

An array of methods are being employed and customized to capture mobile phenomena. Büscher *et al.* list the following clusters of mobile methods (2011a: 8–13): 'observing' movements, 'participating' in movements, mobile video ethnography, time–space diaries, explorations of virtual mobility, imaginations of alternative mobile futures by art and design experimentations, mobile positioning methods, capturing 'atmosphere', studying the active development and performance of 'memory', researching dynamics of places, examining conversations and researching activities and places *en route*. In our work to connect mobilities research to urban design, we put particular emphasis on the embodiment of mobilities and methods, which will help us make noticeable the less tangible aspects of daily mobilities. Moreover, we seek to move beyond mere representation, as the analysis of mobilities is coupled with discussions of potential interventions. In accordance with the designerly ways of thinking, we keep an experimental attitude to the unfolding of potentials for change as we probe deeper into each site and case.

As introduced in Chapter 1, our focus in this book is on articulating mobilities design, with urban design as a particular focus. Urban design is here understood as a practical endeavour of intervention that addresses situated design problems. The scope of urban design is primarily to evoke potentials, to create something new. This includes the very practical and mundane ordering and design of well-functioning urban spaces. So it is important to appreciate that urban design is a combination of knowledge forms and technical skills, as well as having normative underpinnings in relation to actions and experiences enabled or prevented by the choices and interventions made within the realm of urban design. The discipline of urban design is entangled with many other disciplines (Krieger 2009), and likewise it includes a wide variety of ideas about how to deal with the processes of shaping urban environments, with varying emphasis on social, visual, spatial, economic, ecological and political aspects of urban design (see also Tietjen 2011). While aesthetic and technical approaches which see urban design as a purely professional activity are well-established, more responsive and participatory approaches exist which link design objectives with the needs and wishes of users and with the barriers they experience. These approaches constitute a challenge to the distribution of power in the processes of urban design, with more demand added to the direct involvement between users, stakeholders, professional designers and authorities than other established ways of doing urban design can offer (Architecture for Humanity 2006; Oliver *et al.* 2011; Steinø 2005).

An example of the methodological tension between aesthetic, technical and purely professional approaches and more immersed approaches can be seen in the processes of mapping in urban design. While mapping is often a cartographic practice (see Abrams and Hall 2006; Dodge *et al.* 2011) with a strong representational scope, in urban design mapping is also used as a highly creative and evocative operation (Corner 1999b). Urban design mappings are parallel to non-representational approaches, indicating that simply depicting the world is a too-simple conception. Representations such as cartographic maps are sometimes criticized for being a modernistic abstraction that deliberately excludes a multitude of aspects, in that they 'reduce the complex multi-sensuous experience to visually encoded features and then organise and synthesise these into a meaningful whole' (Urry 2000: 88). In urban design and architecture, site mapping can similarly be seen as a methodological and epistemological move to allow the designer to act and intervene in messy and uncertain site conditions. However, the analytical moves in architecture towards abstract order and simplification has a tendency not to be made explicit and reflected upon, thus not providing an explicit modelling method, but rather showing an inclination to conflate what we can know through such tools and concepts with how a site is and works in all its complex doings (Till 2009). Aesthetic and technical approaches to urban design give priority to the object, the master plan, or the function, and in some cases tend to regard sites 'as blank surfaces on which to organize urban functions in efficient and often standardised ways' and reduce 'the innate richness and history of sites … into diagrammatic map-forms' (Marot 1999: 47). Such critique and an exploration of other means of mapping and representation are widely acknowledged in architecture and urban design, where steps have long been taken towards supplementing the abstract representations in maps and architectural drawings with more responsive and inclusive imaging procedures, such as narrative texts, films and photomontages. This bears a resemblance to the declared need of mobile methods to contribute to methodological alternatives: there is a temptation in much of the existing work to restrain and make static the mobile phenomena they seek to understand.

Urban design is more than attention to spaces and materials. The situational experiences of users and mobile subjects are central, hence our attention to actual situations. The more complex, multisensorial and situated experience of cities was in focus with, for example, the French 'Situationists' in the 1950s and 60s who developed the method of '*dérive*' (Corner 1999c; see also Bunschoten *et al.* 2001 for another approach to an explorative study of the city). A *dérive* is a drifting, with an openness to distraction. The Situationists drifted around in the city, following their intuition in their creation of psychogeographic maps that foregrounded new, alternative visions of spaces and relations. Their approach decidedly acknowledged chance and a subjective perspective on field work, and their outcomes were thus closely interrelated with each researcher's attitude and sensitivity towards the city. The advantage was the possibility for daily life and potentially unexplored dimensions of the field to surface. The Situationist ambition was to compete with – and even destabilize – the dominant and established readings of the city and provide the grounds for a '*détournement*', or reversal, of the existing situation. The method therefore replenished a methodological preference for representation with evocation and imagination of alternatives.

Such considerations are also present in ANT studies. In her ANT studies of architecture, Yaneva asserts a concern towards an irreductivist and lively alternative for mapping in relation to architecture. She argues for a shift in inquiries from 'the regime of explanation/causation to the regime of "presentational immediacy"' (2012: 106), and asks:

> How can we collect, familiarize and draw together the practices and objects that make a cosmos visible? How can we draw a 'thick' description of a building to give justice to it as a cosmic 'thing'? How can we visualize not

> what a building is and what it means but what it does and what worlds it is able to enact?
>
> (Ibid.: 67)

The ideas we have outlined here go towards mobilities, embodiment, situations, artefacts' agency and the evocation of alternatives. Against this background, mobilities design methods are not so much about 'freezing' mobile, relational, contingent conditions of mobilities spaces as it is about engaging methodologically, 'with less control' and more experimentation with tendencies and potentialities of specific socio-material situations (see Thrift, in Farías 2010b). We engage in designerly ways of thinking and urban design approaches, with an open mind in an ongoing search for new insights and experiments of new methods. If there were a hallmark characteristic of mobilities design, we would describe it thus: an open attitude towards the complex relationships between materialities, sites, movement, practices and multisensorial experiences. In the rest of this chapter, we will delineate the methods used in the empirical studies of actual mobilities designs. Key to the method assemblage is the aim to research mobilized artefacts through situated analysis and design speculations.

The empirical studies of this book

The following three chapters of this book are centred around three sites in Aalborg East, Denmark. We unfold how mobilities are materialized at these sites, and we unravel how mobilized, designed artefacts work and what they do in the midst of their spatial and temporal engagements (see Chapter 3). The sites are indeed ordinary instances of design for mobilities: a pedestrian and cyclist tunnel, facilitating the segregation of smooth, fast – and dangerous – automobilities from the slow and vulnerable velomobilities and pedestrians; an asphalt parking lot in front of a grocery store; and an informal road crossing, where mobilities intersect in spite of the planning desires to keep them apart.

Aalborg East is a suburban district. The planning of the district, then a modern, new, industrial and residential town, was initiated in the middle of the last century as a means to accommodate the growing population and industrial activities of the city of Aalborg (Rohbrandt 1948). Aalborg East is, as was briefly explained in Chapter 1, built on rational ideals of town and road planning, rooted in the concept of the functional city, as proposed by the CIAM organization and congress in 1933. The zoned and segregated organization of urban functions is a main principle to this method of planning. Four urban functions constitute the components of the city: dwelling, work, leisure, and transport (Krieger 2009; Mumford 2000). Functional planning for transport foregrounds road safety and efficient traffic flow in the organization and design of urban areas. This ideal took an extensive form in the Swedish SCAFT guidelines of 1968, explicating the road-planning principles of Denmark, Holland, and Sweden at that time (Harder 2003). The SCAFT guidelines encompass four central planning recommendations (Hagson 2000):

1 Localization of industries and service facilities, in relation to access via primary traffic connections (easy access to Benefits community facilities);
2 Segregation of motorized traffic from pedestrians and bicyclists in different systems that do not intersect;
3 Differentiation of traffic means and speed within each traffic system; and
4 Clarity, simplicity and uniformity in the design of the traffic environment.

These principles were developed to handle the increasing automobility in urban areas, organizing and facilitating traffic flow with a minimum of conflict and disorder. Within this way of planning and designing the physical world, private motoring has been the central approach to mobility in the city. The widespread system of automobility has initiated and reproduced spaces that were not of any relevance, or even an option, before the advent of the car (Urry 2007). Large urban areas have been built or rebuilt within this functionalist planning agenda. These are carefully organized to accommodate and control the predominance of automobility over other forms of mobility, which can appear as obstacles to seamless travel by car.

The study site is a vivid material manifestation of these principles. Local service facilities are located around the traffic junction with easy access from both traffic systems. In addition, forms, spaces and materials are kept simple and uniform in expression, following the generic design code of SCAFT. The motive behind the simple and uniform design is safety: travellers' overview of the traffic situation and a minimum of disturbances keep their concentration on the traffic (Hagson 2000: 16). In Figure 4.1, we have included a plan diagram of the area where the three sites are located. The diagram is adapted to the SCAFT traffic scheme. It depicts the principal layout of the area around. This layout is easily recognizable, and this site can be regarded a distinct example of a functional typology.

Though not an unambiguous project, the principles of the functional city have been cemented in many urban areas throughout the world. The functional city often seems to be fragmented with buildings dispersed on an open surface, and with different activities in different places. Some of these areas are often referred to as monotonous or people-hostile because of, for example, their vast areas for traffic and open space, stringent repetitive layout and lack of activities in public space.

The methods chosen to approach these mobilities sites work with analysis of what the designed artefacts do in concrete mobile situations and with a designerly experimentation with their potentials. The complex, real life problem of mobilities design at these sites does not let itself conform to disciplinary boundaries. As such, method applications have not been written in stone, external and indifferent to the sites' conditions, but have been customized, i.e. reconfigured, in the relations between them and their purpose, in the interest of making them specific and relevant to mobilities design at these sites (see Lury and Wakeford 2012). Most importantly, and in resonance with mobile methods and non-representational research, we have attempted to work in productive ways with

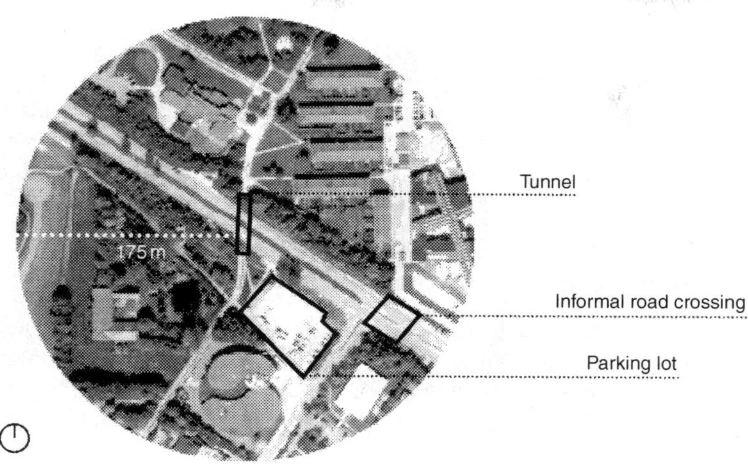

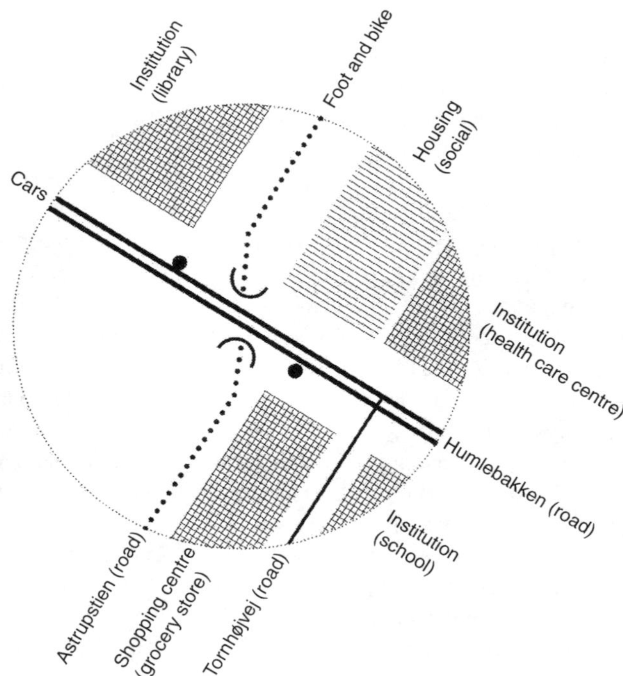

Figure 4.1 Selected study sites of mobilities, Aalborg East, Denmark (diagram: Ditte Bendix Lanng). Top: aerial photo of suburban area with three mobilities sites: tunnel, parking lot, informal road crossing. Bottom: plan diagram of suburban area, adapted from 1968 SCAFT traffic scheme: traffic segregation and functional zoning.

mobilities, interrelations and the imagination of alternatives, searching out methods that allow '[u]ncertainty [to be] valued as a productive state for exploration rather than a condition to be resolved' (ibid.: 10). The research process has been oriented towards making a difference, and methods have been customized to have a transformative capacity, in that they help capture what already is and animate what might be (ibid.: 11). A certain degree of exploration, intuition and even chance plays a role in this methodological approach.

Researching what urban artefacts *do* in mobile situations

As mentioned briefly above, the entwined processes of capturing, analysing and representing existing conditions of a specific site and of identifying its design potentials is sometimes termed 'mapping' (see also Lanng forthcoming). Mapping is a prerequisite of the urban designer's work in imagining and developing alternative futures through design proposals, 'inaugurating new worlds out of old' (Corner 1999b: 252) and actualizing the unseen and unrealized. The mapping of a site and the subsequent design proposal are closely interlinked – what designers draw is shaped by what they see:

> The implications of reciprocity between ways of seeing and ways of acting are immense.... With regard to design, how one maps, draws, conceptualizes, imagines, and projects inevitably conditions what is built and what effects that construction may exercise in time.
>
> (Corner 1999a: 8)

Accordingly, in every urban design process, the chosen design site is subject to 'site knowledge construction' (Burns and Kahn 2005). In other words, a process that focuses on the situational context and 'what is there' at the same time as it is a creative seeking out of 'what could be there'. This brings urban design analytical methods in general, and particularly mapping, as evocative and subjective operations to the foreground. It points to the key interdependencies between the methods, tools and techniques of analysis and the way we design. Hence, when speaking of mapping in urban design, we are not dealing with a cartographic work alone, and certainly not with a neutral representational practice. This point is made vibrant by architect and scholar James Corner in his essay 'The Agency of Mapping: Speculation, Critique and Invention' (1999b). Taking his cue from philosophers Deleuze and Guattari, Corner advocates that, in architectural and design practice, we move beyond mapping as a representational practice of 'tracing' that which is already known, towards mapping as an active experimentation with the actualization of site occurrences, processes, interrelations, and potentials for the future:

> [T]he unfolding agency of mapping is most effective when its capacity for description also sets the conditions for new eidetic and physical worlds to emerge. Unlike tracings that propagate redundancies, mappings discover new worlds within past and present ones; they inaugurate new grounds upon

> the hidden traces of a living context. The capacity to reformulate is the important step. And what already exists is more than just the physical attributes of terrain (topography, rivers, roads, buildings) but includes also the various hidden forces that underlie the workings of a given place.... Through rendering visible multiple and sometimes disparate field conditions, mapping allows for an understanding of terrain as only the surface expression of a complex and dynamic imbroglio of social and natural processes. In visualizing these interrelationships and interactions, mapping itself participates in any future unfoldings.
>
> (Ibid.: 214)

Mapping in this sense is 'doubly operative' (ibid.: 225): it is a selective and exploratory process of 'digging, finding, and exposing' as well as 'relating, connecting, and structuring' with the intention to activate and challenge the architectural imagination of the possibilities at the given site. Through this process a 'map is already a project in the making' (ibid.: 216), Corner asserts. He underlines that while multiple 'dark' issues are related to mapping as a powerful practice of setting the scene for how to see and act, his focus is on the 'world-enriching' potential of mapping in architecture and design (ibid.: 213).

The studies couple urban design mapping with non-representational streams of research. This is done because non-representational research offers a nuanced appreciation of some of the fleeting characteristics of sites, such as 'the contingent, the ephemeral, the vague, fugitive eventfulness of spatial experience' (ibid.: 231) which tend to be less apparent and less representational, and thus difficult, to reverberate in mapping. Non-representational research can help us, with reflection, to better understand the 'more affective, tactile, sensual effects' (Kraftl and Adey 2008: 214) of sites, and foreground the 'capacity of architecture to enable bodies to inhabit it' (ibid.: 213). Furthermore, the studies draw on non-representational research and its drive to 'rupture, unsettle, animate, and reverberate rather than report and represent' (Vannini 2015: 5). Non-representational research is not anti-representational, and, thus, it does not promote that we disregard mapping as a tool to understand existing site conditions. Rather, it helps us deepen our understanding of mapping as more than a mimetic practice of representation – as a kind of 'presentation' in itself. Human geographer Jamie Lorimer (2005) has used the term 'more-than-representational' which also seems to capture this continuum in a design process.

In the chapters that follow, the interaction of materialities and mobilities has been researched through an ethnographic sensitivity to the journeys performed at the sites. Artefacts of mobilities spaces are sought, captured through 'their enactment in contingent practical contexts' (Anderson and Harrison 2010: 7). The journeys at the sites are daily life commutes that follow certain routes and are conducted at certain speeds, using various modes of transportation by specific people, each with their own affordances. The material collected in the studies comes from numerous initial site visits, during which observations of daily journeys were conducted. It also includes desktop studies of planning documents, and dialogues with the local planning authority and other stakeholders. Not least, it includes film-elicitation studies of a handful of journeys that we address in more detail now.

Film elicitations of four daily life journeys at the study site have been a key method through which to learn about what artefacts of mobilities spaces do. With this method, we have attempted to learn about the mobile lives which are lived at the site, paying particular attention to the precognitive sensations of interacting with materialities. Film-elicitation is then meant as a method to analyse the solid artefacts in light of their character as 'relational-material "crossroads" where many different things gather, not just deliberative humans but a diverse range of actors and forces, some of which we know about, some not, and some of which may be just on the edge of awareness' (ibid.: 12). This means integrating, in tangible ways, non-representational sensitivities in the evocative mapping of the study site.

The three studies were carried out as inquiries into different modes and systems of traffic, thereby to some extent seeking to embrace users' diversity in transit spaces. They point to designing with variety according to this diversity – by no means a trivial task, given that multiple, perhaps conflicting, needs should be accommodated and synthesized (see Loukaitou-Sideris 2012; Madanipour 2006). We have travelled with and interviewed two pedestrian schoolgirls aged 13 and 14, a 29-year-old female cyclist, a 33-year-old female bus passenger and a 40-year-old male car driver. In spite of this diversity, this is a narrow study, not representative in terms of some of the lines that would separate users' circumstances from one another's (for example income, ethnicity, education, health etc.) in a more comprehensive study. Its focus is therefore not to broadly expose variations of needs or spatial practices, but rather to dive into a few examples in order to, by means of a detailed sensitivity to some of the situations of those journeys, inquire into the relationship between artefacts and embodied mobilities. In the following paragraphs, we will outline methodological reflections regarding the film-elicitation studies, using one example: the journey home from school, as it is performed by the two schoolgirls, whom we first met in June 2012.

These journeys are indeed ordinary. Many of them are daily commutes: people travel from school by foot or to the supermarket by car, cross the site by bike, or get on the bus. The journey home from school is one such ordinary journey. The mundanity of this journey poses a methodological challenge, or in the words of Spinney:

> A key central problem, however, is that whilst fleeting moments may be representational – that is to say they are fundamental to the creation and reproduction of meaning – their transient nature does not readily lend itself to apprehension through quantitative or verbal accounts.
>
> (2011: 162)

Travellers' knowledge of their own mobilities may be tacit; after all, the journey home from school is just a trivial, everyday movement from one location to the other, 'unreflexive and not necessarily amenable to introspection' (Anderson and Harrison 2010: 7). How, then, to unpack the inhabitation and experience of something that is indeed familiar, and could perhaps best be expressed as 'embodied ways of knowing' (Pink and Mackley 2012)?

Following scholars of ethnography Pink and Mackley (2012), film-elicitation contributes to capturing the journey as a sensory (audio-visual) continuity through a certain environment. Place can be understood as a 'place-event' – open, temporal, unbounded and constituted through entangled pathways (Pink 2008a: 193; Pink and Mackley 2012). They argue that researching place through the film-elicitation method, as an interweaving of processes and entanglements, offers a way to understand how processes, things and persons become interrelated to make place a place-event. In their study of the 'place-event of home', they further argue that the video tour and the researcher become interwoven with other processes in the construction of this place-event, taking part in the place-making. We have used this technique to explore particular, situated and personal experiences of daily life journeys. This knowledge enters the mapping process to deepen the understanding of the less instrumental dimensions of journeys and enlarge individual narratives while allowing practices and multisensorial experiences to come forward. Therefore, the use of video in these accounts is a way to evoke, in the concrete sites, 'some of the more "unspeakable" elements of mobile practices' (Spinney 2009), herein how practices and experiences are co-conditioned by artefacts.

According to Murray (2010), film-elicitation involves two phases: one of video recording (which Pink and Mackley (2012) term 'video-tour') and one of interviewing the participants while watching the video ('follow-up interview' (Pink and Mackley 2012). These two steps are those that involve direct contact with the participants. However, it is also of benefit to include in this reflection other research actions related to this evocative mapping: the analysis of the material and the communication of it.

During the video tour, we attempted to evoke and capture a direct sensory response to the journey and the material environment through which we travelled. As such, the first step of the film-elicitation aimed at an exploration of the participants' phenomenal experiences of everyday mobile life while it was taking place (Murray 2010). The video material also allowed a further exploration: after the recordings, when the participants and researcher viewed the video together at the follow-up interview, and when the researcher returned to the recorded material to recall the journey and its details in the analytical processes. Video can also be used directly for presenting data to readers and viewers. Pink and Mackley argue that it is indeed valuable for this purpose, as it invites 'the viewer to empathetically imagine her or himself into the experience that is suggested by the video sequence' (Pink and Mackley 2012: 4.3). However, due to the format of this book, we will communicate the study through the illustrations included in Chapters 5 to 7. This format of representation is mediated and thus distorted (like all other forms of representation) and we agree that 'when talking to people about the character and sensory make-up there was something that could not be quantified merely through words or descriptions' (Degen 2008: 13). However, the intention here is to do as much justice as possible to personal experiences and practices by situating personal narratives within the stable format of this book (see Larsen and Meged 2012). Following these points, video can be understood as:

> a route through which seeing and hearing can lead researchers and viewers to empathise with and imagine multisensory embodied experiences and not simply the aural and visual worlds of others.
>
> (Pink and Mackley 2012: 4.1)

In other words, Pink and Mackley argue that video can go beyond the direct transmission of image and sound, that the viewer might be able to sense other dimensions of the situation too. For example, the sound of footsteps tells us something about the materiality of paving, and perhaps makes us imagine feeling the paved surface underfoot; a whistling wind may make the viewer recall the feeling of a cold autumn day. As such, the video makes it possible to retain quite a lot of the context of practice (Spinney 2009). Viewing the video might invoke a feeling of 'being there'. This suggests that knowledge about the sites is produced through a form of acquaintance with the environment and the experience when using the video. In our study, the video has been valuable for the follow-up interview and for our analyses. By viewing the video, the participants and the researcher can recall the encounter with the field, attuning themselves once again to that journey, and the repetition of it can provoke a dialogue about other details than those with which they had previously engaged.

In our analyses of the participants' engagement with the environment, the video allowed us to recall 'their world'. The video is therefore also a form of nuanced notation technique, acquainting us with the multisensory embodied experience of the journeys. At the same time, it allowed us to have a distance from the embodied experience, thereby providing the option and context for reflection (Murray 2010). The recordings also gave us the opportunity to dig into the less visible dimensions of travelling (Pink and Mackley 2012). For example, some video clips showed 'live' situations of how social interaction occurred on the journey, as when the participants enthusiastically greeted some school friends we came across or helped a stranger find her way. This allowed us to get a sense of their social interaction beyond the ways they expressed themselves verbally, as well as how they interacted with space and architecture, and to then use it as a shared reference for going deeper into this aspect during the follow-up interview.

The researchers' engaged presence in ethnographic studies is of importance, and this point corresponds to the involved activity of evocative mapping in which the designer is highly productive. Pink stresses the collaborative and reflexive dimensions of the ethnographic research process (Pink 2008a, 2008b; Pink and Mackley 2012). In the film-elicitation study, we have engaged in a collaborative process of producing ethnographic knowledge (Pink 2008b). The video tour and the follow-up interview are conducted in direct contact with the research participants. Through our contact, we encouraged them to collaborate with us and to allow us to learn what they know, feel and do. We have sought to feel the multi-sensoriality of their journey in order to produce – with the school-girls – a sensory and embodied account of the journey. The site knowledge of the two girls, in relation to how they inhabit and experience the site, is thus merely one level of the ethnographic place-making. Other levels come about through our collaboration, our representations and the reception of those representations by you, the reader. The inclusion of the travellers' personal lives, experiences and remarks in this publicly accessible research study demands a respectful, ethical treatment. To accommodate this, we have the informed consent of the participants, have offered them anonymity, and have worked towards an accurate and respectful understanding and representation of the information that they have shared with us. The last point has been addressed in the follow-up interviews, in which the travellers had the opportunity to reconsider and clarify issues from the video tour. It has also been addressed via a series of concluding dialogues, in which we shared the journey narratives with them to get their responses, in particular regarding possible inaccuracies and misinterpretations; these were part of the original research in a PhD thesis (Lanng 2015).

These considerations may be reflected in relation to one particularly interesting approach to the exploration of mobile subjects and their mundane experiences as developed by urban design scholar Gitte Marling. She coins the notion of 'urban songlines' (2003), which is an important source of inspiration when combining the embodied, mobile perspective with mapping of urban form and space. There is a parallel between Marling's urban songlines and the more trivial notion of 'journey', which we use here to embrace a wide spectrum of aspects attached to travelling through the site, foregrounding embodied multisensorial experiences and practices. Her urban songlines stem from Chatwin's report on Australian Aboriginals, who performed 'songlines' – personal and situated narrative trails across the continent. Marling's present-day urban songlines signify the trails that each of us follow in our daily movements in the city, attaching social meaning and experiences of the city to them. In her work with urban songlines, she shows how urban inhabitants move along different routes in the city, taking in different territories. Her work concerns mapping everyday narratives about individuals' movements in the city and the meanings and experiences of urban space and architecture attached to those narratives. Parallel to our intentions here, Marling's method foregrounds the many co-existing ways of inhabiting and experiencing the city, and how it works to orchestrate our everyday lives. In the city, multiple urban songlines come together in a network of journeys across time and space. Through this network, the city is inhabited, experienced and enacted.

Furthermore, the ethnographic study also follows a stream of work in the mobilities turn that explores the embodiment of mobilities, and suggests methods that are capable of making noticeable the less tangible aspects of daily mobilities.

'Move-along' methods are an important part of this field. Büscher and Urry argue that when moving with the research subject, 'researchers are tuned in to the social organisation of "moves"' (2009: 103) and that '[m]obile ethnography draws the researchers into a multitude of mobile, material, embodied practices of making distinctions, relations and places' (ibid.: 105). With the mobile ethnographic approach in this research study, we foreground the embodied dimensions of travelling to understand more about architectures as entangled with mobile practices and experiences at the study site.

Focusing on materialities-in-use by people on the move, we can direct attention to what artefacts do as mediators of multiple experiences and activities when they are enacted through embodied sensorial journeys. These journeys are practices of continuity; when travelling, we do experience spaces not as detached entities but through continuous movements across spatial boundaries, and with attention to adjacent areas, surroundings and backgrounds (Allen 2010). Mapping transit spaces through continuous journeys therefore also directs attention towards the transit spaces as relative to other spaces. Hence, in a concrete way, our studies deal with how 'the material matters' (Fallan 2008: 93) in interaction with those people on the move. In this regard the study has been an exploratory experimentation with how mapping techniques can 'facilitate more dynamic and nuanced analyses of the many and complex interactions of people and things' (ibid.).

Through the focused and narrative ethnographic study of the particular sites outlined above, the following chapters concern a small range of 'mobile situations', which we draw from the empirical material. These situations facilitate a thinking about how designed artefacts of the sites work and what they do. Through the mobile situations, we are allowed to unfold the thoroughly mundane and specific entanglements of designed artefacts. The situatedness and specificity of our account enable our research of the ordinary artefacts in their relational interaction with people and things. The solid artefacts are thus mobilized through researching them in their specific dynamic, mobile assemblages; this is where they are used and experienced, and thus where they exert a significant share of their influence.

Researching what urban artefacts *could* do: speculative design operations as method

Our attention to mobile situations also drives a speculative design work. It facilitates a series of 'What if…?' questions to the status quo of the sites of mobilities. Design is thus central, not only as our networked/hybrid object of investigation but also as a method. Dyrssen's account of 'architectural thinking-making-composing' has been highly motivating (2011). Architectural thinking-making-composing is an active, explorative and spiralling process of associative, intuitive and logical action and thinking derived from art-based research. The design development is not a strategy of rational problem-solving; rather, it points at design as a research practice that, in a problem field of uncertainty, aims to open up a pathway for the future of mobilities design rather than defining a set target (see Ingold 2014). It works as a dynamic assembling of various methods to form a dense field of interwoven analysis and design of these sites. This assemblage leads to the production of 'examples that can reveal new aspects, meaning and questions' (Dyrssen 2011: 227) with which we can address the research topic. In our speculative design operations, an important part of this interrogation is to work with a possible discrepancy between what the designed artefacts do now and what they could do in the future. Thereby we use design as a way to analyse possible deficiencies of existing conditions and identify potentials for other future mobilities designs (or identifying 'problems' and 'potentials', to put it more simply). Design is then thought of as an analytical mode with results 'accomplished through action, by staging, provoking or changing the situation' (ibid.: 229). The answers do not progress linearly from question to answer, but iterate around formulating and responding to the question of how to 'shake up ingrained patterns of thought; provide quick feedback, increased curiosity and discoveries of hidden possibilities; reveal possible links and points that need to be mapped' (ibid.; see also Yaneva 2009b), and they are thus an attempt to be sensitive to 'improvisational possibilities and systematic contributions that, through links and key points, successively connect to other research and follow-up on operations' (ibid.).

Indeed, there is a utopian current to this use of design that relates to a rich stream of scenarios and experiments on mobility and the city pushing the imaginations and discussions about visions for the future (Jensen and Freudendal-Pedersen 2012). We have engaged in hypothetical redesign operations, conducted on the basis of the real situations of the tunnel, the parking lot and the road crossing. Hence, 'the designerly capacity' is used 'to both project an alternative vision for the future and to direct this projection to present repressed conditions from a critical perspective' (Dyrssen 2011: 233). There are consequently two interwoven aspects of the design speculations: a critical challenge of established ways of thinking of and designing artefacts of mobilities spaces; and a 'constructive vision' (Jensen and Freudendal-Pedersen 2012: 200) which is a channel for the exploration of fruitful potentials to think and do otherwise. These two moments of our design speculation align with Dunne and Raby's notion of 'critical design' (2013). They are a form of critique, in that they question and challenge the way designed artefacts of mobilities 'enter our lives and the limitations they place on people' (ibid.: 34). However, they also embrace a wishful speculation about possible futures of our mobile world. The small design speculations are 'testimonials to what could be, but at the same time, they offer alternatives that highlight weaknesses within existing normality' (ibid.: 35).

The 'weaknesses' of the existing design, which our three design speculations concern, are central issues of mobilities design: atmospheres, environmental sustainability and inequalities. In the pursuit of unfolding how these topics are entangled in concrete designs of mobilities, we use design as a driver for 'experimentation, speculation, and the reimagining of everyday life' (ibid.: 31). Learning from Dunne and Raby, then, our design cases aim to be a form of Critical Mobilities Thinking 'translated into materiality. It is about thinking through design rather than through words and using the language and structure of design to engage people' (ibid.: 35). However, though design is imperative to this book, we are hedging our bets by thinking about key issues of mobilities design through both design and words.

Ultimately, design speculation may be powerful enough to work as catalyst for change. Indeed, Dunne and Raby write about feeding the imagination and opening up possibilities. At the risk of sounding lofty, our design speculations would ultimately contribute to the rethinking and remaking of materialities of mobilities. In our work, design speculation happens in a very unpretentious realm. We deal with the utterly mundane – with shouts in the concrete tunnel, with routine parking on asphalt, with a barrier in the central reserve of the road. Our ambition is to balance the need for challenging assumptions of ordinary mobilities design with 'carefully radical' (Latour 2008) speculations, as Dunne and Raby express it:

> Critical design might borrow heavily from art's methods and approaches but that is it. We expect art to be shocking and extreme. Critical design needs to come closer to the everyday; that's where the possibility to disturb lies. A critical design should be demanding, challenging, and if it is going to raise awareness, do so for issues that are not already well known. Safe ideas will not linger in people's minds or challenge prevailing views but if it is too weird, it will be dismissed as art, and if too normal, it will be effortlessly assimilated. If it is labelled as art it is easier to deal with but if it remains design, it is more disturbing; it suggests that the everyday life as we know it could be different, that things could change.
>
> (2013: 43)

Hence, and in accordance with the inventive dimension of mobile methods, with the design investigations and speculation we wish to contribute to mobilizing our conception and concrete reimagination of these mundane sites and artefacts. The design speculations have a modest architectural expression, which oppose an aesthetic approach to elaborate visual design; instead, they cultivate potential within a modest architecture, responsive to ideas of daily life mobilities. Through this modesty, the images, diagrams, photographs and sketches of the following pages can hopefully be used as a more-than-representational material to 'think with' (see Jensen 2014; Latham and McCormack 2009) in mobilities design. These illustrations are representations, but their main purpose is not a representational endeavour. Similar to Corner's point on mapping as an active producer of the world that it is meant to show, Latham and McCormack assert that images cannot provide a reliable tool to depict the moment. However, this does not imply that we give up on either writing, drawing, photographing, filming, mapping or on using design as research and imagination. Instead, we need to rethink the terms of use. Images, Latham and McCormack (2009) argue, have the capacity to evoke affective resonances of their own; they make (new) sense as they present themselves and not solely for what they represent (ibid.: 260). When images of a city are connected or juxtaposed with other images, or other media, ideas or experiences, they exceed the interpretative narrative of which they have been a part; they become 'non-representational participants in the processes and practices of thinking through cities' (ibid.: 253). The design illustrations which we present thus provide us with a 'generative constraint' (ibid.: 260) which can 'move' us, and which we can use to mobilize concepts and develop ideas.

Conclusion

In this chapter we have aimed to show more specifically and presicely what the turn towards design and materialities mean for the choice of empirical methods and practical approaches in the case chapters to follow. We have also included the myriad methodological sensitivities for mobilities design in a more general manner. The nexus between design and mobilities means an orientation towards approaches, mind sets and designerly ways of thinking in which an openness to the mobile, fluid, processual field is crucial; also, an explorative and playful attitude to experiments is a key identifier. However, we are also moving towards a very tangible approach to explore how mobile subjects experience the mundane everyday life spaces in which they move and see the world. Therefore, the creative and material sensibilities of the (urban) design engaged with here is connected to well-known ethographic methods and approaches like site inspections, field studies, go-along interviews and observations. In the three following empirical-cases, this methodological assemblage is deemed neccessary if we are to come closer to the pragmatic key questions driving this work, such as *how are design decisions and interventions staging mobilities?*

We have given an account of the way we engage the material world and turn our explorations into data, as must be expected within a chapter on research method. Our methodological approach has strong links to the theoretical underpinnings of this work. We see a chapter accounting for the practical approaches as an important link to some of the perspectives growing out of this work. As mentioned earlier, we see the emergent mobilities design research field as one of the phases. We have focused our attention in this book on the phase of learning to see, by which we mean bringing a new gaze on the familiar to the forefront. The future phase would then be articulated as an invitation to act. In this latter phase, we see perspectives of future development, with theoretically informed and empirically underpinned design speculations and interventions of a larger scale and complexity than the ones presented in this book. Here, the methods may be developed further in the direction of participartory approaches, future scenario building, as well as 1:1 experimentation with artefacts and materials. However, as we have indicated, this book is an early step in articulating mobilities design as a theoretical and empirical field of explorative analysis and intervention. We have approached the empirical cases with tools and methods deliberately aimed at learning to see mundane sites of mobilities in a situational, critical and experimental mode of research. With this in mind, we now move towards the real test beds – where the action actually is – namely, the sites of mobilities.

5 Tunnel atmospheres

Mobile situation: on the south edge of the tunnel, Aalborg East, Denmark [28 June 2012]

Along their daily walk home from school, two girls pass through a pedestrian and bicyclist tunnel. The tunnel is 42 metres long and facilitates the crossing between a large road and the district's main pathway, segregating the incongruent movements of the smooth, ruled and fast traffic of the insulated 'iron cages' (Urry 2007) from the more vulnerable and slower movements of pedestrians, bicyclists and moped drivers. The two schoolgirls approach the tunnel from the south side of the pathway. Above the south entrance of the tunnel, there is a small strip of grass. Here, the girls sometimes hang out with their friends after school. To reach this upper edge of the tunnel, they climb the steep but short dirt slope, a result of the vertical traffic segregation. On this edge, they sit down and chat. Sometimes they eat snacks bought en route. This place is not designated for breaks; it is simply an excess area in between the road and the path, and the girls have plenty of more formal opportunities for lingering in the local area. However, they like this particular place. It invites spontaneity and allows them to be high above ground and to swing their legs freely. It is a good place for 'just sitting', talking and greeting acquaintances and strangers who pass by, they say. Looking at the affordances of that strip of grass, we might get a hint of the material conditions that stage the mobile situation and invite the girls to engage with this place: it faces south and is often blessed with afternoon sunshine. It is not pre-programmed with any activities but provides an informal setting for them to sit down, appreciate the view of people passing by and be seen themselves, while enjoying the sun on their backs. At the tunnel, when kids climb the steep verge to the strip of grass above the tunnel entrance, they get a rare opportunity to grab the long grass with their hands to propel themselves upwards. This situation seems laden with an atmosphere of youthful fun, spontaneity and togetherness, which works as an attraction to the girls.

Mobile situation: in the middle of the tunnel, Aalborg East, Denmark

Sometimes the girls pass through the tunnel when it is dark. In this situation, they find it scary and they do not like to use it. One of the girls explains why she finds the tunnel scary:

> There is not always light in there. And, when there is light, you cannot see out.... Well, you don't know – you can't exactly see what's on the other side of the tunnel, and you get like: phew! – the heart skips a few beats.
>
> (Interviewee, 5 July 2012)

In this situation, the tunnel seems animated by anxiety, resulting from the lack of visibility. Lights and spatial enclosement are key design features. The lack of light inside the tunnel makes it a dark, long and narrow space and contributes to the girls feeling closed in by the space and to a pressing, affective atmosphere. However, the pressing atmosphere occurs even when the lights are functional inside the tunnel, since this bright light facilitates an overexposed 'frame of visibility' (Thibaud 2001) that contrasts too strongly with the dark exterior. Thus, the movement towards the exit of the tunnel is filled with the nervous anticipation of what, or who, may be out of frame (ibid.) in the darkness. The design of the tunnel edge adds to this anxiety: it is an abrupt transition, in which one tends to temporarily lose the overview of the situation while the eyes are getting used to the change in light, and the shape of the concrete edges could allow somebody to hide behind them. This anxious atmosphere affects the way one of the girls moves around in the area: sometimes she runs through the tunnel to get to the other side as fast as possible; other times she avoids it and chooses another route where she must cross a large road.

Introduction: tunnel atmospheres

The two mobile situations above are drawn from the research study introduced in Chapter 4. The situations exemplify situated, personal and affective inhabitations of a tunnel and point to the atmospheric resonance of this mobilities site. The tunnel is not merely a functional, neutral background upon which mobilities are performed; it is a strongly affectively laden space where multisensorial and emotional relations to the tunnel materialities matter to the mobile experience and use of the place. In one situation, the tunnel is a joyful sensorial fabric for embodied experiences, in another it is animated by a feeling of anxiety. Indeed, the tunnel works as a functional transport artefact: its design scripts shuffle the girls across space at this particular point in the area. However, the girls also show non-conformity to the design's implicit guidelines for mobile behaviour. They *are* channelled through the tunnel and dispersed on the other side, but they also contest the sterile rigidity of the tunnel's functionalist traffic design with their affective engagement with it. With this situational opening, this chapter takes up a persistent issue of urban mobilities design: the atmospheres of the environments for our everyday life mobilities. The chapter addresses this issue through the study of the design of a mundane pedestrian and bicyclist tunnel and explores the designerly staging of ambiguous, atmospheric mobile situations that emerge, when travellers' embodied mobilities enter into relationships with the materialities of the tunnel.

The tunnel is a typical functionalist infrastructural artefact. In Aalborg East, as elsewhere, pedestrian/cyclist underpasses are used to handle the intersection between car traffic and pedestrians. This type of mobilities design is so widespread and ordinary that it may go by almost unnoticed, both in our daily use of it – as a material object 'out there', and in our conceptual understanding of it – as an issue 'in here' (see Latour 2004). Often, a tunnel is merged into our frequently used surroundings as a banal object, which melds into the background of our daily life movements, becomes barely visible and is not considered unnatural in all its ordinariness and ubiquity. Critical urban mobilities design encourages us to reconsider the tunnel's status as a naturalized object and develop a language to engage with it. We need to notice it, unfold our mobile engagements with it, diversify our understanding of it and address its design as more than a taken-for-granted 'tame' technical problem to solve (Rittel and Webber 1973). This focus is on how the tunnel not only rationally affords movements from A to B, but also affords the performance of a myriad of embodied mobilities through its character as an atmospheric urban space in the city, where people meet, and experience and live their lives in multisensorial ways. In alignment with Ingersoll, we think such spaces may be looked upon in a more open-minded way:

> Transportation infrastructures continue to be designed with the positivist ethos of government institutions and thus elicit a certain inevitable determinism that corresponds to the economics of increased mobility. Despite their potential consensus: these interventions are often upsetting and alienating.... Citizens and designers could demand more of infrastructure than just its primary functions.... The difference resides in a promotion of a culture of design, which can make such a work [of infrastructure] congruent rather than hostile to its setting.... To approach infrastructure as art can provide a way of dealing with the violence it interjects into the urban system and become a means of creating civic meaning.
>
> (Ingersoll 2006: 123–4)

We will introduce the tunnel, its rational design and its varied mobile inhabitation, in order to diversify an understanding of it as an ambiguous atmospheric space. Following this, we discuss the concept of atmosphere in relation to urban mobilities design, drawing on theoretical resources related to the architecture and design fields, as well as non-representational and mobilities research. We can think of the tunnel as affording our practices and experiences, as providing the initiating architectural conditions for travellers to temporarily engage with it along the way, to trigger actions and sensations (see Chapter 3). The tunnel atmospheres, we suggest, form and deform when travellers and the tunnel share agency. From the theoretical outset, we tease out an operational, yet essentially simplified, way of addressing the atmospheric design of the tunnel, asking the following speculative questions to the multisensorial qualities of the tunnel: *What if your journey through the tunnel was associated with the scent of wood? What if lights interwove the view of the interior intimate passage with the open expanse? What if you felt compelled to test the tunnel echoes? What if you felt invited to lean against the tunnel wall in conversation during an encounter there?* The chapter closes with a discussion of the ambiguity and power of mobilities sites as atmospheric materialities and with concluding reflections.

The tunnel: organization of traffic, embodied mobilities and atmospheric space

To pedestrians, moped-riders and bicyclists, the tunnel is a key passage to and from the suburban district's main local service centre. It connects dwellings and local service facilities in its proximity, including a grocery store, public school, cultural centre, library and health care facility; bus stops are located at the road-sides right above the tunnel (see Figure 4.1). The tunnel dates back to 1973, and it is a vivid example of how safety and convenience for local travellers had gained a significant part of the considerations in the planning of the district in the mid-twentieth century. The heavy increase in the number of cars in those years nurtured a thorough segregation of modes of traffic, which was a selling feature of this 'new town', as a contemporary local trade magazine states: 'some of the internal footpaths will even be led under the roads, so that mothers do not need to fear when sending their children off to school' (Aalborg Erhvervskontor 1967, our translation; see also Aalborg Town Planning Office 1962).

As a passage between the two sides of the large road, the tunnel facilitates multiple flows. People move through it by bike, foot, motorbike, rollerblades, etc. Some travel alone, others two-by-two or in groups. They travel at different speeds, at different times of day, with different rhythms – to school, from the bus, along the pathway. Journeys through the tunnel embrace accelerations and decelerations, as well as interruptions. While some travellers linger there in some situations, others move through as fast as possible. While some, mostly groups of playful children, enjoy exploring the reverberation of the concrete envelope with loud shouts, others are anxious to reach the light on the other side. Much of the time, the tunnel appears under-used; at other times, many travellers pass through at the same time. It comes into focus as an intense point in the extensive suburban network of paths, roads and adjoining open surfaces, where journeys are dispersed and concentrations of people are rarely found.

The tunnel has an ordinary, functionally efficient design. It is an enclosed, narrow space with walls, ceiling and floor, in which travellers are brought close to materials and to each other. The interior rectangular space of the tunnel is approximately 42 metres long, 6 metres wide and 3.5 metres high. The walls and ceiling are cast in grey concrete. The tunnel often appears dim, with daylight only reaching a short way into it. The floor of the tunnel consists of the path going through it, which is divided in two parts: the asphalt bike path, approximately 3.5 metres wide, and the tiled concrete footpath, approximately 2 metres wide. A narrow dirt-and-grass verge separates the two paths. At each end, the tunnel meets its surroundings with vertical concrete edges. Small lamps illuminate the tunnel when it is dark outside. It is usually a stark contrast to move into or out of the tunnel, with a transition from dark exteriors to bright interiors at night time, and a transition from bright, day-lit exteriors to dim interiors during the day. Though the layers of graffiti in the tunnel were painted over in the spring of 2013 during an official graffiti event arranged by the city's art museum, it still appears somewhat derelict, with its worn walls, broken lamps and heaps of trash.

Like other tunnels, this one is mainly experienced from within. Upon entering the interior space of a tunnel, the effects of weather are transformed, and a clinical artificial light often supersedes daylight, dusk or the darkness of the outdoors (Hasse 2012). This may contribute to an 'empty and cool spatial atmosphere'; in a tunnel an 'aseptic and claustrophobic expression' may be expected (ibid.: 154; our translation). The exit from the tunnel is also affective: during the day, the bright light at the end of the tunnel provides an abrupt transition as one emerges, and at night the sense of the open horizon, the sky and the ability to move more freely constitutes a remarkable shift (ibid.). Such atmospheric descriptions might be indicative of many tunnel experiences, but our situational analysis of this tunnel's design adds nuances to how it feels to travel through a tunnel. In addition to the mobile situations above, many other atmospheric encounters take place. When walking through the enclosed space of the tunnel, for example, one can hear one's own footsteps more clearly, and other sounds reverberate strongly as well. A woman, with whom we travelled through the tunnel, reports how groups of three- to six-year-olds on a trip with their kindergarten classes pass through the tunnel and stamp, shout and clap their hands. The children make a literal sound spectacle, and they, in effect, experiment and play with the space and get to know it while doing so. Their spatial engagement is ludic, filling our interviewee with joy and completely overflowing the content of the tunnel as a dark, narrow space of anxiety. The ludic echoes in the tunnel are made possible by the long concrete envelope. Echo is a sonic effect of reverberation, whereby sounds persist after they have ceased to be emitted (Zardini 2005: 179). Form and materials are very significant to reverberation: halls, squares and tunnels have different sonic qualities, depending on their shapes and materials. The concrete tunnel is a sound-reflecting material as are plaster, glass and marble in their smoothness and hardness, whereas carpeting and fibreglass, for example, are sound-absorbing materials. The enclosed space also affords other activities. It invites the pedestrian schoolgirls in the study to use it as a shelter when it rains, and they are inclined to linger there, chit-chatting with their friends on the journey home.

Sometimes, when this woman exits the tunnel after riding through it by bike, she has a tendency to 'feel at home'. The transition from the enclosed space to the exteriors, with open skies and a change in lights, smells, sounds, views, temperature, etc., at times can invite a remarkable shift in her mobile experience. She has extensive local knowledge and multiple memories of this site and these are significant in mediating her experience. Though we, as visitors to the place, recognize the remarkable spatial and atmospheric shift, we do not have the 'perceptual memory' (Degen and Rose 2012) that she does and thus do not share her association of this situation with a feeling of home. The sudden jolt of sunshine, whether combined with a feeling of home or not, is afforded by the spatial transition. The enclosed space of the tunnel is distinct and encompasses one set of conditions of light, temperature, reverberation and so forth, as we have seen above. The exterior, on the other hand, encompasses a completely different set of material conditions. The abrupt change between these two spaces is indeed a change in experience, and the subject's own movement across this spatial transition is thus of overriding importance to the emergence of atmosphere. Movement, architectural features, and the traveller come together and condition a situated, embodied and multisensorial immersed production and experience of the tunnel atmosphere.

Describing atmospheres of the tunnel is a complex and open-ended task. Due to their inherently non-representational nature, it is not possible to fully transport the sensorial and emotional experiences generated from these atmospheres 'ex situ' (Albertsen 2012). When describing an atmosphere, as Anderson points to, we have to do so by approximation through use of singular adjectives such as pleasant, homely, disgusting, serene, depressing or eerie (2009: 79). Therefore, while atmospheres are difficult to capture, they are indeed ubiquitous and forceful:

> Whilst these atmospheres are invisible, nonrepresentational, they form part of the ubiquitous backdrop of everyday life on the move. However, rather than being inert, background or ephemeral phenomena, atmospheres are forceful and affect the ways in which we inhabit these spaces. As such, affective atmospheres are central to everyday conduct whilst on the move since different atmospheres facilitate and restrict particular practices.
>
> (Bissell 2010: 272)

The acknowledgement of atmospheres as forceful in the shaping of our mobile lives makes it essential in urban mobilities design to sharpen the attention to the affective relations between people, senses, movement and materialities of mobilities. The various fleeting moments of encounter between specific architectures and specific mobile activities and experiences encompass a considerable sensorial heterogeneity. Even in the tunnel, such affective variety exists in spite of the insignificance and uniformity of the architecture. Its mundane, even banal, architecture turns out to 'kindle certain capacities for inhabitation' (Kraftl and Adey 2008: 225). With our special interest in materialities, we will allow ourselves to further de-territorialize the architectural features of these situations 'from their original seamlessness with other things' (Corner 1999c: 230) and seek to sum up how they perform simple, tangible and highly affective affordances to travellers. We will engage the strip of grass above the tunnel, which faces the sun and provides an overview and a comfortable, cosy seat, hence inviting pleasant pausing points. The narrow, long, poorly lit tunnel with low visibility calls for acceleration to get through as fast as possible, or for the choice of another route to avoid the anxiety felt in the tunnel. The reverberating quality of the concrete tunnel envelope invites the thrilling experimentation with sounds, the remarkable shift between the interior and exterior of the tunnel facilitates a sudden sunshine jolt, and the roof of the tunnel offers a rare, sheltered intimate space along the way. Though these few situations are far from forming an exhaustive list (in our study alone multiple other situations occurred), they do give us an indication of the relational, dynamic and affectively charged situations of which the tunnel architecture is part. The tunnel is an ambiguous and dynamic artefact of movement and of multiple sensorial encounters, animated and co-produced by atmospheres (see Figures 5.1–5.6).

To get a better understanding of the tunnel atmospheres and their significance to mobilities design, in the next section we tease out some of the conceptual intricacies of atmosphere through the extensive scholarly work done in relation to atmosphere in architectural and urban design and in mobilities and non-representational research.

Atmosphere: a powerful concept in urban mobilities design

There is no singular meaning, use or clear definition of the concept of atmosphere (Bille *et al.* 2015). Used widely both in colloquial and scholarly language across multiple fields, the concept carries many meanings, stretching from meteorological, the air we breathe or the weather conditions (Ingold 2012: 19) to the 'mood' of a nation or of a certain time period, for example, the 'roaring twenties' (Anderson 2009) to a 'feeling in the air' of an event or a situation, such as a football match (Edensor 2015) or a journey in a train compartment (Bissell 2010). In urban design and architecture, the concept of atmosphere encircles a shared apprehension of the affective relations between people and materialities. To a great extent, architectural and urban design discourse is inflected with allusions of atmosphere, as architect Peter Zumthor articulates here:

> [W]hat do we mean when we speak of architectural quality? It is a question that I have little difficulty in answering.... Quality architecture to me is when a building manages to move me. What on earth is it that moves me? How can I get it into my own work?... How do people design things with such a beautiful, natural presence, things that move me every single time? One word for it is Atmosphere.
>
> (2006: 11)

Although the concept of atmosphere is used to encircle such affective architectural quality between perceiving subjects and the architectural objects of the

Figure 5.1 The enclosed space of the tunnel. Top: the enclosed space of the tunnel, in which travellers are brought close to each other, and to the walls and ceiling, in contrast to the large, open spaces before and after moving through the tunnel. Bottom: alternative body-space proportions: wide, low, and high and narrow spaces (drawings: Hans Bruun Olesen; concept: Ditte Bendix Lanng).

surroundings, atmosphere is neither an unambiguous, uniform phenomenon, nor is it something we can easily produce or design. A significant resource when discussing atmosphere in urban design and architecture (and beyond those disciplines too) is philosopher Gernot Böhme (1993; 1998; 2005; 2013). According to him, the production of atmospheres cannot be ascribed to one thing or one person but to the relationship between multiple elements. Atmospheres take shape as a 'manifestation of the co-presence of subject and object' and are characterized as the 'prototypical "between" phenomenon' (Böhme 1998: 114).

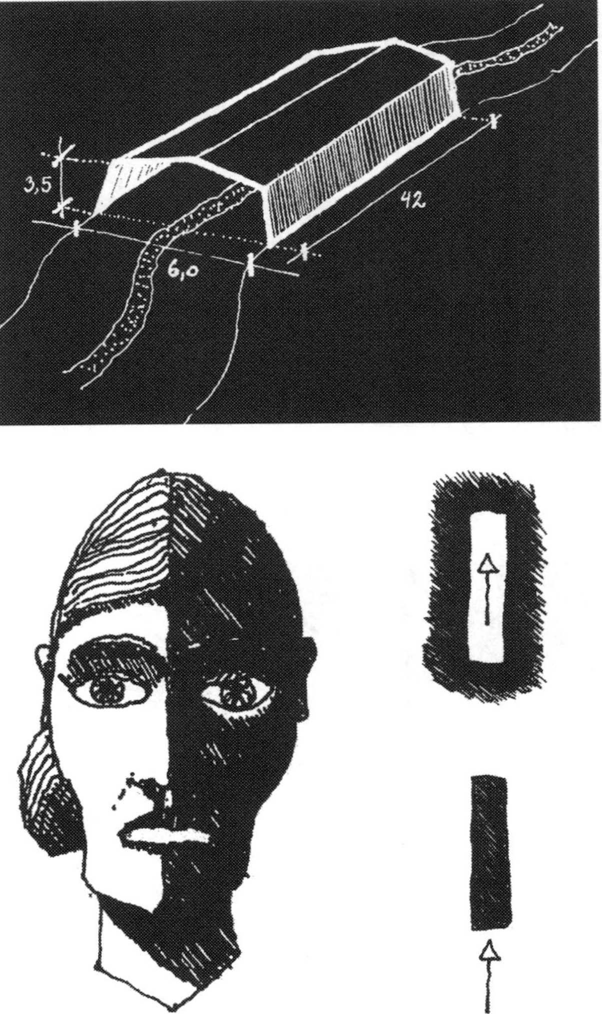

Figure 5.2 Tunnel lightness and darkness. During night time: transition from dark exteriors to lit interiors. During daytime: transition from daylight exteriors to dark interiors (drawings: Hans Bruun Olesen; concept: Ditte Bendix Lanng).

Accordingly, Bille *et al.* find that 'focusing on atmospheres means addressing not simply "experience", but rather the co-existence of embodied experience and the material environment' (2015: 36), and Urry refers to atmosphere as a phenomenon emerging in the sensorial encounter between people and things: 'Atmosphere is in the relationship of peoples and objects. It is something sensed often through movement and experienced in a tactile kind of way, what Thrift

Figure 5.3 The tunnel edge; an appealing place for spontaneity, for seeing and being seen, for swinging feet, facing the sun, and greeting passers-by (drawings: Hans Bruun Olesen; concept: Ditte Bendix Lanng).

terms "nonrepresentational" practices (1996)' (2007: 73). Urry here directs attention to the often-mobile circumstances under which atmospheres are experienced and produced. Such a mobile understanding of atmospheres in urban design implies a process of forming and deforming in and through mobile embodied activities in concrete physical environments, indicating the temporality of urban experience and atmosphere. This is seen, for example, in the work

Figure 5.4 Touching the tunnel wall; could we imagine some smoothness and warmth to the tunnel interior, some expectation that the wall invites leaning and pausing in conversation during an in-the-tunnel encounter? (drawings: Hans Bruun Olesen; concept: Ditte Bendix Lanng).

of Böhme (1993), in which he states that any change might incite the processes of formation and deformation of atmospheres. Likewise, other architectural/design writings on atmosphere, such as Pallasmaa (2011), Thibaud (2011) and Zumthor (2006), acknowledge this fluidity due to the subjective dimension of atmospheres. These writings bring insights into how actors, materialities and architectural effects combine to form atmospheres, but they do so without

Figure 5.5 The tunnel and the elements; a cool, dim concrete container creating shelter from the sun's heat and the rain (drawings: Hans Bruun Olesen; concept: Ditte Bendix Lanng).

placing much emphasis on the essential on-flow and mobility characterizing atmospheric encounters. The direction in many architectural/designerly writings on atmosphere hence infers a relatively stable condition without explicitly accounting for mobilities. However, mobilities research and non-representational research offer a comprehensive and nuanced thinking about atmosphere as explicitly interrelated with mobilities, events, and practices and experiences. It

Figure 5.6 The sounds of the tunnel; at times a silent place, at other times one where mopeds and playful shouts, stamps and claps reverberate in the enclosed space (drawings: Hans Bruun Olesen; concept: Ditte Bendix Lanng).

recognizes the precognitive ways in which we relate to our material environment while performing journeys (Adey 2010; Anderson 2009; Anderson and Harrison 2010; Bissell 2010; MacPherson 2010; Pink and Mackley 2014; Spinney 2009; Thrift 2008; Vannini 2012, 2015).

Scholars of non-representational theory draw on an understanding of atmosphere similar to the one above. According to Anderson, atmospheres emerge in the relational 'assembling of the human bodies, discursive bodies, non-human bodies, and all other bodies that make up everyday situations' (2009: 80). As we have described in Chapter 2 of this book, non-representational theory in particular takes interest in the ephemeral and precognitive realm of sensations, affects, atmospheres and emotions. A cornerstone in non-representational thinking is an inherent, fluid understanding of the world, a dynamic world in constant motion (Anderson and Harrison 2010; Thrift 2008). This encourages a profound analytical sensitivity towards the fluidity and ambivalences of the world and the everyday lives that exist in it. Rather than focusing on the steadiness of routines and habits, it prompts us to focus on the possibilities, contingency and open-endedness for practices, events and situations to play out differently (Edensor 2003: 155). Following this vitalist perspective, human geographer Anderson tells us that the atmospheres we encounter in everyday life are 'never finished, static or at rest' but always 'perpetually forming and deforming, appearing and disappearing, as bodies enter into relation with one another' (2009: 79). As Wind and Lanng argue (2014), an analytical scope inspired by non-representational research towards atmospheres in urban design urges us to go one step further than thinking of atmospheres as the effect of the relational coming together of subjects and objects. A mobilized and non-representative perspective emphasizes atmospheres as continuously being shaped by and reproduced through the intersections of heterogeneous movements and flows of people, things, artefacts, etc., who also act back and affect the very movements and flows they proceed from, as they are co-producers of the sensorial and emotional experiences (Sheller and Urry 2006).

These theoretical approaches to atmosphere are of high relevance to urban mobilities design, in that they theorize the affective quality of the relational encounter between a mobile person and the physical environment. In spite of the complexity of the concept of atmosphere, it remains a powerful tool for description and imagination of those subjective, emotional, embodied and fluid experiences which we have at some places, at some times. Bille *et al.* have argued that we have little reason to question the ontological status of atmosphere; it is rather our methods and language to engage with it that still need precision and development (2015: 33).

As we saw in the mobile situation in the tunnel, atmospheres can be conspicuous. They certainly also can be in embodied encounters with mundane mobilities sites beyond the tunnel example. Some sites may be felt as 'sterile', or even 'gloomy', as Danish poet Søren Ulrik Thomsen expresses in his atmosphere-laden Bukowski-inspired poem, entitled 'The Worst and the Best':

> The worst place after midnight
> is the vast pathway systems of the suburbs
> which connect the sparkling housing blocks
> and in this very moment always oddly empty
> even though you very well feel
> that somebody was here a moment ago
> and that in a moment you will hear footsteps behind your back
>
> (Thomsen 2002, our translation[1])

In spite of such negative connotations of many experiences of mundane sites of mobilities, and in spite of the difficulties connected to a clear usage of the concept, we find that 'atmosphere' can open the field of urban mobilities design to the vital importance of embodiment and senses. Also, it should be noted that in an analytical sense, the term 'atmosphere' has no particular value orientation. In other words, an empirical investigation may find positive or negative senses of atmosphere, but as an analytical concept is has no valorization prior to the empirical exploration. Through our study of the tunnel, we can recognize the relational conception of atmosphere, in which materialities are not uniformly perceived in whatever the situation. The tunnel architecture's mundane and somewhat sterile expression does not only produce homogeneous sterile tunnel atmospheres (see also Anderson 2009); mobile experiences of this place are, on the contrary, multiple and varied. Through the mobile situations reported above, we sense atmosphere as produced in a highly temporal and relational assemblage, of which designed artefacts are only a part. Yet as the sources above suggest, materiality matters to this production. Similar to Zumthor's proposition of how architecture is capable of 'moving' him emotionally and sensorially, Böhme proposes that things themselves project an affective quality on a situation. He writes of the 'ekstases of things': 'it does not relate to the determinations of things, but to the way in which they radiate outwards into space, to their output as generators of atmospheres. Instead of properties, therefore, I speak of ekstases' (2013: 14). The anxious atmosphere of the school girls' passage through the tunnel in the dark, for example, does not solely reside with them but is also shaped by such ekstases, what Thibaud terms the 'affective tonality' (2011) of the physical space of the tunnel.

The effect of atmospheres can be understood as a propensity, 'a pull or a charge that might emerge in a particular space which might (or might not) generate particular events and actions, feelings and emotions' (Bissell 2010: 273). Hence, atmospheres are important to any place, indeed to any piece of urban mobilities design intervention, as they play a prominent role in coshaping how these places are perceived and felt and thereby how they can be used. When we include atmosphere in our discussion of urban mobilities design, we therefore wish to make clear that the designerly 'staging' of mobile situations is evidently not only shaped by the mere functional-practical material form but also in the affective human-non-human configurations of travellers, movement, materialities and other elements. Atmosphere sets the lived, multisensorial world on the agenda of urban mobilities design; it forces us to push our understanding of the physical materialities beyond their solidity and beyond their functional affordances, to their situational affective qualities. As we have addressed in Chapters 1 and 3 of this book (see also Jensen *et al.* 2016), the notion of affordance carries a material emphasis that allows us to focus on the role of designed artefacts in mobile situations. Affordances hone our attention to the dynamic physical and affective encounter between the material environment and its users. And in doing so, the concept of affordance allows us to become attuned to the performativity of the material world: what it *offers* and what it *does*. In his work on affordances, Heft points to what he calls 'attraction' (2010). With this, he emphasizes the affective tonality of a physical environment and thereby highlights that the coupling between the user and the physical environments or designed artefacts is never neutral but charged with an affective pull or push. This indeed resonates with non-representational thinking and Ingold's request for a refocus from 'the material' towards 'materials' in order to sharpen the attention to the multisensorial engagements with the felt and embodied experiences (Ingold 2011). Urry makes an example of this connection between atmosphere and affordance in a different context, in an apparently unspectacular fishing village at the island of Bornholm, Denmark, which 'has the kind of atmosphere such that pleasures and bodily security are afforded to those able to walk about' (2007: 73). What we see here is that atmosphere takes part in defining what a place offers; it exerts power on the concrete situations which play out in a place. Atmospheres can therefore also be regarded in terms of their manipulative authority. The power of atmospheres is used to affect our behaviour and judgement in relation to, for example, consuming products and services (Griffero 2014; see also Böhme 1998). We should not be blind to such use of atmosphere, nor in urban mobilities design, where the authority of atmospheres can be used and perhaps misused in powerful ways. Examples exist in many cities, where atmospheres are deliberately shaped in some tunnels and passageways, where loud and intense music is played to push people through the space and to prevent anybody from taking shelter there: the playing of classical music at rail stations is an example of an explicit attempt to drive away homeless people and drug dealers.

When we acknowledge the relational and temporal character of atmosphere, obviously there are difficulties connected with 'designing atmospheres'. Designing, or making, atmospheres sounds as if we could script anything so messy, rich and ephemeral through design operations and fixities. It is paradoxical, Böhme writes, that 'making' is associated with something tangible – with concrete things – whereas atmosphere is airy and indefinite. Böhme finds that making an atmosphere is 'setting the conditions in which the atmosphere appears' (2013: 10). Elsewhere he discusses how atmosphere is actually what architectural and aesthetic work is all about. Though the architect shapes objects and spaces, this is not what really matters, rather it is 'atmosphere':

> The aesthetics of atmosphere directs attention to what had always taken place in these areas of aesthetic work, though an ontology oriented to the thing had distorted it; the object and the goal of aesthetic work is literally nothing; i.e. that which lies 'between' the spaces.
>
> (Böhme 1998: 115)

Accordingly, our point here is to use atmosphere as an important sensitizing device that contributes to expanding what counts as relevant design consideration in sites of mobilities. When applied to urban mobilities design, atmosphere draws our attention to the diffuse embodied-emotional sensations of mundane mobilities sites and thereby supplements focus on cognitive, semiotic and functional design. Hence, through highlighting atmosphere, we can challenge some of the taken-for-grantedness and invisibility of many a mobilities site, herein the tunnel, where the affective relation between mobile users and the tunnel architecture can indeed comprise a significant share of how they are used and experienced, and merge into the urban environment. Atmosphere therefore points us to target the affective resonance of mobilities sites, and to seek to work with the designerly staging of mobile experiences.

In the following section we will tease out a useful, yet essentially simplified, way of addressing atmosphere in relation to urban mobilities design, unfolding an imaginary alternative future for the tunnel design. To bring an operational order on the affective tonality of spaces in an urban context is obviously not an easy task. Yet, the scholarship of Thibaud and related works in the scholarly interdisciplinary ambiance network (www.ambiances.net) present efforts to work with atmospheres through the heuristic separation of multisensorial ecologies into singular senses. This resonates with Bille *et al.*, who suggest that '[i]n order to get to grips with atmosphere we have to engage more actively and analytically with architecture, colours, lighting, humidity, sound, odour, the texture of things and their mutual juxtaposition' (2015: 36).

What if…? Sensorial ecologies of the tunnel

In the encounter with spaces of mobilities, different sensorial journey experiences coalesce and are embedded in 'sensory ecologies', which, like atmospheres, are relational and dynamic (Thibaud 2011). Sensory ecologies include multiple senses and thereby challenge the dominance of the eye in architecture (Barbara and Perliss 2004; Zardini 2005). They correspond with Böhme's question, '[I]s seeing really the truest means of perceiving architecture? Do we not feel it even more?' (2005: 399). As Urry has argued, pictures and maps have a tendency to reduce the world to a visual text, and the extensive use of such media nurtures a marginalization of the multi-sensuousness of the body and the rich bodily relations to the material world (2000: 92). The dominant role of vision in architecture, and perhaps particularly in the modernist urban project, can possibly even be held responsible for the 'disembodying of people's relationships with space' (ibid.: 103; see also Pallasmaa 2005/1996; Schwarzer 2004). The privilege of the eye links to the sanitization and standardization of the city, which were accelerated with modernist city planning (Zardini 2005). The modernist city is a 'hygienic' city – one in which sounds and smells have been considered disturbing and thus something to be controlled and eliminated. A focus on a more sensorial urbanism, on the other hand, can be regarded as partly a return to the studies and questions raised half a century ago by, for example, Cedric Price, Kevin Lynch, Jane Jacobs, William Whyte, Steen Eiler Rasmussen, and Alison and Peter Smithson (Jacobs and Appleyard 1987; Zardini 2005), with which urban design is often associated. The phenomenological lens on the city foregrounds the lived 'urban experience' and suggests a 'humanised' vocabulary for urban form that depends on sights, sounds, contact and smells of the city, and regards its materials and textures, floor surfaces, facades, style, signs, lights, seating, trees, sun and shade as amenities (Jacobs and Appleyard 1987). A sensorial urbanism thus deals with everyday life and the qualities of atmosphere, nature, environment, the human body and health, and proposes to take into consideration a polyspectrum of the perceptual phenomena that make up the interconnected sensorium of the city beyond the visual regime (Zardini 2005). Aforementioned atmosphere researcher Thibaud captures this in his work on urban spaces:

> Urban spaces provide numerous ambiances to be felt with all the senses. Whether we think of a lively outdoor marketplace or an ordinary parking lot, an attractive historical centre or an accessible subway station, the very way we relate to these places is based on the sensory experience they provide. It is a matter of light and colour, sound, smell, touch and heat, as well as the manner in which we walk and talk, move and look, relate and behave. In other words, urban ambiances always create a subtle interweaving of synaesthesia and kinaesthesia, a complex mixture of percepts and affects, a close relationship between sensations and expressions.
>
> (2011: 1)

To move beyond the visual regime and towards a sensorial urbanism means including other senses in the conceptual as well as analytic and interventionist takes on urban mobilities design. Bodies, mobilities and materialities interrelate in non-quantifiable atmospheres, in which it is arguably not easy to separate different sensorial impressions from one another, or to point out what exactly in the material environment would facilitate distinct sensations. Rather, sensory experiences tend to be closely interconnected, as Zardini addresses (2005: 101): when walking in snow you would know the temperature from the sound of your footsteps; your sensorium works as a whole, not on partial terms, but interconnected. All sensorial information comes together in your perception of the environment. Apart from poetically addressing the sense of movement in a snowy landscape, Schafer importantly exemplifies the 'interconnectedness' of sensory ecologies, including that we feel our bodily actions through feeling the physical environment, as underlined by Shusterman:

> To focus on feeling one's body is to foreground it against its environmental background, which must be somehow felt in order to constitute that experienced background. One cannot feel oneself sitting or standing without feeling that part of the environment upon which one sits or stands. Nor can one feel oneself breathing without feeling the surrounding air we inhale. Such lessons of somatic self-consciousness eventually point toward the vision of an essentially situated, relational, and symbolic self rather than the traditional concept of an autonomous self-grounded in an individual, monadic, indestructible and unchanging soul.
>
> (2008: 8)

Following these points on atmosphere and an analytical engagement with it through multisensorial experiences, we launch an atmospheric reimagination of the tunnel through articulating four sensory variables: the smell, the touch, the sound and the view of the tunnel. These variables enter into the multisensory ecologies of the tunnel and are arguably not easily separated, as discussed above. However, by taking them apart, we can articulate questions of small imaginative dramas of displacement, in which sensory and social experiences from elsewhere are juxtaposed with the mundane realities of the tunnel. These sensory dimensions work to initiate the imagination of rich and tactile practices and experiences. Such richness of mobile inhabitation could include many diverse mobile situations, which embrace heterogeneous engagements between travellers and materialities during their daily life mobilities. The sensorial dimensions of the smell, the sound, the sight and the touch of the tunnel equip us with a multisensorial sensitivity to the design of functional and affective affordances that facilitate embodied journeys. They point towards a multisensorial mobilities design agenda, which aspires to plasticity, tactility and intimacy, in response to the functional city's striving for clarity, uniformity and sanitation (see Howes 2005: 325), which – according to some – has resulted in 'sensory deprivation' and 'sterility' (ibid. referencing Sennett 1994).

The four hypothetical 'What if…?' questions below confront the existing situation in the tunnel and point to material changes that could be done to the tunnel design. They do not suggest an end point for urban mobilities design of the tunnel. Rather, with this multisensorial exploration, we strive to feed a shared, open action space with a starting point for including consideration of atmosphere. Our exposition here is far from comprehensive. For example, it would often be relevant indeed to accentuate the temporality of sensorial issues related to the seasons of the city: the sense of weather, temperature and changing seasons. In Denmark, temperate climate seasons do make a significant difference in the sensorial ecologies of any mobilities site: they change remarkably in a cycle from cool, dark wet and snowy winters to blue-sky springtime to warm and light summers, and finally to wet, windy, grey autumns. This seasonal dynamic can indeed be used as a productive force in architecture and design, as Danish landscape architectural studio SLA has shown, in, for instance, the design for a local park in the northwest of Copenhagen (SLA n.d.).

Smell: what if your journey through the tunnel was associated with the scent of wood?

The attempt to create fragrance-free urban environments in the modern 'hygienic' city has been one of the important instigators of many grand urban projects (Barbara and Perliss 2004: 173), not least the envisioning and construction of the pure, rationally ordered functionalist city (Urry 2000: 99). This rational city was a remarkable transformation from the contagious, crowded, old inner cities, where the odours of the roads were presumably dreadful.

The smell of the tunnel in Aalborg East is not significant. Rather, there seems to be an absence of heavy smells; in spite of its interiority, usually it is a rather fresh place. Motorized traffic is seldom heavy enough to leave a long-lasting odour; occasionally a vague scent of trees, flowers and bushes is present but not often and not heavily; no industries nearby emit odours; there are really no crowds there, where sweat, perfume and food smells becomes overwhelming. Indeed, you might move through this narrow space without feeling embraced by the smell of anything or anybody. The sanitized, almost fragrance-free city has been achieved in the tunnel. Yet, if one is calling for an alternate sensory approach to urbanism, it can be argued, 'odour is an essential component of the character of a place' (Classen 2005: 302). To sharpen our attention in this field of design opportunities, we can begin by imagining the diversity of smells that could challenge our experience of an ordinary tunnel; what if it smelled like a cherry blossom park in Japan, a market bakery in Pakistan or a slaughterhouse in Argentina? (See Classen 2005.) Imagining such unaccustomed scents in the tunnel replaces a notion of instrumental transport with a radical sense of embodiment and invites us to engage in a highly sensorial manner in rethinking this environment of mobilities. The stridently displaced scents mentioned above may not be wished for, but perhaps, in urban mobilities design, we could explore the use of materials with pleasurable smells, such as wood. Wood can have pleasurable, yet discreet, smells, which are most often not associated with the efficient transport trajectories of cities. In Seoul, Korea, the studio 'lokaldesign' designed the Seongsan Tunnel, an underpass of the Hangang River. The interior is clad in wooden lamellas, remarkably changing the space from the conventional concrete interiors of tunnels.

View: what if lights interwove the view of interior, intimate passage with the open expanse?

As travellers, we are not only seeing objects at a distance. We are also mobile observers embedded in the visual environment. Architect and urban designer Gordon Cullen in his account of the 'visual impact' of the 'Townscape' (1961/1996) has considered this. Cullen discusses city design as an 'art of [visual] relationship' (in opposition to the architectural design of isolated buildings), in which the grouping of buildings has a major influence on the visual experience of the city: we move in the spaces between buildings, and the relative location and form of each building or object creates a 'drama of juxtaposition' (ibid.: 9). In our movement through the city, we are part of the urban environment, continuously changing our position and our visual perception of the surroundings. Cullen uses the classical city, with sharp spatial transitions between paths, courtyards, gateways and bending roads, as his exemplifying scheme for the potential visual drama of moving through the city: the existing views and the emerging views, which include the sudden revelations of new views (see Cullen's sketches, ibid.: 17). He is critical towards long, straight roads, pathways and uncontrasting urban forms like those in the functionalist district of Aalborg East. He finds that such urban forms are digested too soon, and thus become 'monotonous'; they lack the drama of juxtaposition and 'slip past us featureless and inert' (ibid.: 9). When moving through the tunnel, Cullen's preferred embedded views are present. Travellers are surrounded by walls and ceiling but are still only slightly exposed to sudden revelations of new views, because of the straight pathway. When moving through the tunnel, many objects and people are seen at a distance, framed by the tunnel's opening, allowing for a distanced 'consumption of a modernist scenery' that might be quickly digested indeed (and, not least, might be found too 'featureless' to be worthy of consumption) (ibid.).

Visuality, movement and architecture, however, are not only interesting when considering the views of objects or the built environment. As we saw in the second mobile situation (i.e. the schoolgirls' anxiety in the tunnel at night), so the visual dimension of social interactions in transit space is relevant, in considering the ways materialities work as tangible mediators of people's visual interrelations. Thibaud (2001) specifies five 'frames of visibility': 'overexposure', which directs our attention to the difference between being a spectator and being an actor; 'enclosure', which allows for short glances between passers-by; 'filtering', which facilitates a shared luminous, atmospheric environment; 'blurring', which reduces the (mutual) visibility; and 'silhouetting', which describes an asymmetrical relationship between passers-by. These considerations direct our attention to the potential for affording visual dramas, with regard both to the view of objects and to the view of people. (See, for example, the project termed 'Måløv Axis' outside Copenhagen, where a light design strategy turns the place into an interesting and attractive site at night time; Jensen 2014: 246.)

Sound: what if you felt compelled to test the tunnel echoes?

In her introduction to the *Danish Landscape Award 2013*, landscape architect Annemarie Lund challenges 'the contemporary mantra of "activation"' (2013: 105, our translation). The theme of the landscape award was 'quiet places', which advocated places with a 'low-voiced' manner and a modesty in their use of architectural or landscape architectural effects, which nonetheless possessed strong 'charisma and integrity' and which were capable of being both filled up and emptied (ibid.). Lund suggests a sensitive will to appreciate the qualities of the 'powerful' acoustic condition of silence (Urry 2000: 101). This is an interesting proposition in relation to the tunnel, where silence, or a sonic state close to it, does occur. As Urry states, 'sound is the result of activity' (ibid.) and activity is far from intense at all times in the tunnel. There are, rather, pockets of time during the day when you can find yourself almost alone here. At night, it can easily be completely empty, and one can be embraced by the sound of silence, with only an occasional sound from afar. In this relatively quiet environment, we might find another case of sanitization of the city, in which many sounds perceived as noise, which were previously an inevitable part of the city, have been separated out. A 'silencing of the modern city' has taken place (Thompson 2005) through functional zoning and traffic segregation, which allow living to be distanced from loud industry, and pedestrian movement to be segregated from roaring cars.

A journey from the bus stop across the steep verge down to the tunnel reveals the transition from the soundscape of heavy traffic on the automobility system's road to the soundscape of low-speed, mixed urban life. Sounds tell us something important about the sensory ecologies of mobilities sites. Thibaud, who has also been occupied with sonic territories, finds sound to be a 'powerful medium to express' these ecologies (Thibaud 2011: 5). In his words, we are 'plunged' into the urban world by 'the density of micro-event, the loss of intervals and pauses, the reverberated sound of enclosed space and the fast pace of street life' (ibid.). As such, sounds might play important parts in specifying places. As such, sounds might play important parts in specifying places; they can be regarded as the sonic equivalent to landmarks, i.e. soundmarks that define places and render their character distinct (Zardini 2005: 63). Above, we reported on the occasion of a playful echo in the tunnel, an experience that points to the reverberation of sounds as one of the landmark features of the tunnel. (For interesting sound designs see the 'melody roads' of Japan (Johnson 2007) and Hemmer's YouTube video (2013).)

Touch: what if you felt inclined to lean against the tunnel wall during a conversation therein?

Touch is central to our relationship with objects and with people. In crowded cities, we do not only touch objects; we also touch other people and are touched by them:

> [I]n all social life we necessarily move amongst bodies within cities which we continuously touch and are touched by, in a kind of reciprocity of contact.... Moreover, unlike the see-er who can look without being seen, the touch-er is of course always touched.
>
> (Urry 2000: 102)

Urry's assertion suggests that the tactile connection between people brings them closer together in a reciprocity of contact that does not necessarily occur between the one who sees and the one being seen. However, in the tunnel, with its low-density inhabitation, the touch of other people is rarely facilitated. There is also the 'object side' of touch: 'we can regard the tactile sense as a delicate instrument for exploring and appreciating the physical world, and objects' properties are learned and felt as they are touched: their texture, strength, scale, contrast, material composition and uses' (Urry 2000: 102). At the tunnel, when kids climb the steep verge to the strip of grass above the tunnel entrance, as we saw in one of the mobile situations above, they get a rare opportunity to grab the long grass with their hands and to move upwards with bodily effort. Apart from this example, it is most commonly the shoe on smooth pavement or the bicycle wheel on the asphalt, or – perhaps – the hand or the back on the concrete wall – that establishes a tactile connection between the traveller and the material environment in the tunnel. The example of the wood-clad interior of the Seongsan Tunnel is demonstrative with its material invitation to touch the smooth and soft wooden walls, to let the hand slide across the lamellas as one walks through, as well as the material invitations to sit down on wooden benches integrated into the design of the tunnel edges.

As such, the tunnel resembles many spaces of mobilities; more often than not, our mobile bodies are met by an asphalt floor. Asphalt is a material which has come to be seen as a symbol of the 'harmful and pervasive effects of traffic', an 'enemy to be defeated if paved roads and walkways are to recapture the diversity of character that was destroyed by the ubiquitous covering of urban surfaces with asphalt' (Zardini 2005: 240). This is a judgement shared by Cullen, who regretfully addresses how the progression of automobility has resulted in 'the suppression of the variety and character in the ground surface' (1961/1996: 121). Before asphalt became ubiquitous, moving around in the city was a dirty and rough endeavour; every mobile urbanite and every vehicle was a 'dust stirrer' (Zardini 2005: 242), and urban promenades were transformed into muddy lanes after just a short rain shower. Asphalt did exist before the car but gained immense success with the progression of automobility. This technology of smoothness and hygiene does not just eliminate the dust, it encapsulates it and is easy to clean; it muffles noise from vehicles, thus sanitizing the sounds and smells of the city. It is also ideal for markings, which became necessary to regulate increasing traffic flow, and it makes surface drainage and repair work easy. It is also cheap. These continuous gap-free surfaces have allowed driving to be a smooth and speedy practice (Zardini 2005). However, asphalt surfaces are not to be understood solely in technical terms, as the 2008 Harvard Graduate Design School project 'On Asphalt' was concerned with:

> The asphalt landscape is the most public of all landscapes, at the same time the most undervalued: it lies invisible and unrecognised as a cultural landscape. Asphalt is also one of the most liberating inventions that shaped the 20th century world. It allows us to fly and drive everywhere we desire – making the entire world accessible to us.... Asphalt touches on a multitude of urban issues such as car culture, accessibility, hydrology, infrastructure, nature, and urban density.
>
> (Harvard Graduate Design School n.d.)

Asphalt, as one of the most extensively used surface materials of the city, is significant to the mobile experience. We may ask, 'What do our feet feel? Or what do we feel when seated in our automobiles or on the saddles of our bicycles?' (Zardini 2005: 214). Through our feet, or our car or bike wheels, we know when the urban floor is irregular or smoothly paved, and we adjust our mobile practices to this condition.

With this interrogation of the smell, view, sound and touch of the tunnel, we have intended to open an action field of atmospheric, multisensorial considerations of mobilities design. Before concluding the chapter, however, we will briefly touch on the relevance of such an approach.

Discussion: powerful atmospheres, ambiguous sites

The tunnel cannot simply be regarded as a stable artefact with one or more atmospheres inherent to it. Rather, it has the potential to 'come alive' as a relational and heterogeneous atmospheric actor when it is multisensorially experienced through daily life mobilities. Thinking through the possible richness of lived mobilities, the atmospheres of the enclosed space of the tunnel, and the inherent potential for social interaction and sensorial pleasures on the move, we can explore how the materiality of the tunnel might invite experiences. Atmosphere, then, becomes a focal concept for supplementing the thorough and developed technical measures and consideration for efficient transport in this functionalist transit space design, with careful concerns for affective lives lived on the way. The design of a pedestrian and bicyclist underpass may satisfy more diverse criteria than functionality of traffic alone.

This proposition points to at least four important discussion points. First, it refers back to the call made by architect Stan Allen (see Chapter 1) that infrastructural design is in need of a new mindset that can surpass the minimum engineering standards and include the wider reach of mobilities sites as capable of triggering diverse urban effects. The urban effects pointed to by Allen should, we argue, include atmospheres and, in turn, their powerful effects on the mobile practices and experiences that can take place in journeys. This suggests, as we have indicated in this chapter, that mobilities design is approached through a rich conception of physical travel, which is elaborately researched in the mobilities turn (for example, Cresswell 2006; Urry 2000, 2007). With this extensive and growing knowledge base, mobilities design targets not only efficient transport from point A to point B but also design for a richness of lived lives on the move – for immediate embodied dwelling-in-motion. Through such attention to embodiment, affect, atmosphere and senses, the privilege of vision in much design and architecture is challenged. This further raises other issues of importance, for example sensitivity towards the diverse bodily affordances of travellers. The embodied capacities with which we encounter mobilities sites differ a lot. An atmospheric mobilities design approach should be developed to include deliberation of the diversity of bodies that inhabit these spaces, some overtly simple categories being children, adults, the elderly, males and females, and people who are differently abled. In Chapter 7, we will touch upon the issue of diverse bodily affordances and abilities, in relation to the unequal design of a road crossing adjacent to the tunnel.

Second, atmospheric considerations included in mobilities design should not be mistaken for a decorative design approach. A tangible example in which the multisensorial potential is realized is a space for aeromobilities, namely Michael Singer's design for Concourse C at Denver International Airport, which is a striking artistic intervention. Singer designed a lush, green garden for this airport space, and it reduces air pollution, adds fresh fragrances and even attracts birds. The materials include wood, stone, concrete and plants. Describing the garden, Singer says that he 'took what would have been a usually antiseptic airport zone, made it smell, made it wet, and made it grow, and gave life that you don't get in places like an airport' (Bukdahl 2011: 50). The airport, sometimes referred to as the example par excellence of modern non-places of mobilities (Cresswell 2006), is an evocative example for the potential to supplement generic smoothness and visual coherence with explicit design considerations for multisensorial embodied mobilities. This is not a simple and unambiguous goal, however. Koolhaas writes of the normative distaste for the homogenization and identity strip-off of the contemporary 'Generic City' in these confrontational terms:

> Specific cities still seriously debate the mistakes of architects – for instance, their proposals to create raised pedestrian networks with tentacles leading from one block to the next as a solution to congestion – but the Generic City simply enjoys the benefits of their inventions: *decks, bridges, tunnels, motorways* – a huge proliferation of the paraphernalia of connection – frequently draped with ferns and flowers as if to ward off its original sin, creating a vegetal congestion more severe than a fifties science-fiction movie.
>
> (1995: 1254)

We recognize the danger of the emphasis on atmosphere leading towards useless drapery to cover up what can be recognized as mistakes of the functional city. However, we maintain that our suggestion is a profound attention to lived lives on the move and to the powerful effects of atmospheres. This means that our association of mobilities design with atmospheres is not about ornament but about the weighty agency of materialities – what mobilities sites do and what they could do to our mobile ways of life (see Chapter 3). Thereby, we highlight the significant performative effect of atmospherically laden materialities on daily life mobilities. As we referred to in Chapter 3, D'Hooghe, among others, has concisely articulated the potential of moving designed artefacts from their isolation as autonomous objets d'art or as utilitarian-only technocratic systems (D'Hooghe 2010) to their entanglement in hybrid sociotechnical networks, which reach across multiple realms. Our inclusion of atmopshere as a persistent issue in mobilities design aims to do just that.

Third, atmospheric considerations do not, of course, confine themselves to the tunnel and similar typologies related to a well-ordered, traffic-segregated (sub) urbanity. We cannot do justice to the immense diversities and intricacies of urban environments around the world, but we can underline that there are overriding differences between the functionalist and 'hygienic' Danish welfare urbanism with which we have worked here and the many cities which are embedded in far different urban formations, and some of which appear noisy, messy, smelly and dirty, with very serious repercussions on well-being, health and safety for the (mobile) inhabitants. Arguably, a sharp control of such multisensorial ecologies is needed in some places.

Fourth, this means that atmospheric mobilities design is not a uniform endeavour, regardless of which mobilities site is in question. It is, rather, a balancing act of responding with insight effectively and sensitively to existing site conditions and challenges. In Chapter 7, we discuss some of the intricate balances that any design intervention must involve, if new or transformed materialities are to succeed in addressing profound challenges. Allen's point on the importance of balancing between control and openness (see Chapter 1) is hugely relevant. The potential of 'open minded' rather than 'single minded' space is at stake here (Walzer 1986). Atmospheric attention in mobilities design can be a strategic means to shape affordances and create connection, difference, vitality, safety, efficiency and possibility, but mobilities cannot be scripted per se. This draws to the front the inherent relationality of mobilities design, which must regard the open and anticipatory nature of infrastructures if these are to proliferate as public spaces.

Conclusion: mobilities design and atmosphere

The concept of atmosphere bears an argument to challenge primarily a 'technical-only' design agenda for sites of mobilities. It also challenges the privileging of vision in much design and advocates re-embodying people's relationship with these sites, of which many are perceived as sterile or gloomy. In this chapter, we have proposed a multisensorial nerve in mobilities design. This means conceptualizing materialities of mobilities sites as part of a sensory urban fabric. Materials and textures of floors, walls and little artefacts are part of this. So are lights, dimensions, vegetation, topographies, shade and sunlight, water, weather and seasonal changes, and animals, to name a few. We have accentuated a relational and mobile conception of atmosphere that corresponds with the 'mobilization' of designed artefacts of mobilities sites, which we addressed in Chapter 3. This highlights the entanglement of materialities in hybrid networks of which atmosphere is a powerful part. Our approach to unpack and diversify the understanding of the atmospheres of the tunnel has accordingly been through the situational focus that is a key part of our approach to mobilites design. Atmospheric mobile situations in the tunnel have been drawn to the foreground; these point to a direct designerly work with situated 'little practices' and multisensorial lived experiences. Embodied mobilities include an abundance of sensorial and physical variation, some of which tend to be more-than-representational, and which go beyond the technical categories of transport modalities. This chapter has opened the operation of mobilities design to a range of considerations beyond the more instrumental, quantitative facts of bodily movement to the less representational affective experiences inherent in performing embodied journeys. Thus, with this chapter, we suggest cultivating insight and foresight into concrete, atmospheric mobile situations, in order to articulate mobilities design in terms of the ways in which it is part of staging affective, embodied mobile ways of life.

From the atmospheric account of tunnel mobilities, we move on to the second empirical narrative that takes place at a well-known scene: the parking lot.

Note

1 *Det værste sted efter midnat, er forstædernes vidtstrakte stisystemer, der forbinder de tindrende boligblokke, og i dette nu altid er underligt øde, skønt man meget vel mærker, at her har nogen netop været, og om lidt vil man bag sin ryg høre skridt.*

6 Sustainable parking lots?

Mobile situation: across the parking lot by foot, Aalborg East, Denmark [21 August 2013]

On her daily bus journey, a woman often gets off at the bus stop right next to the large parking lot of a grocery store. The bus stop is her point of interchange from one mode of mobility to another. It can be a relief for this traveller to be met with a breath of fresh air and the bodily shift from sitting and waiting in the bus to walking, particularly if it has also been a rough ride with abrupt braking, too many people or too much heat. At this point, she shifts from being a passenger to being a pedestrian who is in control of her own kinaesthetic efforts to move forward. She finds it a good place to get off because it is quite welcoming to her embodied walking, with clear path connections that make it safe for her to continue her journey. However, both the bus stop area and the parking lot can appear 'gloomy' at night. She finds that the lights are too sparse in the parking lot, and that makes her feel anxious. When she gets off the bus, she switches off her phone to be attentive to new sensorial impressions. Her primary concern is traffic safety; she wants to be alert to the sounds around her when walking on the paths or across the parking lot. In springtime, when she cannot hear well due to hay fever, she tends to turn around every other second to make sure that there is no moped coming up behind her or a car making a dangerous turn in the parking lot. After getting off the bus, she follows the sloped pathway a little way down, until she walks across the narrow verge and onto the parking lot. Even though it is a more direct route to use the staircase to access the parking lot, she rarely does so because she would end up 'right in the face of the cars'. That feels like an unsafe situation for this traveller, who finds that she never really knows if car drivers are paying attention or not. In the parking lot, they might be occupied with a child on the back seat or a mobile phone they just dropped on the floor. In addition, this woman does not walk that well, and the staircase is an obstacle for her. In winter, the entire area of the parking lot is difficult for her to engage with. It tends to be icy and is not sufficiently salted: 'It's like trying to walk on soap', she says. The parking lot is an open, extended surface where cars can come from many directions and move suddenly. As a slow walker, this traveller experiences this as a rather insecure situation that she has to navigate with great care and attention. The design of the open, surface parking lot allows cars to spread out and drive anywhere. When the lot is less than half full, as is most often the case, there are very few material items that work to organize the routes of cars, and no places where vulnerable travellers, like this woman, are shielded.

Introduction

In this chapter, we will introduce a significant typology of the automobile's infrastructural landscapes: the surface parking lot. Like the other cases in Chapters 5 and 7, the parking lot of our focus is located in Aalborg East (see Chapter 4 for an introduction to the site). It is designed in a conventional way, on the terms of the car, and lies as an open asphalt expanse between important local facilities and along multiple mobility routes. It is, by and large, a utilitarian-only automobility space, which tends to threaten the local area's connectivity, walkability and well-being for people who are not in a car. The above-mentioned mobile situation of a pedestrian's attentive navigation across the lot points to this problem of the parking lot. A human body on the lot is a small, soft entity exposed in the large, open, hard-surfaced space with motorized, slow traffic.

Our account uses this situational and embodied outset to discuss potentials for sustainability in urban mobilities design. Some of the assumed relevant questions to ask to the transition to a more sustainable future of parking lots are: *What if the parking lot afforded more than just storage of cars? What if it supported multiple mobile situations and mixed uses? What if it facilitated local connectivity by inviting pedestrian and bicycle journeys? What if it was a green and enjoyable urban space?*

These questions take their point of departure from ideas about sustainable urban transformation towards a post-carbon, climate-responsive urban environment (see, for example, Ben-Joseph 2012; Dunham-Jones and Williamson 2011; greenparkingcouncil.org). A central effort in urban design is to develop responses to the urgent problems of climate change and resource scarcity. One strategy is the retrofitting of existing urban environments to make them adaptive to present and future environmental challenges. The basic idea of retrofitting is to work with existing structures as a resource for creating sustainable urbanism, herein mobilities, thereby addressing some of the many outdated, environmentally problematic urban spaces and structures of the world. This is an alternative strategy to the clearing of lands for developing new eco-cities which should leave more land in its natural ecological state. Retrofitting distinguishes itself as a type of urban transformation and redevelopment that takes particular advantage of existing buildings, systems and infrastructures and searches to integrate new solutions that were not available at the time of construction. This chapter discusses an environmentally concerned mobilities design agenda, with a basis in the idea that local-sensitive, situational retrofitting of a parking lot can be an important approach to include in the transitioning of a place or a city towards a more sustainable future. This may be a future where we will witness a dramatic decrease in demand for car ownership, coupled with the emergence of driverless vehicles.

Any surface parking lot epitomizes a series of serious environmental concerns. Parking lots are intricately linked to the city of the car, and they make important parts of the automobility system that tends to foster unsustainable car-dependency. In this chapter, we will tease out some of the important environmental problems of parking lots that can reasonably be addressed by mobilities design. Among the problems we address is asphalt, the most common material of the urban floor of parking lots, which has attracted considerable attention in relation to sustainability issues, such as local heating (creating so-called urban heat islands) and flooding. Other key environmental problems include the general underperformance of asphalt, highlighting the mono-functionality and underutilization of some parking lots; they include the barriers for local connectivity that these huge car-prioritized asphalt surfaces often make, the lack of pedestrian-friendly connections and livability. These problems add to forced auto-dependency.

On the other hand, and in line with the view to potentials that the Critical Mobilities Thinking of mobilities design implies, any surface parking lot can also be thought of a resource for evolving towards sustainable futures by redesigning from the basis of existing conditions. These may be physical structures, investments already made or future ones, uses, experiences and local urban life, relations to other places and mobility forms, and the natural processes and systems that may have been subdued or hidden by previous constructions. Parking lots are some of those undesirable urban spaces with much negative, and only little positive, contribution to the surroundings and to the users. However, on the other hand, as Roger Trancik proposes, 'they offer tremendous opportunities to the designer for urban redevelopment and creative infill and for rediscovering the many hidden resources in our cities' (Ben-Joseph 2012: 39). The path we follow in this chapter, then, is a designerly outlook for potentials, beginning with the optimistic note that parking lots can be more than too-large areas of underperforming asphalt: they can be multi-programmed, well-connected, green, sophisticatedly engineered and landscaped urban spaces. They can be 'Critical Points of Contacts' (Jensen and Morelli 2011) along journeys, connecting urban and mobilities networks, and encouraging experiences and meetings, which can support low-carbon ways of life.

Parking lots may indeed be full of potential (and problems), since they are ubiquitous in most corners of the world, and since their design remains largely underdeveloped. The amount of time, energy and creativity that goes into parking lot design is diminutive (Ben-Joseph 2012). Yet, they are an integral part of our currently high-carbon way of life and our cities. Parking lots are some of the enormous amount of heavy mobility structures in the world, which are significant human achievements of imprinting trajectories into the surface of the earth (Urry 2007: 20). Parking lots are organized and designed according to car system features. Rationales and visions about automobilities are frozen in asphalt, grass verges, light poles and the occasional trash bin. They are some of the spatial fixities that have entered into distinct time-spaces with remarkable impacts on patterns of life, and they linger over time, thus continuing to be powerful in co-conditioning our way of life (Urry 2007: 272). Indeed, parking lots make a potentially rich mobilities landscape that must face transformation in the light of the pressing agenda of developing more sustainable cities and lives. For this, we need to develop insight, foresight and design tools. As MIT professor Ben-Joseph expresses it in his book on the significant oversight for designers that the residual spaces of surface parking lots make:

> A successful parking lot is one that integrates its site conditions and context, takes measures to mitigate its impacts on the environment, and gives consideration to aesthetics as well as the driver-parker experience. Designed with conscientious intent, parking lots could actually become significant public spaces, contributing as much to their communities as great boulevards, parks, or plazas. For this to happen, we need to release ourselves from the singular, auto-centric outlook for the use of the lot. We need to reevaluate conventional parking requirements against evolving lifestyles and changing priorities. Above all, we need to accept that parking lots are primary settings for many aspects of public life for Americans, and for a growing number of others across the globe. For something that occupies such a vast amount of land, and is used on a daily basis, the parking lot has received scant attention. It's time to ask: what can a parking lot be? It's time to rethink the lot.
>
> (2012: 136)

Our discussion of parking lot design takes its outset in situational urban mobilities design. Hence, sustainability is addressed through an integrated and context-specific user perspective. This approach implies that we do not offer a formula for retrofitting, but we do provide an integrated lens on parking lot design, elaborating the problems and potentials of its design from the outset of concrete situations. Lived mobile lives are key to mobilities design, not least to sustainable parking lot retrofitting. In the heart of this approach lies Ingold's proclamation, that '[t]he truth is that the propositions of art and architecture, to the extent that they carry force, must be grounded in a profound understanding of the lived world' (Ingold 2011: xi).

In this chapter, we will discuss central sustainability issues of parking lot design. We begin with the introduction of one example of an ordinary parking lot, a conventional asphalt surface in Aalborg East. We will then elaborate on the urban sustainability *problems* that materialize on the parking lot, followed by a section on conventional parking lot design. Then we will reverse the scope and discuss the redesign *potentials* of a more sustainable future for the parking lot, elaborating on the 'What if…?' questions asked above. The chapter closes with a discussion of how the detailed issues of a situational mobilities design of a parking lot matters to the grand challenges of sustainability in section five and a chapter summary and reflection.

Figure 6.1 Top: model showing parking lot location in Aalborg East, Denmark. Bottom: photo with outlined, superimposed inset (illustration: Ditte Bendix Lanng).

A lot of environmental problems

The parking lot is located in the central node of the district of Aalborg East, in front of a large grocery store. It is a traditional-surface parking lot, consisting of a flat, asphalt surface, and has demarcated parking spaces for 100 cars. Each space is 2.5 metres by 5.0 metres. The parking lot's dimensions are approximately 65 metres by 40 metres, or about 2,600 square metres. Entry to and exit from the parking lot by car are facilitated by an access road in the south-eastern corner connected to the local road, Tornhøjvej. Its edges vary. Kerbs and grass verges of diverse topographies mark its boundaries on three sides. Thresholds for pedestrians crossing these boundaries are a staircase, asphalt paths and informal paths. The fourth, south-facing boundary of the parking lot is less manifest, shaped by the asphalt-paved access road. At the horizontal surface of the parking lot, a few light poles, sheds for shopping trolleys and kerbed traffic islands with trash bins protrude from the extensive surface continuity. That is, of course, in addition to the temporarily immobile (parked) cars and the daily life travellers of many kinds.

The parking lot displays a series of environmental problems. First, it is not unique. The parking lot is an omnipresent urban typology, and the environmental problems should be seen in the light of the global ubiquity of surface parking. In 2009, there were 600 million passenger cars in the world, and the number is growing; cars are immobile 95 per cent of the time; and in the US alone, there are 500 million surface parking spaces (Ben-Joseph 2012). Parking spaces cover a lot of space. In the central area of the district of Aalborg East, for example, surface parking takes up 14 per cent of the surface area. In other parts of the world, surface parking appears to be an equally or even more abundant phenomenon, demanding extensive measures of land. In some American cities, they cover more than one third of the land area (ibid.: xix). This shows in the figures for surface parking in various American cities. For example, the suburban strip of Orlando, Florida, has no less than 36 per cent of its area covered by surface parking. The small-town main street of Pulaski, Virginia, has 15 per cent of its surface area taken up with parking (ibid.: 14).

Surface parking is for cars. Many post-war suburbs, in particular, are built on a romance with the car. Cars, as the desired mobility mode across many cities, have received high priority in the organization and design of the suburban landscape. Urban functions are zoned and separated, and their relinkage takes place by means of a hierarchical automobility system. It is typical for the suburban form that large surface parking lots surround single use buildings that are set as solitary objects in a landscape. In the central part of Aalborg East, where the parking lot of our focus is located, this suburban form is vivid, with functions dispersed in a horizontal plan, connected by huge traffic areas, and with in-between spaces functioning as buffer zones (see Figure 6.2). Urban functions housed in buildings and recreational areas cover approximately one-third of the surface area; they are the destinations (including housing, shopping, institutions and cultural spots) which this functionalist layout is designed to cater to.

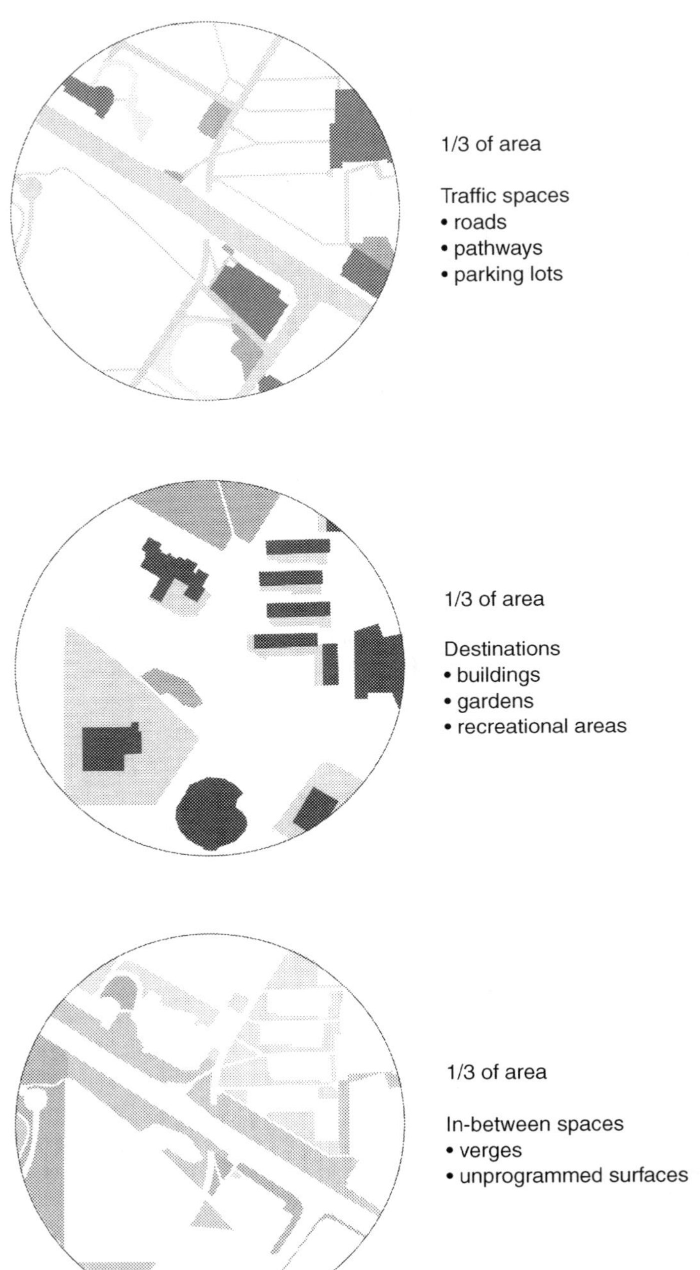

Figure 6.2 Area usage in study site in Aalborg East, Denmark; spatial typologies of the functionalist city (diagram: Ditte Bendix Lanng).

Travelling between these destinations is a necessity; we travel to get from one of these destinations to another; from home to workplace; from school to home. The roads, pathways, parking lots, entrance squares and bus-stop areas comprise this connective urban fabric of mobility spaces. They too cover one-third of the surface area. The last third is covered by in-between spaces, i.e. verges and unprogrammed surfaces. These spaces are often planted with low-maintenance vegetation and they take up a remarkable amount of space, facilitating a spacious feel, relatively long distances between buildings, and an open surround of mobility spaces. The functionalist city is continuously criticized for this type of layout, which is found to foster serious problems such as spatial disintegration, dead borders of parking and huge access roads functioning as barriers to local connectivity and livability, and urban spaces that encourage unsustainable car-dependency and discourage other forms of mobility and urban life.

Parking lots and car-dependency must be seen in the light of the extensive automobility system, which is a common and convenient transport system but also much more than that: it is an 'omnipotent taking over the world' according to Urry (2007: 134). During the twentieth century, the automobility system grew from a fledgling fascination of speed and machinic progress to having profound significance in our world, as a way of life. Urry shows how the automobility system dominates the physical organization and design of places and cities, and how it has great influence on social life, economics and politics, acting as one of the 'enduring systems that provide what we might call the infrastructures of social life' (ibid.: 12). For example, the 24-hour availability and seamlessness of individualized car travel is a highly valued asset of the automobility system, which sets it in contrast to the more inflexible and frictioned mobilities modes of public transport. The 'unbundling' of territories, i.e. the division of spaces for home, work, business, leisure, etc., is induced on our cities by the automobility system (ibid.: 120). Indeed, Urry emphasizes that automobility has initiated and reproduced spaces that were not of any relevance, nor an option, before the car. Therefore, while planning and design are guided by the principle of division, made both possible and necessary by the car, this principle further encourages automobility. The sites of automobility underline the point of how the system of automobility has created new socialities: social life has been locked in to these 'specialized time-spaces' of automobility; city life is often organized and orchestrated by people-hostile environments which Urry terms 'dead car-only environments' (ibid.: 126). We live with and by automobility in negotiating our opportunities for and constraints upon our lives. The car gives us what Urry terms 'a peculiar combination of flexibility and coercion' (ibid.: 119). The flexibility stems from the opportunities to travel wherever (far and near), whenever. In the rise of the automobility system 100 years ago, this liberation from constraints of time and space was a luxury and a fascinating driving force in developing the system. Almost-frictionless movement and unopposed progress were imagined by means of the car. Today, the flexibility seems more like a matter-of-course that rests with most of us (ibid.: 134) and is necessitated by automobility itself (ibid.: 120). As a widespread and all-embracing phenomenon, the immense system of automobility is not just a means of convenience and freedom of individualized seamless mobility but also of coercion. It forces us to live in its instantaneous, compressed time and in those stretched spaces that it has produced. We must live across huge distances in 'complex, harried patterns of social life' (ibid.: 120). The system of automobility tells us what to do, so to speak – it stages our ways of life from above and leaves, in spite of its individualization, only little space for manoeuvring within its forceful system properties.

Asphalt, the prevalent paving material of extensive parking-lot surfaces, has in itself gained considerable attention and critique (for example, see Erell *et al.* 2011; Zardini 2005). Most often, asphalt does not comply with environmental standards and does not invite social exchange to happen, not to mention the sensorial richness of travelling which we addressed in the previous chapters. Asphalt, often in large unshaded expanses on parking lots, contributes to the 'urban heat island' effect. This refers to the increased temperature of hard-surfaced urban environments in comparison to countrysides with vegetation. On the parking lot, when the sun warms the hard, dark and heat-absorbing surface, local air temperatures rise considerably. When huge urban areas are asphalted, mitigated environmental effects become weighty. They include smog elevation, higher energy demand for cooling and compromised health and comfort for people. Though the problem is more pressing in warmer countries, even temperate climate countries like Denmark experience the urban heat island effect, which is expected to increase with the anticipation of warmer summers ahead.[1] When parked cars are left to bake in the sun, they too are significant polluters, emitting contaminants and compromising air quality and health. Traditional asphalt parking lot surfaces also have negative impacts on storm-water run-off and water quality. These surfaces are impervious, and do not allow rainwater and snowmelt to be absorbed into the soil below. Environmental effects are rapid run-off that can cause flooding and hold the risk of pollutants being carried into streams and lakes. Impaired water quality is an effect, as water carries heavy metals, bacteria and other pollutants. With an increase in heavy rainfalls, the problem with storm-water and flooding has risen in recent years, triggering demands for climate-adaptive mobilities design.

The magnitude of these environmental problems grows with the tendency to oversupply parking spaces, and the 'underperformance' of asphalt (Dunham-Jones and Williamson 2011). A large part of the time, parking spaces are vacant. For example, experiences from the US show that in an average day, thousands of spaces are empty. This is the case in Maryland in the downtown areas of Silver Spring and Bethesda, where the Montgomery County Department of Transportation has documented that over 40 per cent of downtown's 9,500 parking spaces are vacant all the time.[2] This is particularly evident in large commercial lots surrounding malls. In Kansas, the tendency to build too much parking has been documented; here, minimum parking ratios have required more parking than is actually needed (Mid-America Regional Council n.d.). Minimum ratios were adopted by many cities in the 1950s and 60s to supply the growing number of cars with parking. Today, however, minimum ratios often remain, even though these do not reflect the actual demand for parking. With many parking spaces sitting vacant most of the time, these areas underperform, so to speak. This leaves parking lots as non-productive components of the urban landscape: mono-functional, overbuilt and often underwhelming, if not alienating, in their expression.

Conventional parking lot design

The environmental impacts of parking lots have often been addressed vaguely in parking-lot design guidelines as well as planning strategies, and little renewal of guidelines and strategies has been implemented so far. While optimization of space usage and vehicular flow are often achieved through design standards, city ordinances in, for example, the US from the 1960s onwards have specified accurate minimum requirements for dimensions, construction, ingress and egress, while landscaping, accessibility criteria and other environmental concerns have only nominally and gradually been integrated into formal regulations (Ben-Joseph 2012). The Danish design of parking lots does not differ much from the US approach. In Denmark, contemporary principles for parking-lot planning and design reveal that functional-programmatic considerations remain dominant on the agenda for the materialization of the widespread phenomenon of surface parking. Mainly municipal authorities through local-planning ordinances regulate Danish designs of parking lots. The Danish Road Directorate (2011, 2012) has formulated a set of national instructive guidelines. These guidelines do contain considerations for, vegetation, lighting, double use, etc., but only in vague and brief terms. In the original (and still valid) local plan for the area of the parking lot in Aalborg East, the design for parking has not been explicitly managed; only the ambiguous phrase of a 'proper appearance' of unbuilt areas has formally directed its design (Aalborg Municipality 1980). However, newer municipal documents address this design issue in less vague terms. The most distinct example with regard to this case is the 2004 Aalborg municipal Architectural Policy. It contains a section on traffic spaces and points out both a dilemma and an under-used potential for the design of these spaces:

> The challenge lies in creating cohesion between infrastructure, urban and rural spaces, and creating original and functional solutions that benefit both the traffic and the surroundings.... The city's different types of traffic spaces shall in general be infused with more aspects in relation to usage and experience so that their interaction with the buildings and structures in the surrounding district is improved. This can be achieved through a very deliberate choice of vegetation, physical cross-section, construction materials, lighting and other urban furniture.
>
> (Aalborg Municipality 2004: 12)

In spite of good intentions, these guidelines and regulations leave the parking lot designer with minimal instructions, formal knowledge, tools and power to integrate consideration for the environment in parking-lot design, and parking-lot design largely remains underdeveloped. As Ben-Joseph remarks, 'Planners, designers, developers, and the public rarely pay attention to the design of parking lots' (2012: xx). The ubiquitous landscapes of parking have become naturalized and absorbed into everyday life without too many questions. However, as we will show in the next section, demonstration projects are being designed, employing innovative technologies and a raised awareness of the significance of parking for our cities and mobilities. Further, we will show how a situational mobilities design approach offers a way to capture and deal with the problems and potentials so that these are made tangible, workable and persistent to the designer, who is not necessarily the professional alone, but may include multiple other actors in co-creation processes.

What if....? A parking lot's potentials for sustainable retrofitting

Let us return to the 'What if ...?' questions we articulated in the beginning of this: *What if the parking lot afforded more than just storage of cars? What if it supported multiple mobile situations and mixed uses? What if it facilitated local connectivity by inviting pedestrian and bicycle journeys? What if it was a green and enjoyable urban space?* These questions emanate from a locally sensitive and integrated approach to sustainable transformation. Yet, this is by far the only strategy to employ when redesigning our material surroundings as we could imagine, for example, transforming the surface parking lot to a park or building new structures there. Dunham-Jones and Williamson (2011) suggest such redevelopment as a strategy to respond to environmental challenges of suburban districts. 'Redevelopment' in their work refers to building on existing parking lots, mostly located in suburban centres, and in the context of urban visions towards a compact, walkable, connected mix of functions and urban spaces to support less auto-dependent and more socially engaged patterns of life. Current municipal planning of the parking lot in Aalborg East is promoting a similar redevelopment direction for this suburban node. If plans are realized, the entire area will be densified and infused with new functions that mix with existing ones. Such radical redevelopment is one answer to the question of what a more sustainable future of parking lots could be. It is an extensive strategy that bears resemblance to the *tabula rasa* strategies of many French suburban transformations, in which huge parts of post-war suburbs have been completely redeveloped to new urban patterns of low-rise, high-density buildings, streets with sidewalks and small shops, and urban squares (Bjørn 2008). In such redevelopments, surface parking lots are most often replaced by lots with less parking spaces due to better public transport links, by street parking and by parking garages above and below ground.

However, as suggested above, the path we will take here diverges from this answer. We will address the condition of the many places where surface parking lots will not be replaced in the near future, i.e. where surface parking lots will remain a relevant typology. In addition, we will thus concentrate on a less extensive retrofitting that keeps car parking as a central function. Surface parking has proven hardy, and it is cheap. In Denmark, construction costs for a traditional parking lot are 20,000–30,000 DKR per space (approximately US$3,000–5,000). In comparison, a conventional monofunctional multi-storey car park costs 150,000–175,000 DKR per space (or US$25,000–30,000), and a parking facility under a building reach a staggering 200,000–300,000 DKR per space (US$30,000–50,000) (Realdania By 2014). The overall assumption is that it will remain a design task to deal with surface parking for some time yet. The car will have to be parked, whether its driverless, powered by fossil fuel, hydrogen or solar, and therefore '[t]he question of where we park it and how we design spaces for it remains as essential as questions about the types of cars we will use in the future' (Ben-Joseph 2012: xii). In addition, as already noted, surface parking is already ubiquitous. The sheer extent of extant parking lots, similar all over the world, but located in many varying contexts, demands that we develop not only one but multiple retrofitting answers to mitigate adverse environmental effects. If surface parking remains relevant, the design of parking lots does too.

Parking lots have the potential to be redesigned with a series of concrete and available sustainability technologies, engineering and landscaping concepts, which can reduce the environmental impacts listed above (see Realdania By 2014; Toronto City Planning 2013; United States Environmental Protection Agency 2008 for hands-on guidelines and examples). These include a number of possibilities for retrofitting. The reduction of parking space dimensions, as even a modest decrease can add up to save unnecessary surfacing: Kansas has allowed the building of compact parking spaces, reducing sizes from almost 3 by 6 metres to 2.3 by 4.6 metres. The planting of shade trees (and the planning ordinances to ensure it) and use of cool pavements to mitigate the urban heat island effect is another option. The use of permeable/porous pavements, such as turf grids, porous asphalt or open-jointed pavers, allows rainwater to filter through to the soil below, reducing run-off problems. Balanced and efficient lighting (such as with LED technology) increases safety and comfort and reduces energy consumption. Another possibility is the incorporation of bio-retention areas, such as bioswales and overflow ponds, and absorbent landscaping to maximize shade, storm-water and water quality benefits, and circulation. Various parking lots exist where some or more of such sustainable technologies and concepts are in use. In New Jersey, for example, the US Environmental Protection Agency has constructed an experimental parking lot to demonstrate the use of pavements and rain gardens that mitigate problems of storm-water flooding (Realdania By 2014: 88).[3] The project incorporates three types of paving systems, and the objective is to monitor and compare their abilities to reduce negative effects of storm-water run-off, including stream-bank erosion, contamination of water sources and harm to aquatic plant and animal life. The sub-base material of the parking lot is reused, crushed local concrete. Rainwater is drained off from the pavement and the rain gardens surrounding the parking lot filter it for contaminants before it is absorbed into the water-supply system.

Other demonstration projects are being made with energy-producing parking lots. Examples include a Sainsbury's store in Gloucester, England, where kinetic energy plates have been installed (Realdania By 2014: 68), and in France, where car manufacturer Renault has installed solar panels on several of their parking lots, which in total cover the energy demand of 15,000 people (ibid.: 82). Parking is also part of the wider planning endeavours of the PlaNYC, New York City's development and retrofitting initiatives towards a sustainable and resilient city. Here also, landscape-engineered solutions for managing storm-water/rain-water, such as pervious paving, bioswales and other water efficient landscaping, are being used. An example is the Remsen Hall Forecourt, where an existing impervious parking lot separated the main square from the entrance. To create a pedestrian-friendly space and to mitigate storm-water effects, the parking lot was retrofitted with permeable pavers, rain gardens and bioswales (PlaNYC Environmental Protection 2012: 30). This last example demonstrates that concepts and technologies can be combined into a retrofit that integrates technological sustainability innovations with design concepts for promoting other aspects of sustainable urban environments. These can include walkability, connectivity, multiple uses and urban livability. If parking lots were sustainable, not only would technological retrofitting play a role, in addition, their significance as urban spaces and interfaces of segregated mobility systems, with social and cultural significance for the city and its users, would also be taken into account. As advocated by professor and landscape architect Elizabeth Mossop, the design of ubiquitous infrastructural spaces, such as parking lots, needs to meet more demands than high standards of technical (environmental) efficiency:

> [A] reexamination of infrastructural spaces involves the recognition that all types of space are valuable, not just the privileged spaces of more traditional parks and squares, and they must therefore be inhabitable in a meaningful way. This requires the rethinking of the monofunctional realm of infrastructure and its rescue from the limbo of urban devastation to recognize its role as a part of the formal inhabited city. Designers need to engage with this infrastructural landscape: mundane parking facilities, difficult spaces under elevated roads, complex transit interchanges, and landscapes generated by waste processes.
>
> (2006: 171)

Some parking lots enjoy central locations and have the potential to become key spaces. Parking lots can be a resource along our journeys; they can work as those Critical Points of Contact in the urban and mobilities networks, which enable journeys to be carried on. To a much wider extent than the monofunctional and monocultural lots, they can perform as the necessary key points that connect various mobility systems, for example by making the shifts between car and public transit, foot or bike accessible, easy and enjoyable, as we know it from best-practice park-and-ride facilities. They can be public spaces that invite connectivity, social exchange and urban life.

The parking lot in Aalborg East exposes some of this potential. It is centrally located in the district's node, where mobility systems meet and vital common functions such as grocery shopping, library, health facilities, school and children's day care are located but not all well-connected. The parking lot lies as a square in front of several of these functions, facilitating a contact point between the wider local and regional car-based mobility system, the local destinations and the well-developed local system of pathways for pedestrians and cyclists. As a car driver, this is the space you see from the large road, and it is the space you encounter when you get off the main road. As a bus passenger, you get off the bus in the narrow verge in between the parking lot and the large road, and the easiest way to reach the grocery store or the school is by crossing the lot, as we saw it in the mobile situation reported in the opening of this chapter. As a pupil at the public school, you cross the lot on your way from the pathway system to the school entrance. These mobilities patterns foster many and diverse routes through the parking lot. Though inhabitation is sparsely seen, over time the parking lot is criss-crossed by flows of pedestrians, car drivers, bicyclists and other travellers who use the open surface to reach their destinations (see Figure 6.3). These travellers form a diverse group of people who perform mobilities in variations of modalities, rhythms and social and sensorial engagements. The parking lot is part of the private property of the shopping centre, with a distinct temporal rhythm of occupation peaking around late afternoon on weekdays, when more people tend to go shopping. It is also used for parking outside of open hours when, for example, events are held at the public school next to the store. Parked cars tend to be primarily in the south-eastern part of the lot, forming a distinct pattern of occupation: cars circle around on one side of the lot,

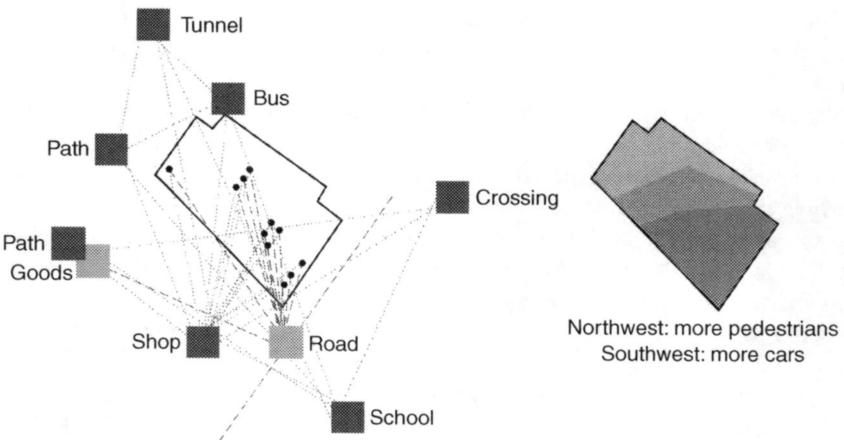

Figure 6.3 Patterns of inhabitation of the parking lot. Left: point-to-point connections of motorized traffic, pedestrians and cyclists, and switches between car and foot. Right: occupational pattern (diagram: Ditte Bendix Lanng).

whereas the majority of pedestrian flows tend to be on the other side. A particularly regularly travelled flow route for pedestrians leads across the parking lot from its far north-western corner to the far south-eastern corner. The journeys of this route are conducted by passengers from the bus who arrive from the city centre and head for the grocery store, school or day care institutions south of the parking lot, just as the woman in our mobile situation. So although the parking lot is sparsely and episodically inhabited, each journey is performed within a pulsating network of co-existing mobile situations. It is an arena of changing formations of mobile and (temporarily) immobile people and things, which fosters subtle 'negotiations in motion' (Jensen 2010a, 2010b). Such mobile negotiations can happen when the bus passengers arrive and trot across the asphalt surface, on the way exchanging subtle and nuanced signs with car drivers about turns and halts.

At localities where routes intersect or overlap, they shape temporary 'social condensers' for travellers who flow in and out of different 'mobile withs' (Jensen 2009). These can include small travel groups, such as two kids who playfully stumble across the kerb-side of the parking lot, or an unplanned meeting between acquaintances on their way. They also include the 'long goodbyes' of our two schoolgirls. They perform their journey home from school across the lot on a daily basis. On their way, they are likely to be caught up in conversation with their co-travelling friends at crossroad places before they must continue in different directions. They like to linger at such places, delving into a long goodbye, talking together, not really motivated to leave. One important place of crossroads is on the edge of the parking lot, where some travellers would need to continue to the bus stop, others to the tunnel or south along the pathway. It is also a place for chance encounters for travellers who come from different directions. One of the schoolgirls vividly explains the simple presence of the crossroads as orchestrating the way that these become the places where they tend to linger: 'It's right here that we have to go in different directions [...] so it's right here that we gather' (interviewee, 5 July 2012). The crossroads are simple intersections of pathways or informal routes. These intersections have not been designed for lingering or meeting as such, but nevertheless they pull travellers together before pushing them in different directions again, forming tiny nodes of dynamic proximity in the vast space.

As the surface material of the parking lot, asphalt is practical for driving and for manoeuvring shopping carts. However, the material is also active in co-conditioning mobilities on the lot in other ways. The two schoolgirls recall how the parking lot surface could be a facility for ludic activities. When they were younger, they enjoyed this place, as it gave them the chance to play on wheels: '[W]e used to come here and just cycle or skate or something like that, and just go round. It was great, because it's such a large place [...] such a plane surface; there aren't any pebbles', one of them reported (5 July 2012). As the girl points to here, the simple architectural feature of a smooth, planar, extensive asphalt surface invites not only parking, car driving and easy pushing of shopping trolleys but also this ludic activity. In parking lot designs, this asset of asphalt has been explored. For instance, a Berlin parking lot, designed by 'Topotek 1' in a housing development at Flämingstrasse, integrates a children's playground by superimposing signs, codes and colours known from road markings on the unvarying asphalt surface. The architects articulate their intention with the design:

> In this way, the polyvalent parking area, traversed by routes leading to the building, creates a graphic landscape in which the lines that delimit spaces alternate and overlap with a system of more complex signs offering opportunities for open space. The result is an aesthetic of conflict designed to foster, day after day, new negotiations on the very interpretation of space.
>
> (www.topotek1.de)

As we addressed with the situational opening of this chapter, the parking lot is designed on the terms of the car, even though this utilitarian-only automobility space tends to threaten the local area's connectivity, walkability and well-being for people who are not in a car. However, the mobile situations reported above demonstrate that this parking lot is not solely a detached monocultural and utilitarian-only space. Though the parking lot itself does not contain formal architectural features to support its affordances of culturally, affectively and socially important daily life mobilities, the mobile urban life does thrive to some extent. This points to the potential of the parking lot to be a 'mobile agora' (Jensen 2009: 151). It is part of the continuous urban fabric of the neighbourhood, and it has significance in how journeys are performed in the district. In the continuities and discontinuities of daily life mobilities, the parking lot plays a very concrete role in staging these mobilities. The parking lot's location and spatial relation matter in this role. Its edges and the adjacent spaces in its periphery, such as the bus-stop area and the entrance plaza of the shopping centre, shape it as an ambiguous public space and as a Critical Point of Contact in the area. Arguably, this is not the case for every parking lot, and the potential for parking lots to perform as important public spaces may be particularly significant in suburban areas where traditional public spaces, such as inner city squares, are rare. Urban life in the suburb takes place in relation to mundane activities in residual spaces. The daily meetings and the experiences at the bus stop or at the parking lot in front of the grocery store are important parts of life in the city. Design attention should therefore also be paid to unfolding the possibility for supporting the 'public domain' (Hajer and Reijndorp 2001) that a parking lot has; it is a combined connective and disruptive in-between space, in order to support places of human interaction that relink the divided zones and mobility systems of functionalist planning (see Figure 6.4). A parking lot is, potentially, more than a facility for parking cars. It is one of the ambiguous mobility places of rest, activity, meeting, experience and consumption (Urry 2007: 148), where design may afford possibilities for travellers to cultivate the 'precious gift of travel time' (Vannini 2012: 194) and develop meaningful social practices and experiences.

1

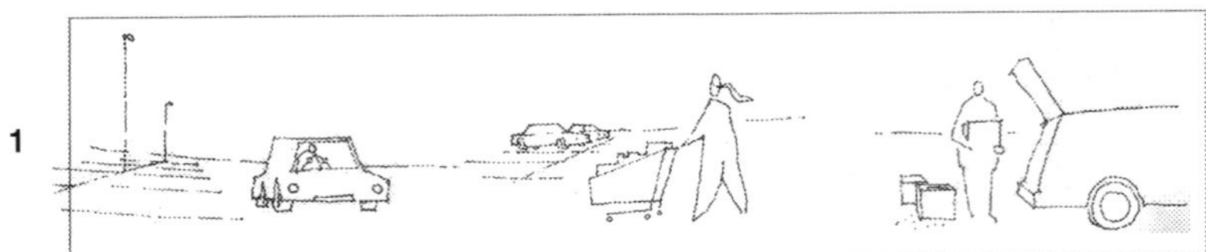

Straight from A to B

Enter by car – park – walk to shop – walk to car – exit by car

Modalities: car, foot

2

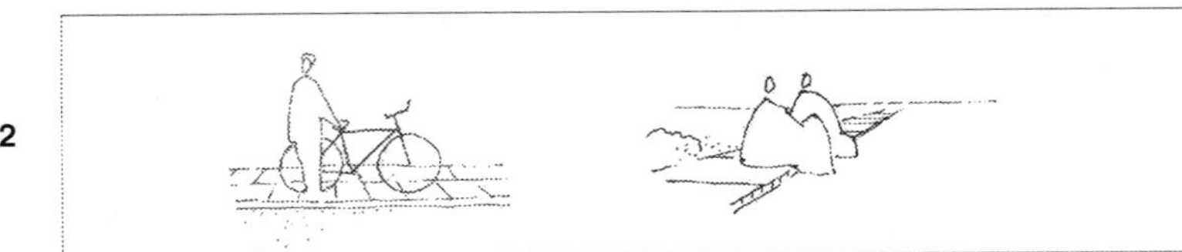

Lingering (on the edge)

Sit down or hang out (for a break or a meeting with an acquaintance)

Modalities: foot, bike, moped, wheelchair

3

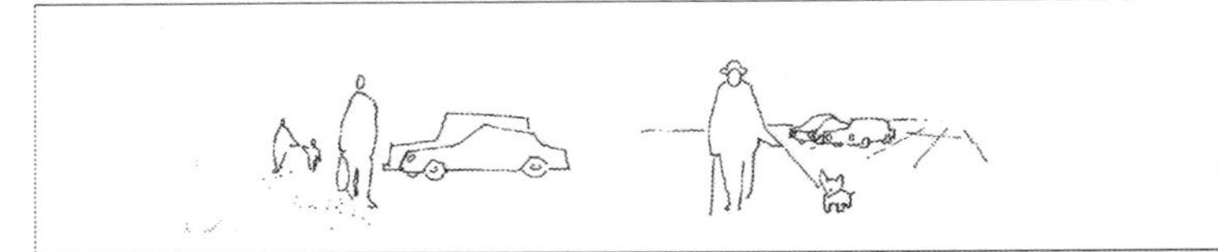

Crossing with the flow

Get off bus – walk across lot in a dispersed group – enter shop/school

Modalities: foot

4

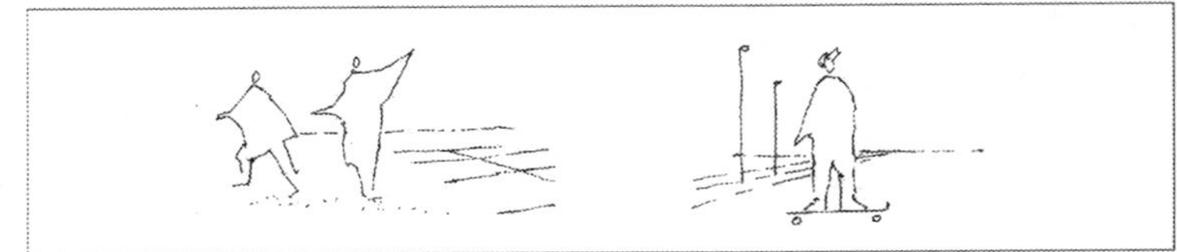

Ludic

Recreational activities on the surface

Modalities: rollerblades, foot, bike, skateboard

5

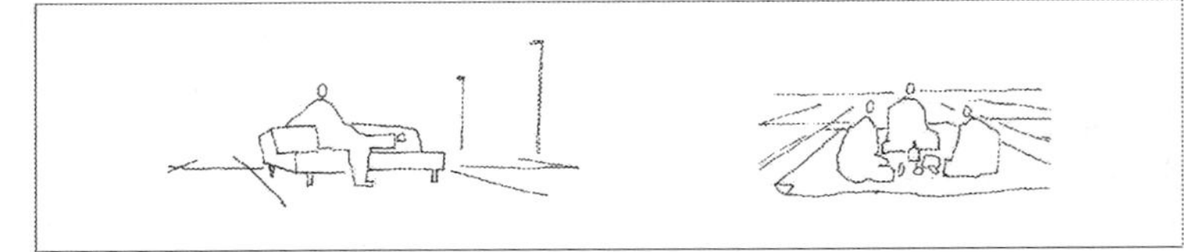

Park(ing) Day

Furnished parking booth, plants, events, encounters

Modalities: foot, bike, wheelchair, skateboard

Figure 6.4 A catalogue of mobile situations that do or could occur on the parking lot (drawings: Hans Bruun Olesen; concept: Ditte Bendix Lanng).

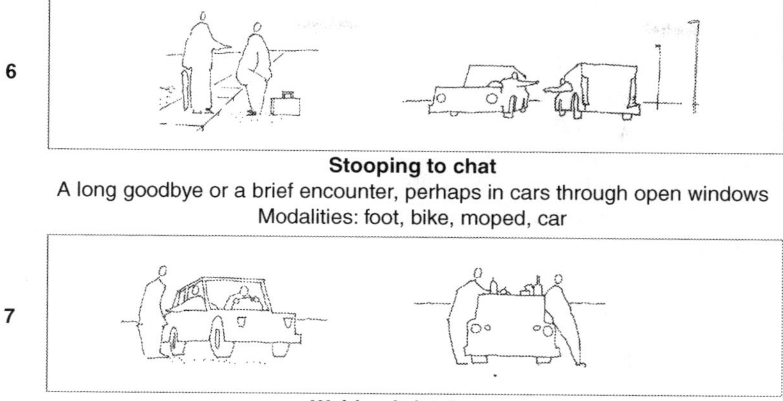

Stooping to chat
A long goodbye or a brief encounter, perhaps in cars through open windows
Modalities: foot, bike, moped, car

Waiting in/at the car
A temporary stop, maybe with the motor on, perhaps a lunch break
Modalities: car, foot

Figure 6.4 Continued.

Using the potential of the parking lot as a central and more sustainable space in the area and in the mobility systems demands an integrated transformation approach, which uses both technological innovations and the recognition of the parking lot as an urban space where users' daily life mobilities can be performed in appreciated and sustainable ways. The parking lot can be a place that exceeds its one-dimensional role as unsustainable, monocultural and car-dependent. The potential is to search for ways to develop it into a heterogeneous and vibrant urban component with significance for the neighbourhood, and for journey connectivity and experiences. A place to start could be transforming a few per cent of the parking spaces to little gardens on the extensive asphalt surface (since there is an oversupply of spaces, except for a few peak hours per year). The parking spaces could be spread out on the surface, to provide a network of traffic islands to ease the connectivity for non-car travellers in the daily life use of the lot. The spaces could also work as demonstrations of sustainable landscaping elements, integrating some or more of the technologies and concepts mentioned above. They could possibly work as small multisensorial features that add a richness of materials and effects to the asphalt: sounds, plants, smells, rubber, shadows, shelters, wood, water, concrete and dirt, perhaps then introducing new affordances for meetings, sensorial pleasure, fun and sustainable mobility choices. This brief, imagined retrofitting is a simple and open concept that explores the thriving of daily life mobile situations with their cultural and social indeterminacy and heterogeneity, as an overlayering of a parking lot monoculture. Such a design concept does not work with replacing the existing logics of surface parking. It works, instead, with exploring a space of opportunities for retrofitting within these logics, in order to supplement the utilitarian-only layout with considerations for sustainability. Figure 6.5 is an image of an initial, simple mock-up of a single-parking space reconfiguration on the parking lot in Aalborg East. The concept of 'Parklets' as well as the annual international open-source event, 'Park(ing) Day' (www.parkingday.org), similarly reject the idea of utilitarian parking monoculture and expose the multiple possibilities of how to take over single-parking spaces. Park(ing) Day takes place on the third Friday of September every year. In 2011, more than 900 parking spots across six continents were redesigned into imaginative public spaces for a day by artists, designers and other citizens.

Figure 6.5 A parking space retrofit at the lot in Aalborg East, Denmark (photo: Ditte Bendix Lanng).

With an urban mobilities design approach, a sustainable parking lot retrofitting is an integrative effort of balancing the utilitarian and short-run cost-effective demand for efficient surface parking with a strategic and concrete consideration for the environment, beginning with the low-carbon mobile situations, which the parking lot design should stage. An example of a parking lot retrofit that integrates several such objectives is the award-winning project Edwards Gardens/Toronto Botanical Garden Sustainable Parking Lot Retrofit in Toronto.[4] Schollon & Company Inc. conducted the retrofit of the deteriorated parking lot as a pilot project by the Toronto and Region Conversation Authority and the City of Toronto to demonstrate sustainable parking lot technologies. The design is developed on a multi-object approach, including the mitigation of storm-water impacts on a nearby creek, the enhancement of a tree canopy, the improvement of circulation, pedestrian access and safety, and the complementation of the interpretive and educational programmes of the botanical garden. Permeable pavers on parking spaces and walkways, integration of bioswales, traditional storm-water management, extensive plantings and public art are included in the project. The retrofit has limited the parking lot's impact on the creek, including eliminating further erosion of the banks adjacent to the parking lot, and has improved the water quality of storm-water. The result has reduced the urban heat island effect, provided better wayfinding for users, and improved safety in the winter due to the reduction of ice and snow build-up on permeable pavers. Another example is the climate-adapted parking area of the town hall square at Viborg, Denmark, designed by LIW planning. The design is distinctive as it rejects the idea of utilitarian monoculture and combines the parking lot with the traditional core urban functions in a hybrid area that includes the town hall and its square, a park and parking. It integrates rainwater basins and solar cells with possibilities for urban life, including taking breaks, sports and experiences. The functions are organized side by side and on top of each other in a mosaic of intimate spaces and large surfaces, with different materials and uses throughout the day and year (Ravn 2015; Realdania By 2014: 76).

However, in light of the overarching problems of climate change and resource scarcity, parking lot meeting places, mobility connections, storm-water management, pervious asphalt, LED lighting and the other technologies and concepts which have been mentioned cannot function in isolation. This integrated retrofitting approach is just one element in an incremental transition towards sustainable and resilient cities. In the next section, we will briefly discuss other important aspects of sustainable parking lot design, as well as discussing how situational mobilities design really can be a resource for sustainable urbanism and mobilities.

Discussion: does it matter?

It is fair to question whether sustainable retrofitting of parking lots can have any significant reach or impact on the grand challenges of a more sustainable future. Urry, for example, argues that we are 'locked in' to the precarious automobility (2007). Automobility is a path-dependent pattern in which social life, economics and power are so intricately intertwined that it seems irreversible. The car alone is not what is so significant; rather it is the complexity of tightly knitted interconnections between coevolving, coadapting things, agents, power and money that makes the system, sustains it and reproduces it:

> The car is interlinked with licensing authorities; traffic police; petrol refining and distribution; road-building and maintenance; hotels, road side service areas and motels; car sales and repair shops ... suburban and green-field house-buildings sites; retailing and leisure complexes; advertising and marketing; and urban design and planning so as to ensure uninterrupted movement.... These interlinkages are 'locked in' and have helped to ensure that this system has increasingly spread around the world.... Billions of agents and thousands of organizations have co-evolved and adapted to that remaking of the system of automobility as it spread like a virus around the globe.
>
> (Urry 2007: 116–17)

With such a powerful complex, it is very difficult to imagine, let alone carry through, realistic alternatives to automobility, even though this system has evident and very serious disadvantages beyond the ones described in this chapter (for example, exhaustion of resources, pollution and vast amounts of casualties). However, as Urry also asserts the 'days of steel and petroleum automobility are numbered' (ibid.: 285), and a tipping point to not only a different vision of an alternative post-car mobilities nexus, but also concrete actions towards realization, may be ahead.

In Chapter 2, we pointed to the 'radically careful, or carefully radical' promise of design, argued for by Latour (2008). Modesty and attention to detail were some of the key traits for this promise, which does not directly offer itself to grand systems and challenges. Yet, in this chapter we have dealt with small mobile situations of parking lots, and we have teased out some of the 'many nitty-gritty, material-performative details that are so important to both architects' design and users' experiences' (Kraftl and Adey 2008: 214). We have suggested small material changes that could be done to the parking lot to accommodate steps on the way to a more sustainable future. Following Urry's concept of 'lock-in', such materialities may be able to co-evolve and coadapt with multiple other entities to add up to form a tipping point for a sustainable nexus. Parking lots do play an elaborate role for cities and mobilities in the automobility system, and the material small-scale design of the mobile situations should be regarded in association with a variety of other careful detailing and more or less modest issues that contribute to staging mobilities of parking lots. Let us foreground three important issues.

First, it is highly relevant to broaden the attention from the small-scale design approach we have addressed above to include many more planning and policy possibilities for sustainable staging of parking lot situations. These include deliberate parking strategies, such as Smart Parking. Between 8 and 74 per cent of car traffic in busy urban areas is caused by drivers looking for parking. In Denmark, the number is approximately 30 per cent. In many places in the world, Smart

Parking is being used to reduce these numbers and to address pollution and problems with road safety. In Los Angeles, for example, the City is installing single space parking detection (SDD) on the roads to give drivers information about vacant spaces. The solution gives reliable data in real time but is rather costly (1,000–1,500 DKR per space for a six-year sensor life). A much less costly option is to let users provide the information to each other through apps. Another Smart Parking intervention is seen in San Francisco, where parking rates have been made dynamic, so that the price is regulated according to demand (on a monthly basis). An app gives car drivers an overview of where a vacant space is and the price of it (Realdania By 2014: 90).

Planning and policy interventions to support more sustainable parking also include deliberate zoning amendments. In New York City's large-scale ambitions through the PlaNYC, parking lots play a role in improving water quality, for instance. The work with Green Infrastructure Plans (PlaNYC 2010, 2012) concerns improvement of water quality through integration of green infrastructures. Parking lots add up to 6 per cent of New York City's impervious area, and apart from material design alternatives in public demonstration projects (see above), the City enacted zoning amendments in 2008 that entail commercial and communal parking lots to construct interior and edge landscaping which works as storm-water bio-retention basins.

The supply of parking handled by maximum and minimum ratios is another relevant tool for planning and policy staging of more sustainable parking. As referred to above, tendencies to oversupply parking can be traced. In many central urban areas in Denmark, minimum requirements have been replaced by maximum requirements, thereby reversing the hierarchy between car-users and other mobility modes, responding to the problems with oversupply, and mitigating increased car-dependency.

The cheapness of establishing and using parking can also be reviewed. In his work on 'the high cost of free parking', Shoup (2005) points to the question of who is paying for parking, and thus for its environmental impacts. He asserts that free or cheap parking is a way to subsidize the automobility system, and thus it enters a cycle to reinforce car-dependency. An (over-)supply of free or cheap parking encourages driving by making it cheaper and more convenient, whereas it discourages (through barriers, pedestrian-hostility, bad connectivity) other more sustainable modes of mobilities. However, we must add (not at least in the light of the theme of the following chapters) that economic incentives aiming to reduce transportation carry the risk of social bias and exclusion.

Second, the intersection between mobilities design and sustainability is surely not just relevant for suburban parking lots. Our chapter was based on this, but the term 'suburb' is not key, since suburbs exist in many varying and challenging versions in the world. Mobilities design and sustainable parking lots should be considered in relation to the multicantered dynamics of urban areas – with networks and hybridization of suburban and urban patterns and ways of life. If we stay with parking, we should also look to parking garages, which increasingly are developed as more than concrete eyesores into inviting, efficient and iconic urban elements.[5]

Indeed, multiple other mobility structures, sites and systems, such as roads and streets are relevant to consider through the lens of sustainable mobilities design. An example is the notion of complete streets, related to New Urbanism and public transit networks and interchanges, e.g. train stations and bus stops. A transport interchange can be considered as 'a gateway to sustainable development' (Edwards 2010: 3) and its embedded sustainable, social, cultural and aesthetic matters can be pointed to when considering mobile situations. As with many mobilities sites, the potential for making use of sustainable technologies and concepts is far from exhausted: 'There are surprisingly few examples of eco-design of railway and bus stations, and airport and ferry terminals' (ibid.: 2). Furthermore, design for velomobilities and pedestrian mobilities is apposite. Design that invites sustainable modes of mobilities includes deliberate attention to staging mobile situations by bike or foot, for instance, in ways that are convenient, safe, experiential, fun, etc. The Danish capital of Copenhagen is often praised as a bike-friendly city par excellence, with its sophisticated and extensive network of wide bicycle lanes, including, for example, the programming of traffic lights with so-called green waves that give priority to bicyclist flows in rush hours. We may even talk of 'bicycletecture', which is architecture devoted to afford bicycling (Fleming 2012).

Third, and in continuation of such devotion to afford sustainable mobile ways of life, we reiterate mobilities design's commitment to the agency of designed materialities, which we addressed in Chapter 3. In the networked relations of mobile situations, designed materialities *do* stuff. Our use of the concept of affordances to aid capturing these doings may, in a practical context of mobilities design and among design and planning professionals, be related to the concepts of 'nudging', or, 'behavioural design'. These refer to the technique of influencing people in specific situations to adjust their choices or behaviour (see www.behaviouraldesignlab.org). Concrete situational design solutions maybe developed with the intention of making people choose more sustainable ways of mobile life. As our current mobilities design effort is occupied with an open exploration of key concepts and ways of thinking and aim to develop design consideration from concrete site-specific mobile situations, we have avoided delineating general principles of sustainable mobilities design, which we see in New Urbanism, for example. However, in associating mobilities design with nudging, it is persistent to highlight that the correlation between urban form and the use of design formulas is debated. The mitigated effects of New Urbanist interventions are going through some controversy, both in relation to the explicit intentions of, as an example, encouraging walking or physical activity and to possible consequences such as gentrification and raised inequality (Ellis 2002; Lund 2003; Rodríguez *et al.* 2006).

Conclusion: mobilities design and sustainability

With a mobilities design approach, sustainable parking-lot retrofitting is an integrative effort of balancing the utilitarian demand for efficient surface parking with strategic as well as concrete considerations for the environment, in this case the low-carbon mobile situations and patterns of life that the parking lot should support. Situational mobilities design offers a certain approach to sustainable urbanism and mobilities, which begins with concrete situations where materialities and lived mobile lives come together. This approach highlights problems and potentials for more sustainable user choices, embedded in the materialities, which we have discussed in relation to connectivity, barriers and the coercion or promotion of various modes of mobilities, etc. The 'What if . . .?' questions point to mobile situations – to the daily shift between mobility systems, to the pleasure of inhabiting a parking lot, and to the engineered sustainable landscaping which can support it. With the integration of such multiple issues and objectives, which are present in the situation, mobilities design provides an argument in favour of a cross-disciplinary effort for sustainability. Clearly, many professional expert fields are needed when the ambition is to merge insight into cultural, ecological, technological, social and political formations in the design of some of our residual spaces.

From exploring the theme of sustainability through the artefact of the parking lot, we next turn to the issue of inequality as it becomes manifest at a road crossing.

Notes

1 curis.ku.dk/ws/files/34391374/UHI_i_K_benhavn_25_august_2010_GRAS_LIFE_1.pdf.
2 http//:greatergreaterwashington.org (accessed November 27 2015).
3 www2.epa.gov/water-research/experimental-permeable-pavement-parking-lot-and-rain-garden-stormwater-management
4 www.csla-aapc.ca/awards-atlas/edwards-gardens-sustainable-parking-lot-retrofit; www.rvanderson.com/index.php/news-events/item/351-edwards-gardens-sustainable-parking-lot-demonstrates-low-impact-development-techniques (accessed 15 September 2015); http://oala.ca/edwards-gardens-sustainable-parking-lot-retrofit/
5 www.greenparkingcouncil.org/structures-and-places/design-matters/

7 Road-crossing inequalities

Mobile situation: cycling across the road, Aalborg East, Denmark [28 September 2012]

An elderly man waits for a break in the flow of fast traffic on a big road. He is on his bike, ready to cross when the opportunity presents itself (see Figure 7.1). It quickly does, as cars are not that numerous on this road and because they come in groups, depending on the traffic signals further west downhill and uphill to the east. This particular place is not a designated crossing and the man is therefore left to his own devices to negotiate his way across the road. In the middle of the road, there is a narrow strip of grass and dirt and a passage through it for turning cars. Here the man can stop and give way to the passing cars. At times in heavy traffic, cars drive by in front of him and behind him, and he waits on the central

Figure 7.1 Crossing the road by bike (photo: Ditte Bendix Lanng).

reserve to seize the chance to get across. He is on his way to the area around the newly built health-care centre on the opposite side of the road. If he followed the designated bike path, he would have to make a detour of at least 300 metres to go through the tunnel, so he chooses to act against the design scripts of the large road, as do many other local pedestrians and cyclists.

Introduction: how fast should Grandma run?

> [M]achines, structures, and systems of modern material culture can be accurately judged not only for their contributions of efficiency and productivity, not merely for their positive and negative environmental side effects, but also for the ways in which they can embody specific forms of power and authority.
>
> (Winner 1980: 121)

This chapter is based on the fact that 'mobilities are incredibly uneven and differentiated' (Adey 2010: 87). In *Critical Mass: Transport, Environment and Society in the Twenty-first Century*, transport scholar John Whitelegg fleshes out the significance of social stratification to mobilities design by referring to a comparison between the time one needs to cross on a green light as a pedestrian in the two German cities of Hamburg and Kassel (1997: 134). By using a cartoon and the question 'How fast should grandma run?', Whitelegg imminently addresses the core issue of this chapter. The pictures show an elderly woman at a zebra crossing with a green light. In the one situation (Hamburg), the woman would have to cross the road with a speed of 2.3 km/h to reach the other side while the light is still green. In the other situation (Kassel), she would have to cross the road with a speed of 9.3 km/h to reach the other side while the light is still green. In the latter image, the woman runs (with her cane). Whitelegg presents the image in the following manner:

> [The image] shows that traffic engineers have intervened to give priority to drivers at the expense of elderly pedestrians. A deliberate decision has been taken to steal time from the grandma (in this example) and give it to the motorist. All traffic engineering and infrastructure planning embodies the theft of time in some shape or form and its redistribution to wealthier groups.
>
> (1997: 133)

Values and norms are embedded within design principles and ideas, as well as being enshrined in the very materialities of urban mobilities design. This is clearly brought out in Whitelegg's image of the situational dependencies and linkages between a piece of design code, specified by a traffic engineer in accordance with a larger scheme of seamless car-mobility, and the situational practice of pedestrians or cyclists coping with movement within such coded systems. His striking image shapes our attention to the lack of neutrality to mobilities infrastructures and leads to a clear picture of the significance of design trade-offs which have to be made and which have real, situational effects. 'Stealing time' from one user group to another has become a key issue within the mobility differentiations inscribed into everyday life infrastructures. Furthermore, Whitelegg's image and the mobile situation from the road crossing in Aalborg East reported above show that priority of one type of mobilities users over others comes at the expense of safety and comfort. This might indeed have repercussions for how places are used, which routes and modes of mobilities are chosen by users (by those who have a choice), and how mobilities are felt. It points to mobilities design's embedding in questions of politics, such as whose mobilities are staged in better ways than others, and how materialities match the (bodily) affordances of users. In fact, such design priorities are tied into the '[k]notty issues of mobilities and politics' (Adey 2010: 85), which include questions of difference, access, exclusion and marginality. Hence, the universal and ordinary design of the mobile situation above may be a window into some of the very wide societal implications of mobility and infrastructure provision, as exemplified by Adey:

> Just as some people might have better access to mobility, once gained, they may use their mobility to reinforce and improve their social standing. Those who can afford to drive a car, for instance, or can afford a toll-road perhaps, may be given greater opportunities for employment, while, say, someone who couldn't afford it might not. The ultimate issue here then is much more than a recognition of difference; it is rather how those differences are reflected and come to reinforce societal inequalities and differences.
>
> (2010: 93)

Around the world, each street crossing, road dimensioning and traffic-light code carries a load of choices, normativity and priority between user groups. This is an obvious effect of multiple user groups often needing to share the same space. The zero-sum game of infrastructure provision is, however, not a simple matter of deducing values into design. Choices are made. This is the situation in Aalborg East, where the segregation of mobility modes was inscribed into the design doctrine of functionalist urban planning, not in order to exclude low-income groups or less-abled citizens as such, but in accordance with a vision of creating a highly efficient and seamless traffic machine. Speed and connections across distances, most often by car, were seen as a promise of progress, involving ideological associations of mobility with universalism and freedom (see Adey 2010). However – and this is not just confined to the case of the road crossing – mobilities design is not neutral. As Adey argues, mobilities cannot be treated in depoliticized and universal ways; it is a deception that we can have free and equal mobility (2010). In the traffic segregation system of Aalborg East, we see an instance of how a particular design produces inflexible effects and serious consequences, in that surface crossings of the roads were defined as unwanted practices.

This particular road in Aalborg East is a long, straight corridor connecting central city parts with eastern city parts. Along its route, it cuts through the district of Aalborg East, with a few side roads, designed as cul-de-sacs, facilitating car access into the local residential areas and servicing facilities. When driving along the road by car, the suburban district is less visible. The road is elevated in the terrain, and buildings and activity sites of the suburb are hidden behind dense verge vegetation. The suburb, on the other hand, turns its back on the road and has its own local pathway system for pedestrians and cyclists to access facilities and residential areas. Therefore, the road is not designed for pedestrians to cross. Nonetheless, they do (see Figure 7.2). At the site where the cycling man crosses the road, the road is approximately 27 metres wide. Many people cross the road in this area, and informal dirt paths along the road and in the median strip show where the preferred routes are. The predominant materials of the informal crossing area are asphalt, earth and grass. These materials do not invite pedestrians and cyclists to cross here, as it is uncomfortable and dangerous due to roaring cars and the muddy and slippery roadsides after rainfall, which make people walk directly on the road. Still people cross, some in vividly dangerous mobile situations in which they run across at the last moment with cars approaching. At walking speed, it takes approximately 17 seconds to cross the road: 13 seconds on the road lanes and 4 seconds on the median strip. What seems to have produced this transgressive and dangerous state of affairs is that the car infrastructure is actually better connected to local facilities than the walking/cycling pathway infrastructure is. The nearest formal crossing point of the road is the

Figure 7.2 Crossing the road by foot (photo: Ditte Bendix Lanng).

tunnel, which is not far away but still far enough to be deselected as the better option for many travellers. The traffic segregation does not leave much room for flexible route choices, as the lack of sidewalks and paths leading directly into parking lots or roads illustrates. Having said this, we also readily recognize that the slow-moving suburban dweller in Aalborg East has a completely different social situation than the inhabitant of a favela in Rio or a shanty town in Johannesburg. The discussion of inequality is of course relative to their actual contexts, but at the same time we acknowledge that there are situations and cases with a much graver dimensions. These sites might also be explored in a mobilities design analysis and they would raise a very different set of issues.

In sum, this piece of the road is the site of a conflictual co-existence of the directional flow of car traffic and of the cross-directional flow of vulnerable pedestrians and bicyclists. The number of informal crossings appears to have increased with the new public facilities built adjacent to the road, causing many people to have errands across the road. The physical environment of the road, its width, uniformity and sparse signage, has very little indication for car drivers that this is a place where vulnerable travellers might cross, and the crossing travellers face a huge barrier to their local mobilities as they must move close to the cars without much safe space or time. Thus, and in accordance with mobilities design speculations on alternatives and potentials, this place epitomizes concrete questions of equality and mobilities design priorities, such as: *What if mobile hierarchies were reversed? What if the local connectivity and urban coherence were the main design priorities? What if the road crossing afforded a dynamic rhythm of safe and experiential flows of both cars and pedestrians/cyclists? Or, what if slow-speed local mobilities did not produce friction for smooth and fast regional flows?*

This chapter discusses the theme of mobilities design and inequalities, first by addressing how sites of mobilities are underpinned by and organized around values and normative principles which stage mobilities in accordance with particular interests and visions. Following this discussion, we unfold two mobile situations: the automobility situation of a car driver along the linear and orderly regional road, and the local and tactile situation of two crossing pedestrians. These mobile situations intersect and co-exist in our particular road space in Aalborg East. From this report on mobile situations within the segregated mobility systems, we unfold a redesign speculation on possibilities of rethinking the informal road crossing. Next we open a discussion of the politics of artefacts in mobilities design, including the significant inequalities, which occur when mobile situations are staged (and relationships between people are therefore engineered). We conclude with some relevant reflections.

Imaginary mobile subject types – design for the transported traveller

The fundamental questions of access to infrastructure provision, social justice and equality have an already well-established basis within planning theory and human geography in general (Davis 1990; Flyvbjerg 1998; Harvey 1996; Healey 1997; Jensen and Freudendal-Pedersen 2012; Jensen and Richardson 2004). Based on the initial claims by French philosopher Henri Lefebvre of 'the right to the city' (1996), American geographer Ed Soja has argued for 'spatial justice' and 'a transformative politics of difference' in relation to urban planning (2000: 409). Along the same line of argument planning theorists, Sandercock (2003) and Friedmann (2002) argue for a politics of multiplex heterogeneity and multiplicity, in which the multiple subjects and voices of the city should be included into decision processes. The utopian dimension to such thinking aside (Jensen and Freudendal-Pedersen 2012), such noble aspirations have often proved to be fairly absent from urban and infrastructure planning (Flyvbjerg 1998; Graham and Marvin 2001). In our effort to articulate the key theme of equality of mobilities design, we will discuss the mobile subjects which populate the systems and spaces which mobilities design engages.

Mobilities scholars argue that transport mobilities rest on an assumption of a universal and disembodied mobile subject. 'Transport' appears to be single-mindedly concerned with efficient movement from A to B, and according to Ingold, it is characterized 'by the dissolution of the intimate bond that [...] couples locomotion and perception' (2007: 78). Rather than moving by oneself, 'the transported traveller' is a generic passenger who is passively moved from place to place (ibid.; see also Adey 2010; Bissell 2010; Cresswell 2006). Transport means 'to carry across' and assumes that '[n]ot so much bodily movement is involved here, unless you are one of those doing the carrying' (Scheldeman 2011: 129). This 'hegemonic discourse of transport policy' erases differences of age, gender, embodied capacities and other social or biological characteristics of the mobile subjects (Adey 2010: 114). The imagination of a universal subject has serious implications for those who are different from the imagining. Richardson and Jensen address how 'mobile subject types' are created as imaginary categories from which plans and designs can be developed by professionals. By this is meant 'the production of relatively clear and well defined categories of imagined mobile citizens in the sociotechnical nexus of infrastructure systems' (2008: 218). Accordingly, mobility systems are designed for particular imagined citizens, and plans and maps are drawn up to match planners' and policy maker's imaginings of how such types of citizens might move in time and space. The assemblage of roadscape artefacts (asphalt, lanes, curbs, etc.) and the mobile subjects points to the road-crossing example as one that favours particular bodies and particular modes of mobility. In the minds of planners and politicians, an imaginary mobile subject has been envisioned at some point during the plan's gestation process. The road thus materializes with a particular version of a space of action for humans. The affordances imagined to be ideal (or at least wishful from the value base of the planning process) may play out differently in the end.

In the decades around the 1960s in the city of Aalborg, high priority was given to planning principles that could accommodate the need for car driving to not be in conflict with pedestrian traffic (see Aalborg Town Planning Office 1962). In the 'Disposition Plan' for the new town of Aalborg East that was published in the late 1960s, this came forth in tangible terms (Aalborg Town Planning Office 1967). The new satellite town for 20,000 people was planned on farmland east of the existing city. In the plan, the new town was divided into three residential areas and a large industrial area east of these. As is the case today, in the actual layout, each of these areas is surrounded by main roads. Each area is also cut through by one such road. The aim, as stated in the plan document, was to locate a local centre in the very middle of the area while also allowing high accessibility for both individual and collective traffic. Local pathways cross the road network to ensure accessibility to the local centre from the two residential parts of each area. Hence, the pedestrian circulation in each area was planned to make it safe from car traffic. Apart from the local centre with shops, each area was provided with all the shared facilities that had to be located within walking distance and with the local population as their functional foundation (ibid.: 4). In this system, careful consideration was given to the daily circulation of the future population of the new town. Traffic segregation relying on the definition of categories of mobile subjects was the means. Efforts were put into planning short distances between, for example, work places in the industrial areas, childcare facilities, schools, shopping facilities and green areas. A report on the general planning of Aalborg, which was published a few years later, shows that the functionalist planning project was not blind to the needs and wishes of its users (Peter Bredsdorffs Tegnestue A/S 1973). The report covers traffic planning in detail, with a section on 'design of pathways', for instance. Here, specific consideration for the behavioural patterns of bicyclists and pedestrians is encouraged, leading to guidelines such as the shortest route possible, level-free pathways, protection against climate with lee against the wind along the pathway, and roof-covered sections. As we will show in detail later, however, this imagination of the mobilities of bicyclists and pedestrians does not comply with the mobile inhabitation of the site today.

A particular issue, which is not catered to in many imaginary mobile subject types, is the embodied capacities of the mobile subjects themselves. Next to material resources like money, these are of vital importance. In the words of Elliott and Urry:

> physical travel involves lumpy, fragile, aged, gendered, racialized bodies. Such bodies encounter other bodies, objects and the physical world multisensuously. Travel always involves *corporeal* movement and forms of pleasure and pain. Such bodies perform themselves in-between direct sensation of the 'other' and various 'sensescapes'. Bodies are not fixed and given, but involve performances, especially to fold notions of movement, nature, taste and desire into and through the body. Bodies navigate backwards and forwards between directly sensing the external world as they move bodily in and through it and experiencing discursively mediated sensescapes that signify social taste and distinction, ideology and meaning. The body especially senses as it *moves*. Important here is that sense of movement, the 'mechanics of space', of touch, such as feet on the pavement or

> the mountain path, hands on a rock face or the steering wheel. There are thus various assemblages of humans, objects, technologies and scripts that contingently produce durability and stability of mobility.
>
> (2010: 16)

There is an emerging literature on themes of gender differences (see Adey 2010) and of ableness, impairment and social exclusion within mobilities (Campbell 2008; Dolmage 2015; Shawchuck 2014). Kaufmann *et al.*'s (2004) work on 'motility' as the potential for being mobile connected to both material resources, cognitive capabilities, and embodied capacities may be included in this discussion. Access to mobility and use of mobilities infrastructures are not equal, but are produced by biological and social characteristics, among other shaping factors: 'Can you drive? Do you drive? Can you afford to drive? Do you use public transport? Do you take walking down the street for granted or find it a struggle?' (Adey 2010: 84). In this literature, impairment is understood in its relationality and temporality, and, at least partially, constructed through the very design of the physical environment: 'spaces socially and materially construct disability by failing to enable their user's *different* needs' (ibid.: 112). Sawchuck argues that:

> Impairment is neither simply subjective, nor medical, nor a part of the built environment. It is a state of perpetual being that is relational, contingent, material and temporal. It reminds us, all of us, of how our existence as bodily subjects is never fixed, but in constant transition. Not all conditions of impairments are the same. They may be distinguishable on the basis of 'type', as identified by formal agencies for medical or insurance purposes, but also to provide needed assistance. However, they may also be understood in temporal terms. If we are impaired, or become impaired occasionally, temporally, suddenly, gradually or permanently, it is not the same context of with the same consequences. There are degrees of impairment – or disability – that intersect with our capacities to harness the resources we need to continue to move, engage, and be with and in different environmental contexts.
>
> (2014: 417)

Disability studies thus invoke not so much the question of whether or not one is impaired and what that means to everyday life mobilities as much as they actualize the question '*To what degree am I impaired?*' This may change over the day depending on the system and its 'requirements' or over life phases, from little mobility over maximum human capacity to lack of mobility in old age (see Fisker 2011). The answer to this question is context specific and dependent on the practices we are engaging in the material world, and often such capacities may even shift as we move through mobility systems and infrastructural landscapes with differential-mobility affordances. This can be illustrated through the mobile situation reported above. On the separated bike lanes, the man on his bike is in command, but here on the surface he is in danger and will have to give way to the cars.

Often the underpinning question for mobilities design ('*What affords this mobile situation?*') thus embeds a set of dilemmas and ambivalences, since design decisions paving the way for some may be impeding for others. As many mobilities design issues are embedded within public spaces, these dilemmas and ambivalences touch upon the wider values connecting to the city as an open and accessible space, a site of agoras where the infrastructures play a vital role for an equal distribution of mobility provisions. Such dilemmas or even conflicts may obviously be connected immediately to the types of mobile subjects present at, for instance, the road crossing (and thus might refer to car versus bike, or bike versus pedestrian). However, the ambivalences of mobilities design also reach across scales and manifest themselves in oppositions between regional commuters in high speed, who have no particular local engagement or interest in the areas passed by, versus local inhabitants concerned about safe routes to school, good public spaces and quality in design. As already noted, the multiple sensorial experiences may also play out differently. At the road crossing, the mobile subject will be exposed to the high-speed design, the fast vehicles and the aesthetics of a corridor where interaction is minimized to mutual glances of reciprocity as cars speed by. Importantly, mobility differentials exist not only in regards to issues of age, gender or impairment. We should observe that road spaces and mobile subject types cannot easily be generalized around the world; a vivid example pointing to some of the variations across geographies and cultures are 'spaces of Indian motoring' (Adey 2010: 185–6). Whereas Westernized roads (and particularly the functionalist city ideal) are associated with orderly, controlled and linear movement, much more hustle and bustle goes on on many Indian roads. Here people, animals and vehicles cross the roads in many directions, roads are lined with many sorts of industries and services (repair shops, coffee shops, dentists, hairdressers …), and sound- and smell-scapes can often be intense, composite and even cacophonic.

In the next section, we provide an insight into the actual mobile subjects of the crossing, their mobile situations inclusive of embodied experiences, and spatial practicings related to their regional and local movements and atttachments.

A regional car driver in the road corridor

One of our interviewees, a middle-aged man, commutes along the road by car. The route is very familiar terrain to this traveller. He finds it to be rather featureless and does not enjoy the drive. He tells us that he focuses on getting 'from A to B', devoting his attention to the traffic flow, red traffic lights and braking buses, and also on thinking about what to do when he gets home or problem-solving things for work (move-along and follow-up interviews, 15 and 26 October 2012).

Few artefacts in the physical environment that he drives through extend any invitation for him to take notice of them. The area around the informal road crossing does not present any local distinctiveness perceptible to this car driver. Even though this is actually the very urban centre of the district, the universal linear road design and its optimization for motorized flow is maintained without interruption. This is the nature of traffic segregation, with its principle of order, uniformity and simplicity and thus a minimum of disturbances for driving traffic. In Figure 7.3, a look through the windscreen of the driver's car, we get a sense of the visual engagement with the environment facilitated by the drive. It is a panoramic perception of space in which we see the surroundings as a 'continuous blur' made possible by the high-speed movement (Cresswell 2006: 5). The photo shows a traffic landscape designed for motion by car: a smooth space without either much to distract or much to experience. The dense foliage of the verge vegetation, the speed limit sign, the lamps posts and the planar, asphalt surface facilitate what the driver finds to be a kind of frictionless driving in a corridor designated for movement by car only. Far different from the low-speed, pedestrian-oriented urban environments of the city before modernism, this can be characterized as 'an architecture of mobility par excellence' (ibid.: 51).

The man finds himself stuck in the car, and this seems to affect his attitude towards his daily commute. He regrets that he has to take part in what has elsewhere been called the 'fatiguing effects of routine travel' that seem to 'deplete the capacity of the body to experience more positive effects' (Bissell 2010: 277). In spite of the obvious flexibility of the car – the 'instantaneous time' it affords (Urry 2004) – the driver finds himself, in this mobile situation, highly aware of the limits imposed upon him by the automobility system:

> Consider the relatively individualistic and autonomous act of driving down a road. Before we can even get going, just as one feels the gentle click of

Figure 7.3 Through the windscreen; approaching the informal road crossing (photo: Ditte Bendix Lanng).

> the seatbelt into its socket, one's sense of freedom and expression may immediately slip away. The driver must consciously or unconsciously be directed by a host of limits and directions that he or she must bear in mind.
>
> (Adey 2010: 83)

The interviewee feels trapped in the tightly controlled domain of the car, unable to challenge his routinized practices from within the insulated capsule. He says:

> You are really cut off from the world around you. You don't know if it's a warmer or a colder day, you don't get any different smells or anything.... You're just not really engaged with the world around you. You're just, you know, insulated in a bubble.

Unlike the time when he lived in the city centre and was able to walk to work, he now finds himself confined to certain kinds of spatial knowings. He regrets how his sensory engagement with the environment is limited to a virtual 'tv screen', though he does actually appreciate special views, for example visual marks of changing seasons, such as blooming daffodils along the road and the dramatic visual overview from the top of the road on a misty day. The driver also regrets that he cannot choose among a large number of routes, to let chance and mood lead him as he can when walking, and he misses the exercise, fresh air and potential surprises. Instead he needs to travel the linearity of the few tarmac routes, and this makes him feel desensitized and automatized. His experience aligns with many critical comments on the distancing and insensate nature of car driving, such as that of Jacobs and Appleyard who, in their urban design manifesto, assert that big cities where 'massive transportation systems are segregated for single travel modes ... make people feel irrelevant' (1987: 79). The driver favours walking to the perceived dullness and unnaturalness of driving. He seems to experience the car forcing upon him distantiation, even alienation, from the environment and from his options of inhabiting the city in an engaged and lively manner. His account thus also corresponds to what Edensor sums up as 'the supposedly dystopian nature of the commuter's journey':

> The routine daily commute by car has become a popular signifier of contemporary alienation connoting work-bound single drivers detached from community and alienated from their own nature, dulled by the compulsion to move swiftly and uneventfully toward their destination.
>
> (2003: 152)

Edensor reports his own daily car drive, which he finds to be 'rich in mundane comfort and sensation, replete with small pleasures and diverging incidents and thoughts' (ibid.: 151). At first glance our interviewee's experience appears to be in stark contrast to this, yet Edensor's scholarly illumination of the embodied sensory dimensions of car driving does acknowledge this man's experience. These include the highly mediated sensorial experience behind the windscreen and also the profound embodiment of driving, which surfaces in, for example, his experience of the drive as an annoying 'start-stop-start-stop' rhythmic discontinuity, demanding his body to be ever on the lookout. Additionally, the interviewee feels that he is equipped with only a reduced repertoire of driver-to-driver interaction (see Thrift 2004: 47), and he finds himself, with some frustration, able to communicate only by limited means, such as the sounding of the horn and, perhaps, like many other drivers, an aggressive use of brake lights, hand gestures, etc. This does not, however, make driving completely asocial and desensitizing (Edensor 2003). But, following Thrift, such practices of car driving 'constitute a radically different set of spatial practicings of the city' than walking (2004: 41). This is not necessarily a less valuable experience but perhaps rather another type, which composes its own 'complex everyday ecology of driving' (ibid.: 48), which can 'be as rich and convoluted as that of walking' (ibid.: 45). As Sheller notes, experiences of car driving are 'neither located solely within the person nor produced solely by the car as a moving object, but occur as a circulation of affects between (different) persons, (different) cars, and historically situated car cultures and geographies of mobility' (2004: 227). The interviewee's dwelling-in-motion in the car (as a driver-car-environment hybrid) certainly reconfigures his socialities and experiences from those of walking. The circulation of affects between the car, with its speed, sound insulation, climate control and so on, the driver and the roadscape, unquestionably intermediates his inhabitation of the road in far different ways than a crossing traveller's slow and exposed engagement does. This difference, produced by the perceived lack of features during the car drive, seems to have convinced this particular driver that no potential for a more positive travel experience exists. Nonetheless, it is possible to detect narrow gaps in his explicitly instrumental spatial practicings of this spatial stretch during the drive: he enjoys the drive through the countryside, he appreciates the trees and fields, and on his other commuting route he even occasionally feels inclined to make a stop at the cement-factory pond, which he treasures as it 'even on the dullest day is a little ray of sunshine'. This suggests that in spite of his urge to reach home as fast as possible, he is open to the potentials for experience and joy along his drive, which can be encompassed within a little improvization in the spur of the moment. Or in the words of Jensen *et al.*:

> As people string together activity chains, they are not only choosing routes, but also moving between different affective experiences of mobility, and thereby managing their own emotional geographies in relation to places and other family members.
>
> (2014: 13)

In tracing and enlarging such under-used potential, we could follow Edensor's reconsideration of the supposedly generic, alienating, sterile, boring serialized functionality of automobile time-spaces (2003) and try to imagine redesign potentials that would enable car driving in other ways, perhaps thereby inviting drivers like this man to like their routine journeys better. The imagination of such potential could follow both Edensor's and Thrift's arguments for alternative sensorial capacities of the hybridization of the driver and the car, which acknowledges modes of 'augmented' embodiment and is based on the fact that '[t]he car driver dwells-on-the-paved-road and is not separated from its multiple sensuousness' (Urry 2007: 125). A tangible example of an exploration of this potential is that if you drive at the right speed along the Melody Road of Gunma in Japan, grooves cut into the concrete surface allow you to play the tune 'Memories of Summer' with your car and the road as the hybrid instrument. The story goes that it was a Japanese road worker who accidentally scraped some markings into a road with a bulldozer. When he drove over them, he realized that they produced a variety of tones. Depending on how far apart the grooves were, the pitch of the sound varied. A team from the Hokkaido Industrial Research Institute has subsequently developed and built a number of Japanese musical road surfaces, or 'melody roads', using the hybrid drivers-cars to play music as they travel.[1] This example underlines the fact that, though car driving seems to favour the visual sense, it does not obliterate other ways of sensing (Edensor 2003). As Thrift argues, the increase of automobility in the city (perhaps at the expense of other mobilities) might not mean the demise of rich sensorial and social practicings of the city: 'new spaces for action are continually being opened up as old ones are closed down' (2004: 54).

Local pedestrians beyond and across the road

Turning to the mobility routes of slower local journeys, from which the large road is formally segregated by its location across and above them, it seems we are in another world. The schoolgirls in our study are slowly, sensously and tactilely present in these spaces, in ways which differ remarkably from the car driving we observed above. As pedestrians, they interact in a very direct way with the materialities of the place. They take notice of, use and appreciate trees blooming, the tactile qualities of the asphalt, the shelter of the tunnel and the informal opportunities to pause. They cheerily tell us how they tend to get absorbed in good conversations with their friends and forget what is around them, as, for example, when none of the kids in the group notice that they have entered the grocery store until they find themselves inside the building, only then realizing that nobody had any errands there (move-a-long and follow-up interview 28 June and 5 July 2012). This social togetherness of co-travelling relates to the temporal aspects of their journey, which has neither a very long nor a short duration. Rather, it can be stretched in time: it can be quicker or longer, depending on the casual social lingerings. Sometimes, one of the girls tells us, the trip home takes 40 minutes when she chooses the long, strolling route to spend time on a nice chat with her friends. In comparison, her most direct way home from school takes three to five minutes at a steady walking pace. But this fast journey is the unusual choice; speed is seldom something steady or important on their journey. Rather, it is not uncommon that each of the several pauses on the way adds another five or ten minutes to the journey duration. This happens when the two girls find that they have no obligations encouraging them to hurry. In these carefree situations, they let occasion and their inclination to social togetherness guide the speed. This suggests that there is a high degree of individuality to the rhythm of their journey. Or, at least, that it is a matter of a decision among the travel companions (or the 'mobile withs'), who on their way shape a small mobile and social collective with its own irregular pace, taking in space and time as they go. Yet there is no doubt that there is an overall institutionalized rhythm to the journey home from school: the most steady thing about it is that it takes place on weekdays around three o'clock, when the school day ends, more or less in synchronization with Danish society's common school hours. On this journey, it is the end point that is more open in temporal terms, and there is no doubt that the girls enjoy it when nothing like bus schedules or after-school working obligations makes them hurry.

As we reported in Chapter 5, the tunnel atmosphere can have some drawbacks for one of the girls, in that she finds the tunnel scary at night; it is one of her reasons for regularly choosing to cross the big road, where there is no designated crossing. She often walks that way, across the road, when it is dark and she needs to go home after her babysitting job, but also in the daytime because it is the easy and fast way home from school. She recognizes that some danger is connected with stepping onto the road with fast cars going by. Her father does not like her crossing the road there, and she is not allowed to do it if she is walking with her younger brothers and sisters. It is 'kind of wild', she acknowledges:

> Well, you walk across the one lane, and then there are still cars on the other. And then you stand there waiting; there is such a narrow piece of grass where you should walk and wait. And cars drive in front of you and behind you.

Still, it is a perfectly common thing to do, she explains. To the other girl, it is too 'frightening' to walk across the road at that point. She has done it a few times and found that it demands more 'guts' than she likes. So she sticks to the designated underpass and marked crossings when she needs to cross the big road.

The schoolgirls give us an impression of the diffusion of mobilities inside the pedestrian system. Though they are surely supposed to walk along certain routes in accordance with the design as an organizing frame for their mobilities practices and experiences, the girls may well cut across the system and make their own choices based on their own rationales, which are not necessarily coincident with the traffic-planning rationales of segregation for the sake of safe and efficient movement. This leads them to inhabit the local area in rich sensorial and social ways and to contest the universalism and rigidity of the functionalist traffic design. Though few things in the mundane architecture suggest that this area should invite urban life (although there is a bench here and there), the girls certainly inhabit it as such. The area reveals itself, to some extent, as a self-programming and self-organizing territory, which they are able to inhabit for their own situated journeys, rich and tactile experiences, and various social interactions, even though it is not designed for that as such. Really, the area's rather loose and spacious frame, not rigidly controlling their mobilities, seems inviting to the girls, as it gives them opportunities for informal, personal and situated inhabitation. From their local, slow-speed situations, the place is far more than a functional machine for living and moving. It is 'a layered location replete with human histories and memories.... It is about connections, what surrounds it, what formed it, what happened there, what will happen there' (Lippard 1997: 7). These characteristics of the local place and the local mobilities are extended to the road as the girls move there, and the road crossing becomes much more than a point in practical circulation; it is part of the local area with ambiguous and diverse daily life mobilities.

The road crossing is thus a complex, layered point, which challenges the imagination of categories of mobile subject types. Here, people on the move co-exist and intersect in diverse states of mobile inhabitation, which span, at least from the personal approximation of space so vividly performed by the school-girls, to the regional car driver's experience of a liminal sensation of distance and detachment. However, what we see in terms of design is a road space materializing social processes of inequality and exclusion, as it clearly favours the particular mobile subject type of the car driver.

What if...? Conflicts and trade-offs in the design of a road crossing

The key principle of segregation, inherent in the very idea of modernist urban planning, has been challenged by recent urban planning and design proposals for transformation of traffic-segregated districts. Here, the focus is the lack of activity and the value of interacting flows in cul-de-sac urban structures, which are often monofunctional areas without vibrant urban atmospheres, where buildings turn their backs on the infrastructures, and there are no 'eyes on the street' (Jacobs 1961), which in turn leads to problems of insecurity. By intentionally leading people through housing areas, for instance, the proposed strategy is to create more interaction (Bjørn 2008). The downside to such rethinking of the logics of traffic segregation is that safety and comfort may be jeopardized if pathways and slow-speed local roads leading to schools and other institutions are opened to through-going car traffic. As with much other urban planning and design, we face a situational weighing of pros and cons. When designing a road crossing, similar priorities have to be made. The spatial and temporal co-existence between fast, motorized mobilities and soft, vulnerable mobilities can cause high conflict mobile situations, as 'car travel interrupts the taskscapes of others (pedestrians, children going to school) ... whose daily routines are obstacles to the high-speed traffic that cuts mercilessly through slower-moving pathways and dwellings' (Urry 2007: 123). Below we will follow up upon the 'What if ...?' questions articulated in the beginning of the chapter and discuss some of the very concrete potentials and implications of reworking the hierarchy between modes of movement. The questions are: *What if mobile hierarchies were reversed? What if the local connectivity and varied urban space were the main design priority? What if the road crossing afforded a dynamic rhythm of safe and experiential flows of both cars and pedestrians/cyclists? Or, what if slow-speed local mobilities did not produce friction for smooth and fast regional flows?*

These questions point to variants of trading off considerations for through-going traffic and local connectivity across the road barrier (and, importantly, any answer to these questions comes with the risk of generating other or new inequalities; see Madanipour 2006). They point to the fundamental decision about whether traffic segregation should be maintained and strengthened through design features which can afford the connectivity and comfort needed to actually invite crossing people to stop the transgressive and dangerous behaviour. They also can invite discussion as to whether the principle of traffic segregation should be overruled by a new mobile and urban logic, where the many surface crossings which happen today are staged by a formal design, thus compromising the preference of speed and frictionless passability for car flows. In the latter case, the logics of the mobilities systems are radically changed and new formal relationships between cars and pedestrians, local and regional concerns are being inserted. A new formal surface crossing would follow this idea (see Figure 7.4) and should provide the needed safety as well as introduce a new orientation in

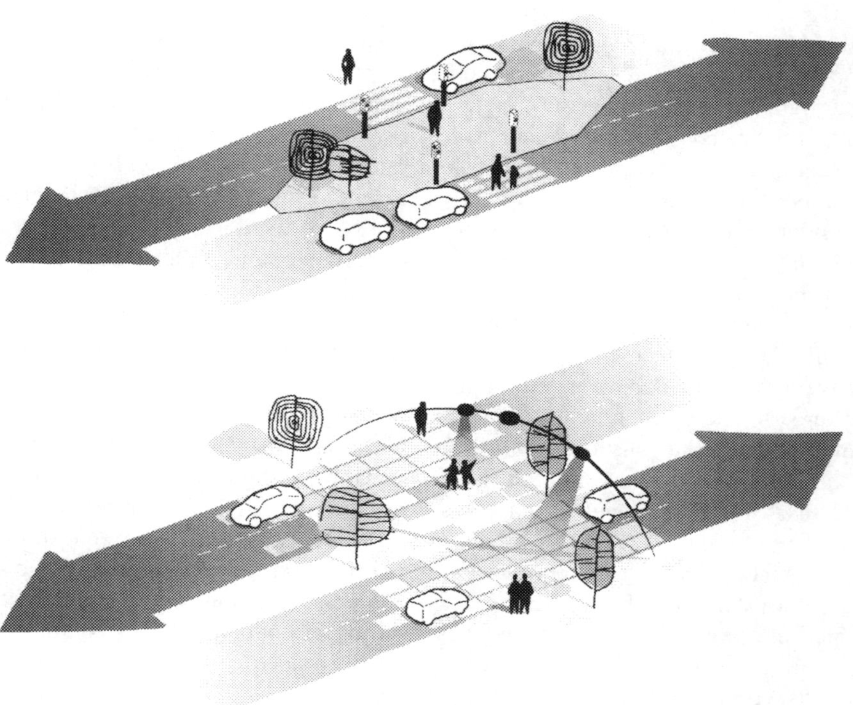

Figure 7.4 Formal road crossing sketches (drawings: Jeppe Krogstrup Jensen).

the local district. It could address a host of mobile situations of both car-users and crossing pedestrians and cyclists through introducing design features that afford a change in geosemiotics to make drivers aware of this Critical Point of Contact and make crossing travellers be and feel less exposed, providing them with a fast, easy and enjoyable link in the local environment.

A material intervention to facilitate such a new intersection could be a narrowing of the road and a change of speed limits, what is sometimes referred to as a 'road diet'. Such a design alters the concrete affordances of the environment for the users, and, in line with Whitelegg's teasing out of the priorities given to car drivers (see above), it shortens the width of the road and thus the time and distance for the crossing pedestrian. A road diet at this site would also remarkably change the semiotics for the users, communicating to car drivers that they are driving through an active suburban centre. The dimension of the road is a signifier of the mobile hierarchy. A large road with several or many lanes and high speed are in many cases relatively more difficult, unsafe and uncomfortable to cross, and clearly show that drivers enjoy top priority.

Yet, there are also design features other than dimensions that can contribute to altering the hierarchy and handle the co-existence of diverse mobilities at a road crossing. For example, new urban elements and materials could be introduced onto the road and on the roadsides. Today, the asphalt and the dirt-and-grass verges are the materials that form the road corridor. However, new affordances of the environment, which extend the district's local slow-speed, urban mobile life onto the road, could be introduced by a broader variety of tactile and visually appealing materials and lights. New pavement, greenery and colours could shape a distinct urban space across the road, with a significant and easily accessible 'urban floor' and with effects for both car drivers and pedestrians and cyclists. Such a design would supersede the strict segregation with a mixed situation, where pedestrians would enjoy priority rights. The 'Stadtlounge' (urban lounge) in St. Gallen, Switzerland, is an example of a daring and artistic design that works to facilitate the co-existence of slow-speed vehicles and people. It is an inner town area of mixed traffic, covered with 4,000 square metres of soft, red granulated rubber. This bold material covers every available surface, including the entire urban floor, the urban furniture, drains, a fountain and a car. Commentators are expressive in their attitude towards the sensuous qualities of this design, which creates an outdoor 'public living room' (Krauel 2009). It is positively interpreted as a symbolic gesture of place-making which gives everyone the privilege of moving on a red carpet (Bickers 2011). It might be regarded as an insertion of conceptual art which propagates unfamiliarity in the familiar or, oppositely, homely familiarity in the public outdoors. The use of the red colour is considered distinct and powerful, in that it invokes a strong affectional expression for the people using it and provides a 'dazzling' appearance, 'like entering another world' (Bickers 2011). Other design features, such as playful and performative components, could likewise contribute to altering the logics of the existing crossing.

The opposite approach to abate the conflicts on the road is to maintain, or rather to re-establish and strengthen, the traffic segregation and not compromise the use of the road as a main through-going effective route for cars (see Figure 7.5). A tunnel could be built (perhaps intentionally avoiding the dark and gloomy expression of the nearby tunnel; see Chapter 5). With an urban mobilities design approach it could for example be connected to the surface level in a green and widened median strip at the road with a perforation allowing light to reach down, and even people to move up and down. Such a design would work to lessen the barrier effect of the road with planting and perhaps even to abate noise. It could give drivers an altered window into the suburb, thereby interweaving the local and regional, fast and slow mobilities, while maintaining the segregation. Another option would be to lead crossing flows above the road on a bridge structure. Just as the tunnel can be more than an efficient flow space, a bridge can be a sculptural landmark which affords several uses, is rich in experiences, and is joyful for both crossing

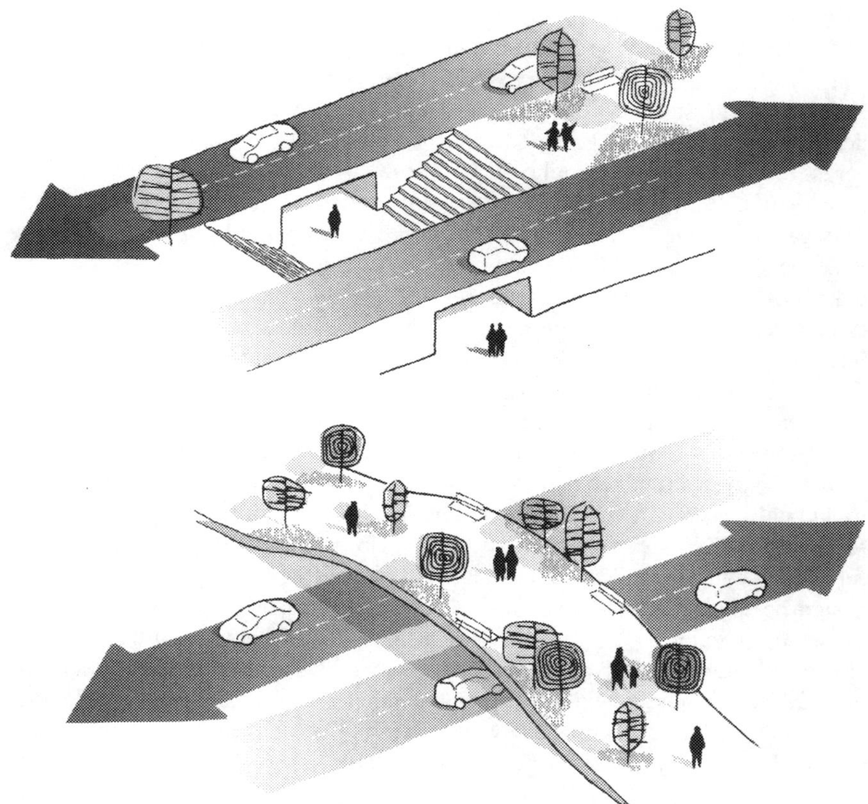

Figure 7.5 Bridging or tunnelling the road (drawings: Jeppe Krogstrup Jensen).

travellers and road users, who observe it from afar and from below. As structural engineer Cecil Balmond says about his design for the Pedro and Inés footbridge in Coimbra, Portugal:

> Now you may think the point of a bridge is to get from A to B as quickly as possible. And, in fact, many bridges are built so everyone feels a need to rush across. But there are actually many other things you can do on a bridge: you can linger on it, you can keep a lookout on it, you can chat on it. So I built my bridge to be functional, to get across, but slowly – it zigzags. It's not just one-dimensional but multidimensional. You see, this bridge is an invitation to discover it for yourself.
>
> (Rauterberg 2012: 23)

In the design of this bridge, Balmond demonstrates a crossover effort to approach a mundane artefact of movement with 'multidimensional' considerations. He recognizes the bridge as a hybrid artefact that must meet multiple concerns related to functional efficiency, interconnectivity and accessibility, aesthetic quality, structural durability, the accommodation of lives on the move and so on. With such hybridity, the bridge enters into heterogeneous relationships with the city of Coimbra as an active part of the local urban fabric.

Bridges may also be designed as landscapes, extending the terrain. Such design can ease the effort needed from pedestrians and cyclists to go up to get across the road. The road could even be lowered into the terrain and turned into a road tunnel, which would give absolute priority to local mobilities in the segregated system. One renowned example is the Seattle Olympic Sculpture Park, which opened in 2007. In this project, lead architects Weiss and Manfredi developed a neatly designed Z-shaped park as a connecting topography across three separate parcels, bridging a four-lane arterial road and a train track, and linking the city and the bay. Integrating as diverse functions and programmes as an exhibition pavilion, public art, a beach, a water habitat, storm-water management and a pedestrian infrastructure, the park is intended to be a 'hybrid landform' (Weiss and Manfredi 2015: 22). In particular, the architects regard the continuous pedestrian promenade as a nerve in the project as it 'thickens this traditionally scenographic and monofunctional device into an armature for art, recreation, and environmental remediation' (ibid.: 52). This work, with multifunctional hybridity, serves as an inspiration and vocalizer of the mobilities design perspective we address, which highlights crossover efforts from picturesque and functional design approaches to the entangled agency of materialities. However, the Seattle Olympic Sculpture Park falls short in demonstrating how the hardest and most inflexible infrastructures may be approached in novel ways. Prior to the construction of the new connection, the highway and the train track impaired the urban landscape, as do many large infrastructures in cities. The project's response to this challenge was to cover these barriers with physical bridges, thus working on the terms of segregation in ways similar to conventional functional planning.

These typologies present variations within a design for an intersection between automobilities and pedestrians/cyclists. Admittedly, neither of the typologies is a total solution to the informal crossing situation. Rather, they all concretize and promote important questions related to equalities and mobilities design. The materialities of mobilities design reveal an understanding of the 'politics of things' (Latour and Weibel 2005). The dead and solid objects are assembled into frames for life and affect us both on the level of the calculated and conscious as well as on the affectual level, where physical features of the built environment create atmospheres that may slip below our immediate intellectual processing but make all the difference in the world (see Chapter 5). The materialities of a new road crossing, as discussed, raise at least four topics in relation to politics, mobilities and design. One would concern 'gentrification' and here the issues are connected to 'travelling ideas' of urban development (Tait and Jensen 2007) such as New Urbanism, 'walkability' and neo-traditionalism. What may look like a favouring of community connectivity in fact carries the risk of new social segregation, gentrification, marginalization and exclusion. Often, the neo-traditionalist pedestrian havens need high-speed car-dependent systems to sustain and facilitate them. A second topic is a return to the issue of impairment and the embodied practices related to mobilities. The affordances that materialize in the nexus between the body and the physical site actualize a number of questions to any mobilities design intervention. Can all bodies move equally with the same efforts in the site? Can all bodies access the sites of mobilities? How does the impairment of less-abled bodies manifest itself in social practices of withdrawal, less usage or other subtle forms of exclusion? (Consider the slow, mildly impaired traveller from Chapter 6 who pointed to her anxieties connected to crossing the parking lot.) We may speak of 'The city for whom?' and issues of appropriation and co-creation. Mobilities design stages everyday life of mobile subjects, and the more or less clear decisions affecting the bodies on the move may link to larger questions of prioritization, public spending of funding and other 'macro issues'. Would it be a solution for the elderly man we saw crossing the road on his bike to create a safe crossing dedicated to bikes on the surface? Alternatively, would he feel alienated and disinterested in solutions that, seen from his perspective, are expressions of top-down bureaucracy? The spaces of mobilities and design are filled with limits, borders, hierarchies and stratifications. Finally, and with significance for the three other topics, we will underline that some of these mobilities designs may risk leading to new imbalances in the search to abate others. This is a condition inherent to any mobilities design intervention:

> Any new development is a challenge to an existing context, able to unsettle an often fragile balance or undermine and displace the vulnerable.... Is urban design helping or hindering social development; improving quality of life for all or for a few? Does it address social polarization and exclusion or does it exacerbate these?
>
> (Madanipour 2006: 189)

Discussion: the politics of artefacts in mobilities design

Madanipour's questioning of the democratizing force of new urban design developments, as well as the issues of inequality demonstrated above, pushes us to seek critical insight into mobilities design politics. The staging of mobile situations by design encompasses possibilities for many ways of 'engineering relationships among people' (Winner 1980: 124). Winner refers to the example of the extraordinarily low bridges of parkways at Long Island, New York, as one instance of seemingly unconspicuous designed mobilities artefacts:

> Even those who happened to notice this structural peculiarity would not be inclined to attach any special meaning to it. In our accustomed way of looking at things like roads and bridges we see the details of form as innocuous, and seldom give them a second thought.
>
> (1980: 123)

The issue is that a bus cannot pass under these bridges, and this design carries a purpose beyond the immediate use, namely to organize who have access to an attractive recreational facility outside New York. Winner reports how New York's master builder from the 1920s to 1970s, Robert Moses, privileged '[a] utomobile owning whites of "upper" and "comfortable middle" classes [as Moses called them]' and accommodated free use of the parkways for recreation and commuting. Conversely,

> [p]oor people and blacks, who normally used public transit, were kept off the roads because the twelve-foot tall buses could not get through the overpasses. One consequence was to limit access of racial minorities and low-income groups to Jones Beach, Moses's widely acclaimed public park.
>
> (1980: 123)

Many other examples of mobilities design's stratification of the city exist, such as the elevated skytrains of Bangkok, which facilitate smooth and comfortable movement for the wealthier citizens, above the city's often chaotic traffic situation on the streets (Jensen 2007, 2013). Furthermore, mundane and widespread typologies, such as bus stops, have a tendency to produce severe inequalities, in that they can work as barriers to the transport access they are supposed to accommodate. This comes about when, say, traces of delinquency and deficiency of shelter make such waiting spaces incredibly 'inhospitable to women riders, who are faced with the potential hazard of waiting for a bus at night' (Adey 2010: 113). An explicitly tragic example of inequality and mobilities design, which bring us back to the informal road crossing, is referenced by Graham and Marvin (2001): in 1995 in Buffalo, New York, a female pedestrian was killed by a truck as she tried to cross the busy highway, which was located between the bus stop and the mall where she worked. The woman required public transport to get to work, but the mall had been designed for automobiles, and the stop for the bus service that she needed to use daily was located across the seven-lane highway.

These examples demonstrate that mobilities artefacts, mundane and indiscernible perhaps, may encompass serious political purposes or repercussions, in and beyond their immediate use. Winner points to instances of artefacts 'in which the very process of technical development is so thoroughly biased in a particular direction that it regularly produces results counted as wonderful breakthroughs by some social interests and crushing setbacks by others' (1980: 125). Following Winner, we may suggest that none of the alternative physical designs or arrangements of the road crossing outlined in the section above would make a difference significant to the pattern of power and authority embedded in the already-existing design. The road and its interlinkage with the automobility system (Urry 2007; see Chapter 6) is a technology which demands its social environment to be constructed in a particular way. We may say that if we accept the private car, we also accept, for example, to be forced to live in an instantaneous and compressed timeframe and in stretched spaces across huge distances in 'complex, harried patterns of social life' (Urry 2007: 120), with or without access to a car ourselves. A well-designed bridge or underpass or urban space does not substantially address this condition.

Furthermore, the system of automobilities may be, as part of its intricate nexus of interests and organizations to sustain and develop it, an example of one of the 'many large technical systems [which] are in fact highly compatible with centralised, hierarchical management control' (Winner 1980: 132). With regard to mobilities design of the road crossing, the infrastructure provision, including the road construction, coding of traffic lights, formal crossing options, etc. is dealt with through a centralized public authority, which exerts certain ideas of the better solutions. Yet, another stream of mobilities design intervention may emerge, countering such a top-down approach. We may imagine creative and inclusive processes of co-design where the hard materiality of objects and surfaces will be the very materiality upon which creative processes of imaginary alternative uses can be played out. The design choices related to the redesign of the road crossing re-actualizes infrastructures and the agoras of the contemporary city. They may be articulated as sites of deliberation, discussion and more or less utopian imaginaries. Sites and artefacts of mobilities may carry the potential for creative co-creation and a change in existing practices. Many mobilities sites may be received as relatively 'openminded' spaces (Walzer 1986), in that they may work as some of the transitions and in-between spaces where 'public-domain experiences (confrontation with otherness, a change in perspective, an exchange)' can be imagined (Hajer and Reijndorp 2001: 129; see Chapter 1). For now, let us end this section with reiterating Allen's suggestion of 'infrastructural urbanism' as a 'material practice' (1999; see Chapter 3). Connecting mobilities design as a material practice with the theme of inequalities and with ideas of co-design, Allen's focus on the performance of infrastructures gains new significance, since they evolve over time and space (as an opposition to the production of autonomous objects) and architecture/design 'as an activity that works in and among the world of things' (1999: 52). He writes that

> material practices do not attempt to control or predetermine meaning.... Material practices are not about expression – expressing either the point of view of an author or of the collective will of a society; rather they condense, transform, and materialize concepts.
>
> (Ibid.: 53)

Though Allen states that infrastructure is about division, allocation, locks and gates, and that it is 'a mistake to think that infrastructures can in a utopian way enable new freedoms' (ibid.: 55), he maintains that they 'are flexible and anticipatory ... a loose envelope of contraints ... which ... works strategically, but ... encourages tactical improvisation' (ibid.: 54–5). By exploring the plethora of mobile practices taking place even in the relatively inconspicuous road space, we have sensed the potential for change and rethinking. In particular, this becomes relevant if we consider the openness and unpredictability of many mobilities spaces, which Chapters 5 through 7 of this book have all touched upon. Mobilities sites may be particularly potential-laden as public territories of movement and exchange, and mobilities design may evolve to produce insights and answers to practice as a co-designer in such processes:

> The question then is how to design for unpredictability and excess.... The city is an intense locus of innovation, its collective creativity always in advance of the disciplines of architecture or urbanism that attempt to control it.
>
> (Allen 2010: 37–8)

Conclusion: urban mobilities design and inequalities

Issues of inequality, power and politics are embedded in any mobilities design intervention. In this chapter, we have attempted to indicate this and illustrate its significance. We have pointed to some of the important dimensions of the knotty issue of mobilities, politics and design and have exemplified this entanglement by an ordinary, informal road crossing, manifest in the dilemma that the design staging of convenient mobilities for some produces immobilities for others. The design decisions and layout of the particular space embed specific priorities about hierarchy and safety, and we have addressed issues of inequality connected to the different modalities as well as to the adversarial relationship between local and regional concerns at stake. Mobilities are underpinned by and organized around values and normative principles, staging mobilities in accordance with particular interests and visions for the city. Any urban mobilities design intervention inherently has conflicts, dilemmas and priorities in relation to different users and mobile subjects which must co-exist. The situational approach of mobilities design pays careful attention to how travellers must and are enabled to negotiate their daily life mobilities, thus concretizing and specifying power issues and drawing attention to their very material manifestation.

We have reported in detail on two instances of mobile inhabitations of the road crossing: a regional car driver and local pedestrians. These instances show that mobilities are arguably not universal in this space, and they furthermore unfold some of the many intricacies inherent in mobile practices and experiences which reach far beyond this particular stretch of road. The attention to users inherent in these accounts thus points to differentials in mobilities design, and to the politics of material affordances. In mobilities design, this user-focus is important, as it highlights the 'primacy of position' (Adey 2010: 93) and challenges the imaginary mobile subject types, upon which much transport infrastructure is based. What may be concluded about certain sites and about users of infrastructures ultimately informs how these materialities are designed (and thus how mobilities design sustains, consolidates, accelerates, or opposes patterns of power, inequality and authority). Adey's practical, methodical advice to pay attention to whose accounts are being allowed for, and what kinds of travellers are being heard, is indeed relevant to mobilities design. So while this can be received as a call to remedy a neglect of actual users' needs in infrastructure design and, through this, to address some inequalities, we also pointed towards how materialities of mobilities are inherently political, beyond their immediate use. Materialities of mobilities may demand that social environment be constructed in a particular way, and the staging from above of mobile situations is often dealt with through a top-down authority. Mobilities sites may carry the potential to challenge these conditions and become territories for alternative spatial organization, social interaction and use. They do not simply articulate issues of efficiency, safety, aesthetics and visual design, they can also perform as vehicles to problematize, and perhaps even resolve, issues related to the underlying value bases, social hierarchies and power geometries that are engraved into the hard materialities.

From this last empirical exploration into the territory of mobilities design, we now want to close the circle and return to our initial questions with general concluding remarks and reflections upon the future perspectives of this work.

Note

1 www.guardian.co.uk/world/2007/nov/13/japan.gadgets

8 Conclusions and perspectives

As we have now reached the end of our exploratory journey into the design of contemporary urban, everyday life mobilities, we shall wrap up arguments, identify conclusions and point to future perspectives. In the first section, we deal with the overall research question and the sub-thematic answers arrived at. In the second section, we focus on the research perspectives coming out of this work. We will engage with the repercussions for future research activities and the future research agenda for mobilities design. The final section is dedicated even more directly to the interface with design practice.

Conclusions

The overall research question guiding this work was the pragmatic enquiry: '*How are design decisions and interventions staging mobilities – or how are they preventing particular mobilities?*' Our route to the book's specific focus has been through earlier work (Jensen 2013, 2014; Lanng 2015). In this work, we have worked through a situational mobilities approach to empirically explore how tangible materialities make a key dimension in the assembled effects of a staging of mobile situations from above, through design decisions and interventions, as well as from below, through decisions and acts of mobile subjects on the ground. From the earlier work, we identified mobilities design as an emerging field within the broader mobilities turn, and we accentuated the potentials for urban design, and other design fields, to embrace the growing knowledge on mobilities. This book has been dedicated to articulating what this may mean in both conceptual/theoretical and empirical/practical terms. Thus, by entertaining the research question, we explored the nexus between mobilities theory and urban design, including designerly ways of thinking. The underpinning rationale of the mobilities turn is that all the myriads of different movements we are embedded in have more than their mere physical effects of displacement, aggregation and movement. Thus the one-liner credo of the mobilities turn: *Mobilities is more than A to B!* The repercussions of these complex mobilities in different directions such as social networks, capital formation, politics, planning and environment are important on their own. But the 'more than A to B' claim also touches how the 'more than' effects of mobilities touch deep into the way we inhabit the material world, the way we interact socially, and the way we think of ourselves in the midst of all this. So instead of speaking of transport as the displacement of things, people and goods, the mobilities turn articulates the wider-reaching term 'mobilities' generating a non-sedentary research agenda for exploring the fact that sociality is defined by flows and movement (and their obstructions).

Our focus in this book is on coupling mobilities research with urban design. Here, urban design is understood as a practical endeavour of architectural intervention that addresses situated design problems. The scope of urban design is primarily to anticipate well-functioning urban environments, to evoke potentials and to create something new. A pragmatic interdisciplinarity characterizes urban design, which assembles concepts and frames of thought from elsewhere, when it is found to be useful in handling specific design problems. In order to shape urban environments for the many, including the multiple, diverging values and interests of authorities, private developers and users, and to influence technical measures to produce, build and maintain spaces, urban design considers aspects of both social and natural sciences. Creating urban design in practice, then, requires a sensibility and acceptance of multiple sources of input. In such an interdisciplinary field, urban design is a morphing and diverse effort, with the common pursuit of finding ways to spatially accommodate an ever-changing urban condition. While aesthetic and technical approaches to urban design as a purely professional activity are well-established, more responsive and participatory approaches also exist, which explicitly link design objectives with the needs, wishes and barriers of users. In our articulation of mobilities design, we lean towards streams of urban design which targets the active and relational performativity, concrete as well as strategic, of designed materialities and open, inclusive design processes.

The notion of mobilities design means not only that we are looking at design, but also that we are engaging with designerly ways of thinking. With this emphasis, we approach the evocative attitudes and creative processes that designers use. The basic frame of understanding is the situational understanding of real, everyday life mobilities. Moreover, we pose the question of how design stages those particular mobilities. Therefore, we are touching upon multiple design decisions and interventions across a number of technologies, artefacts, built environments and sites. Though urban design has been our tentative motivation from which we have embarked on the journey into the land of mobilities design, it is relevant to discuss buildings and public pathways. But we should also pay attention to algorithms of traffic-light intervals, apps guiding people through the means of a new digital layer of information, the user-technology interface of all sorts of contemporary infrastructural systems, etc. Hence, rather than looking at urban design as such or architecture proper (both of which incorporate mobilities design), we open up the perspective utilizing the broader notion of design to understand the choices and decisions taken elsewhere, which shape the situational context. Furthermore, when engaging with designerly ways of thinking, we are promoting a utopian flood of ideas about mobilities design. We envision a rich stream of scenarios and experiments on mobility and the city, which stimulate the imagination and discussions about visions for the future. As a research field, mobilities design aims to capitalize on an ongoing, reflective oscillation between theory and practice, in which designerly ways of thinking and making is the nexus. Mobilities design is therefore not a strategy for rational problem-solving but is instead an indicator of design as a research practice. In an uncertainty-ridden field, it seeks to present a pathway for the future of the associations of materialities and mobilities rather than to define a set target.

Through these three perspectives – the mobilities turn, urban design and designerly ways of thinking – we have engaged in a conceptual discussion of the theoretical status of mobilities design. And through three empirical cases, we have scrutinized mobilities design in the light of the key themes of atmospheres, sustainability, and inequalities by means of some mundane typologies of mobilities' materialities: a pedestrian's/cyclist's tunnel, a surface parking lot and an informal road crossing. This we did with a non-abstract approach, working our way towards how atmospheres, sustainability and inequality are epitomized in mobile everyday life situations afforded by particular mobilities designs. En route, a designerly experimental approach has been our companion to the mobilities turn/urban design conceptualization and theorization. In this manner, we have examplified how research may be conducted on the borderline between academic analysis and designerly exploration, in addition to establishing an academic argument for the emerging mobilities design field.

With the theoretical discussion in Chapters 2 and 3, we primarily wanted to show how the nexus of the mobilities turn and design may be fruitfully conceptualized to aid our engagement with materialities of mobilities. In Chapter 2, we argued for a new material turn in mobilities research. With this we engage with designerly ways of thinking and the resultant sensitivity to tangible materials and spaces, and experimental and evocative attitudes. From this we also connected to a tentative discussion about design, ethics, normativity and public involvement. Our proposal for a mobilities design research agenda embraces two moments, of which the former is the better elaborated at this stage. This first moment is concerned with learning to see infrastructural physical spaces of everyday life mobilities as more than instrumental sites of material displacement. The latter moment points to invitations to act, in particular an opening towards professionals across disciplines, such as traffic engineering, architecture, urban design, planning etc., as well as to a contribution to public engagement. From this double-phased strategy and the call for a materially sensitive approach in mobilities research, we presented the underpinning ideas for such a new field. In our understanding, a research agenda for mobilities design must re-orient the theoretical understanding of matter, materials and spatiality, and indeed take its inspiration from sources like urban design, pragmatism and non-representational approaches. Hence, the ontological and epistemological discussion connected to non-representational approaches and its dynamic, precognitive, relational, vital and situational understanding of materialities illustrated an important influence on mobilities design. The classic philosophical position of pragmatism, with its experimentalist ethos, was discussed as another important source of inspiration. We concluded Chapter 2 with a call for a material pragmatism, in which the situational understanding of mobilities is coupled to designerly ways of thinking (including imaginary questioning, 'What if ...?') and multisensorial and embodied dimensions of mobilities.

In Chapter 3 we continued the theoretical and conceptual investigation, arguing for what we termed 'mobilizing' the designed artefact. We thus took one step closer to the stuff that makes up the mobile situations of everyday life mobilities. In particular, we have been influenced by networked ideas about the situational composition, focusing on what designed artefacts afford in mobile situations. In alignment with the notions of assemblages and actor-networks, we emphasized the question of the agency of artefacts and emphazised how a mobile situation not only relies on a complex relationship between human and non-human entities, but also that volumes, voids, surfaces and sites may do or offer certain things in the mobilities relationships. It is the mobilizing of designed artefacts that lead us to understand this complexity. Even the most mundane mobilities artefacts, such as a parking lot's asphalt surface, a pedestrian tunnel, or an informal road crossing, are only poorly addressed with a terminology of sedentarism and placelessness, and we therefore aimed at conceptualizing materialities of mobilities as networked, relational and active hybrids and as contributors to a nuanced and dynamic work with solid artefacts of mobilities. Such a mobilized conceptualization of materialities in mobilities design is necessary in order to embrace their significance and potential – to nurture the understanding of these designed artefacts in their entanglement in hybrid sociotechnical networks, which reach across multiple realms, and to research them in the midst of ongoing mobilities, mundane and unnoticed as they may be. The chapter ended with a discussion of what we termed the 'politics of stuff' as a way of addressing the relationship between materialities and the social, and how such policies (in the broadest sense of the term) may help inform, measure or contest the mobilities affordances of designed artefacts. Using tunnels, parking lots and road crossings are dynamic and multidimensional situational events that may be redescribed and repoliticized by a politics of stuff articulating how things matter.

In Chapter 4 we focused on methodological matters in the crossfield between mobilities mobilities research and urban design. It was a bridging chapter between the theoretical landscape of mobilities design and the empirical case analysis of this book. The research and practice field of mobilities design calls for methods, which can capture its socio-material hybridity, its dynamics (movement), and its designerly disposition towards intervention and change. We emphasized approaches to mapping and data production which lie in the methodological tension field between aesthetic, technical and purely professional approaches and more participartory, inventive, immersed and evocative approaches. We also presented the three empirical sites of analysis: the tunnel, the parking lot and the road crossing. The wider context and area for the three sites was presented, and the underpinning planning and design philosophies of 1970s suburban development was put forward. Furthermore, the methods selected and customized for the analytical study of these empirical cases were explicated: ethnographic methods of site-specific and case-oriented accounts, as well as qualitative research interviews, go-along interviews, and film elicitations. These methods lend themselves particularly well to situational mobilities analysis with its focus on the specific, concrete and actual practices, aiding our pragmatic research of what urban artefacts do in mobile situations. By widening the questioning from what sites, things and spaces are towards what they do, we explored the agencies of artefacts and illustrated some of the complexities of mobilities design, which demand new concepts and new material sensitivities. We further discussed how to research what urban artefacts could do, foregrounding speculative design operations as method. Our attention to mobile situations in this book drives speculative design work. This has facilitated a series of 'What if …?' questions as to the status quo of the sites of mobilities. Design is thus central in mobilities design, not only as the networked and hybrid object of investigation, but also as the method and a driver for reimagination. We addressed how, ultimately, design speculation may be powerful enough to work as a catalyst for change. It may feed the imagination and open up possibilities for the rethinking and remaking of materialities of mobilities, and thus connect to our aforementioned ambition about invitations to act. The design speculations here have a modest architectural expression, which oppose an aesthetic approach to elaborate visual design and instead cultivate potential within an unpretentious architecture responsive to ideas of daily life mobilities. The method of design speculation is thus more-than-representational, intended to move us, mobilize concepts and develop ideas and reimaginations. Such use of design not only draws a line back to the discussion of the agency of artefacts but also to the idea of critical design as an illustration of designerly ways of thinking.

We moved towards the empirical analysis with Chapter 5. With a situational opening of mundane events in the tunnel, we exemplified situated, personal and affective inhabitations of this artefact and pointed to the atmospheric resonance of this mobilities site. A main conclusion from this work is that the tunnel (or any other artefact for that matter) cannot be grasped as a stable artefact with a particular affective resonance ascribed to it. Rather, the tunnel has the potential to come alive as a relational and heterogeneous atmospheric actor when it is experienced with multiple senses. Thinking through the possible richness of lived mobilities, the atmospheres of the enclosed space of the tunnel, and the inherent potential for social interaction and sensorial engagement on the move, we elaborated on how the materiality of the tunnel affords a variety of practices and experiences. Furthermore, we articulated hypothetical 'What if …?' questions, which confront the existing situation in the tunnel and point to material changes that could be done to the tunnel design, thereby exploring and speculating on alternative materialities of mobilities. The concept of atmosphere challenges the privileging of vision in much design and advocates a re-embodiment of people's relationship with these sites, many of which are perceived as sterile or gloomy. In the chapter, we thus proposed a multisensorial nerve in mobilities design, regarding materialities of mobilities sites as part of a sensory urban fabric. Tangible materialities are the focus: materials and textures of floors, walls and little artefacts are part of this, as well as lights, dimensions, vegetation, topographies, shade and sun, water, weather, seasonal changes and animals, to name a few. Importantly, the association of mobilities design with atmospheres is not about visual ornament but about the weighty agency of materialities: what mobilities sites do and what they could do to our mobile ways of life. Atmospheres are powerful; the concept highlights the significant performative effect of emotionally and sensorially laden materialities on daily life mobilities. Atmosphere, then, has potential as a focal concept for supplementing the thorough and developed technical measures and consideration for efficient transport in this functionalist transit space design, with careful concerns for affective lives lived on the way. The design of a pedestrian and bicyclist underpass may satisfy more diverse criteria than functionality of traffic alone, exemplifying the call for design of mundane infrastructures to surpass minimum engineering standards. Moreover, this could also include the wider reach of mobilities sites as capable of triggering diverse urban effects, including atmospheres' powerful effects on the mobile practices and experiences that can take place along journeys.

In Chapter 6 we turned to another mobilities design typology, the parking lot, as the material artefact in focus and with the thematic framing of sustainability. Pondering the possible sustainability of an ordinary, asphalted parking lot, we emphasized ecologies of circuits and flows. Multiple sustainability problems are inherent in the surface parking lot; it is, by large, a utilitarian-only space, which tends to threaten the local area's connectivity, walkability and well-being for people who are not in a car; it also fosters auto-dependency. The analysed mobile situations show how a human body on the lot is a small, soft entity exposed in the large, open, hard-surfaced space with motorized, slow traffic. The chapter explored ideas about sustainable urban transformation towards a post-carbon, climate-responsive urban environment, tying in mobilities design with the development of responses to the urgent problems of climate change and resource scarcity. It focused on the strategy of retrofitting various outdated, environmentally problematic urban spaces and structures in the world to make them adaptive to present and future environmental challenges. An environmentally concerned mobilities design agenda can have a point of departure in the idea that local-sensitive, situational adaptation of a parking lot can be an important approach to include in the transitioning of a place or a city towards a more sustainable future. In the analysis, we saw how microecologies of water and heat (as two examples of the material ecologies present at the parking lot) inform certain mobile practices. Moreover, we illustrated how these vast surface landscapes carry the potential to become new interaction spaces and public-meeting places. The analysis thus connects the material ecologies of matter and meanings into the hybrid geography of the retrofitted parking lot. With an urban mobilities design approach, sustainable parking lot retrofitting is an integrative effort of balancing the utilitarian demand for efficient surface parking with a strategic and concrete consideration for the environment, herein the mobile situations lived on the lot, and the low-carbon patterns of life which the parking lot should support. The chapter was based on a suburban parking lot, but the term 'suburb' is not key, since suburbs exist in many varying and challenging versions in the world. Mobilities design should be considered in relation to the multicentred dynamics of urban areas – with networks and hybridization of suburban and urban patterns and ways of life. Based on this chapter, we find that situational mobilities design offers an important approach to sustainable urbanism and mobilities. Its outset in the concrete situation puts focus on materiality and lived lives, which we find in larger and more abstract discussions of sustainability. It highlights problems and potentials for more sustainable user choices, embedded in the materialities and in relation to connectivity, barriers and the coercion or promotion of various modes of mobilities, etc. 'What if …?' questions about the sustainable future of the parking lot supported this approach, by pointing to the daily shifts between mobility systems, to the possible pleasure of inhabiting a parking lot and to the engineered sustainable landscaping which can support it.

In Chapter 7 we turned to the final mobilities design typology included in this book, the road crossing. In this chapter, we wanted to explore the large societal issue of inequalities with a minute focus on an actual situation. Values and norms are embedded within design principles and ideas, as well as being enshrined into the very materialities of mobilities design. As a reflection of a larger theme of social stratification and materialization of unevenness into the hard infrastrucures of contemporary society, the analysis of the road crossing shows that mobilities design is not neutral. Mobilities design cannot be treated in depoliticized and universal ways. With the traffic-segregation system, of which the informal road crossing is part, we see an instance of how a particular design produces inflexible effects and serious consequences, in that surface crossings of the roads were defined as unwanted practices. We showed how this piece of the road is a site of a conflictual co-existence of the directional flow of car traffic and of the cross-directional flow of vulnerable pedestrians and bicyclists; this highlights the mobile situations of a regional car driver in the road corridor and the mobile whereabouts of two local pedestrians. The assemblage of roadscape artefacts (asphalt, lanes, curbs, etc.) and the mobile subjects point to the road-crossing example as one that favours particular bodies and particular modes of mobility. We argued that the road thus materializes with a particular version of a space of action for humans. The material affordances imagined to be ideal (or at least wishful from the value base of the planning process) may play out differently in practice, highlighting how mobilities cannot be scripted by design per se. Still, the design for mobile situations encompasses many ways of staging possibilities and relationships between people from above, and we considered alternatives through design speculations, pointing to some of the conflicts and trade-offs in the very tangible design of a road crossing. However, it may be that none of the alternative physical designs or arrangements of the road crossing can succeed in making a difference significant to the pattern of power and authority embedded in the already-existing design, illustrating an important limitation to such concrete design. The presence of the road and its interlinkage with the automobility system require a technology which demands its social environment to be constructed in a particular way. We may say, that if we accept the private car, we also accept, for example, to be forced to live in an instantaneous compressed time and in stretched spaces across huge distances, with or without access to a car ourselves. A well-designed bridge or underpass or urban space do not substantially address this condition. We also pointed to the importance of future democratic mobilities design approaches. The road crossing design is dealt with through a centralized public authority, which exerts certain ideas of the better solutions. Yet, another stream of mobilities design intervention may emerge, countering such a top-down approach. We may imagine creative and inclusive processes of co-design, where the hard materiality of objects and surfaces will be the very materiality upon which creative processes of imaginary alternative uses can be played out. Mundane mobilities sites may be articulated as sites of deliberation, discussion and more or less utopian imaginings. Connecting mobilities design as a material practice with the theme of inequalities and with ideas of co-design, we proposed to explore mobilities sites as potential-laden public territories of movement and exchange.

The general conclusion is thus that the new and emerging field of mobilties design carries potential for reinvigorating mobilities research with a new sensitivity to the material and the physcial. And, in turn, that concrete design of materialities of mobilities may benefit from a mobilized, situational approach, highlighting the embeddedness of any designed artefact of mobilities in important societal issues and processes of mobilities. Mobilities design is not a uniform endeavour, regardless of which mobilities site is in question. Rather, it is a balancing act of responding with insight and sensitivity to existing site conditions and challenges. In Chapter 7, we discussed some of the intricate balances that any design intervention must regard, and whether new or transformed materialities should succeed in addressing profound challenges. We find that the interaction between urban design and mobilities research is one of mutual benefit, and that this interaction can have repercussions for a number of fields, themes and areas of concern in the future.

Research perspectives

From the outset of articulating mobilities design as a new research field, we were conscious of potential controversy about and ambivalence toward our ambition to contribute to research and practice simultaneously. We see our work in this book as an illustration of a Critical Mobilities Thinking, with a double focus on problems and potentials. This dualism is reflected in the contributions to conceptualization as an exploration of the designerly ways of thinking and how they offer a lot to the potential-seeking discussions. The problems (or dark sides) are equally addressed in the conceptualization, and in particular we have illustrated how issues of inequality and sustainability are connected to concrete situations and practical design. The emerging research agenda connected to mobilities design may be connected to the moments of both learning to see and the invitation to act which we have proposed throughout the book. In light of that, he future of mobilities design research will be about refining ways of seeing, as well as seeking out ever-more precise and sophisticated theoretical frames, and being connected to processes of design. In such processes of design, democratic approaches will be of relevance, as will engagement with the general public and with professionals and practitioners across the diverse fields. Regarding the invitation to act moment of the research strategy, this leads to a larger discussion of what it means to mobilize designed artefacts and how this may have importance for our interpretation of the mundane sites of situational mobilities. Our discussion of a politics of stuff and the chasing out of new potentials for activities, programmes and practices within the stages of everyday life mobilities point towards connecting mobilities design to knowledge of co-design, co-creation, new public spheres and citizen engagement.

The research undertaken has a number of interfaces to the public debates and deliberations about the design of spaces, the workings of cities and the public domains of infrastructural landscapes. As such, we see a whole set of connections to the political coming out of this work. It has been an ambition with this work to show how mundane spaces and trivial design typologies may be much more than what they seem. Here, we share the agenda focusing on a 'politics of visibility', articulated by Crang and Graham (2007). The potential of the politics of visibility, when connected to mobilities design, is to explore and illustrate the mundane spaces of the everyday life. However, we are not only thinking of the merry potentials connected to design options. We indeed see a task for the future of mobilities design research to engage with the hidden powers and social exclusions that permeate the materialities of infrastructural landscapes. Here, we are on par with other attempts to 'making things public' (Latour and Weibel 2005). In connection to the politics of visibility and new ways of seeing the familiar spaces and designs, we see a 'politics of design' emerging that engages with the multiplicity of publics (ibid.) and the hetereogeneous dimensions of public spheres in general, and in particular with the potential of exploring notions of mobile agoras, where political identities and voices are shaped and sharpened. The contemporary infrastructural landscapes are public spaces, and we need to engage with their problems and potentials as such. Finally, we argued for a politics of stuff as a way of mobilizing the insights evoked by our material sensitivity. The way things work, the way artefacts afford particular practices, and the way sites are scenes of interaction need to be made clear from the point of view of a politics of stuff. Our call for a politics of design and the shaping of awareness of the repercussions of design decisions and interventions within mobilities design have affinities with the 'Critical Engineering Manifesto' (Oliver *et al.* 2011) and with the 'Design like you give a damn' project (Architecture for Humanity 2006). Like these, we wish to make a call for understanding the new materialities of mobilities as inherently political.

A final dimension of the research perspectives we want to touch upon is the visions and imaginaries of the future. What are the future scenarios of mobilities design as a venue for discussion of mobile atmospheres, sustainabilities and inequalities? Needless to say, the car has played a large role as a 'locked-in' technology (Urry 2007), shaping mobilities design for several decades, and our work is in many respects tangential with the discussion of *After the Car* (Dennis and Urry 2009), for example. We may ask how this research matters by arguing that mobilities design faces a multidimensional task with a wide variety of environmental-societal issues (which differ in persistency in different contexts). The future of mobilities design research must take part in a work towards more sustainable transport choices, less pollution, 'good' communities, safe, appreciated, and even fun mobility experiences, and cities with integrated ecological systems of plants, water and animals, and resilience.

The future of mobilities design practice

Coming to the end, we want to address design practice. How may mobilities design engage with the multiplicity of relevant design professionals involved in urban planning, urban design, architecture and traffic planning? One possibility for engaging with these multiple professions is the multidiciplinary spirit embedded in mobilities design. As with the origin of the mobilities turn, the mobilities design perspective we have harnessed in this work needs to draw on many disciplines and many frames of thinking. This turns out to be of significance in relation to mobilities design practices, which we have implemented through a number of mobilities design workshops with municipalities, engineering companies and architectural companies over the last several years. For instance, our Mobilities Design Group, under the Centre for Mobilities and Urban Studies (C-MUS) at Aalborg University, has signed a formal collaboration agreement with the local municipality of Aalborg. Accordingly, we meet frequently with planners, architects, and engineers from the municipality to discuss concrete projects in the city and how to use and advance the mobilities design approach to these topical issues. In this line of engagement with practice, we have also given guest lectures and set up a workshop at the Danish Town Planning Institute on mobilities design. We see willing participation in endeavours such as these as an emerging interest in the field. Arguably this interest does not grow out of academic interest in new theories. Rather, we have found, the mobilities turn in general and the framing of mobilities design in particular offer a fresh platform for communication for professionals who may have heretofore found themselves locked into governmental silos of traffic engineering or public space design, for example. By engaging with the mobilities design field and applying its concepts and approaches, our partners from practice have enthusiastically taken on this mindset to work with the unfamiliar, the potentials and the problems within familiar mobilities and materialities.

Ahead lies 'roadwork', with mutually influencing and new conceptual challenges and practical explorations. The refinement of arguments, the tuning of methods and the experiences of ameliorated experiments are on the horizon, as we close the pages of these nascent reflections on and articulations of the emerging field of mobilities design.

Bibliography

Aalborg Erhvervskontor (1967) *Aalborg Viser Vej.* Aalborg Stiftsbogtrykkeri.

Aalborg Municipality (1980) *Lokalplan 08–009 for institutionsområde Tornhøj*, Aalborg: Aalborg Kommune.

Aalborg Municipality (2004) *Architectural Policy: For an Attractive and Vigorous Urban Environment*, Aalborg: Aalborg Kommune.

Aalborg Town Planning Office (1962) *Byplanarbejdet i Aalborg*, Aalborg: Aalborg Kommune.

Aalborg Town Planning Office (1967) *Aalborg Byplan*, Aalborg: Aalborg Kommune.

Abrams, J. and Hall, P. (eds) (2006) *Else/Where: Mapping – New Cartographies of Networks and Territories*, University of Minnesota Press.

Adey, P. (2010) *Mobility*, Abingdon: Routledge.

Adey, P., Bissell, D., Hannam, K., Merriman, P. and Sheller, M. (eds) (2014) *The Routledge Handbook of Mobilities*, London: Routledge, pp. 409–20.

Albertsen, N. (2012) Gesturing atmospheres. Conference paper, *Ambiances in action/Ambiances en acte(s) – International Congress on Ambiances*, Montreal 2012, pp. 69–74.

Allen, J. (2008) Pragmatism and power, or the power to make a difference in a radically contingent world, *Geoforum*, **39** (2008), pp. 1613–24.

Allen, S. (1999) *Points and Lines: Diagrams and Projects for the City*, New York: Princeton Architectural Press.

Allen, S. (2010) Landscape infrastructures. In Stoll, K. and Lloyd, S. (eds) *Infrastructure as Architecture: Designing Composite Networks*, Berlin: Jovis Verlag. pp. 36–45.

Amin, A. and Thrift, N. (2002) *Cities: Reimagining the Urban*, Cambridge: Polity.

Anderson, B. (2009) Affective atmospheres, *Emotion, Space and Society*, **2**(2), pp. 77–81.

Anderson, B. and Harrison, P. (eds) (2010) *Taking-Place: Non-representational Theories and Geography*, Farnham: Ashgate.

Anderson, B. and Wylie, J. (2009) On geography and materiality, *Environment & Planning A*, **41** (2009), pp. 318–35.

Andrade, V., Smith, S. and Lanng, D. B. (eds) (2012) *Musings: An Urban Design Anthology*. Aalborg: Aalborg University Press.

Architecture for Humanity (2006) *Design Like You Give a Damn: Architectural Responses to Humanitarian Crisis*, London: Thames & Hudson.

Arefi, M. (1999) Non-place and placelessness as narratives of loss: rethinking the notion of place, *Journal of Urban Design*, **4**(2), pp. 179–93.

Augé, M. (1995) *Non-places: An Introduction to Supermodernity*, London: Verso.

Bacon, M. (2012) *Pragmatism: An Introduction*, Cambridge: Polity.

Bærenholdt, J. O., Büscher, M., Scheuer, J. D. and Simonsen, J. (eds) (2010) Perspectives on design research. *Design Research: Synergies from Interdisciplinary Perspectives*, London: Routledge, pp. 1–15.

Barbara, A. and Perliss, A. (2004) *Invisible Architecture: Experiencing Places through the Sense of Smell*, Milano: Skira.

Barnes, T. J. (2008) American pragmatism: towards a geographical introduction, *Geoforum*, **39**, pp. 1542–54.

Bender, T. (2010) Postscript: reassembling the city: networks and urban imageries. In Farías, I. and Bender, T. (eds) *Urban Assemblages: How Actor-Network Theory Changes Urban Studies*, New York: Routledge. pp. 303–24.

Ben-Joseph, E. (2012) *ReThinking a Lot: The Design and Culture of Parking*, Massachusetts: MIT Press.

Bennett, J. (2010) *Vibrant Matter – A Political Ecology of Things*, Durham: Duke University Press.

Bernstein, J. (1988) Pragmatism, pluralism and the healing of wounds, *Proceedings and Addresses of the American Philosophical Association*, **63**(3), pp. 5–18.

Bertolini, L. (2006) Fostering urbanity in a mobile society: linking concepts and practices, *Journal of Urban Design*, **11**(3), pp. 319–34.

Bickers, P. (2011) Caressing space: Pipilotti Rist interviewed by Patricia Bickers, *Art Monthly* (350).

Bille, M., Bjerregaard, P. and Sørensen, T. F. (2015) Staging atmospheres: materiality, culture and the texture of the in-between, *Emotion, Space and Society*, **15**, pp. 31–8.

Bissell, D. (2010) Passenger mobilities: affective atmospheres and the sociality of public transport, *Environment and Planning D*, **28**, pp. 270–89.

Bjørn, N. (ed.) (2008) *Arkitektur der forandrer – fra ghetto til velfungerende byområde*, Copenhagen: Gads Forlag.

Bogost, I. (2012) *Alien Phenomenology, or What's It Like To Be a Thing?*, Minneapolis: University of Minnesota Press.

Böhme, G. (1993) Atmosphere as the fundamental concept of a new aesthetics, *Thesis Eleven*, **36**, pp. 113–26.

Böhme, G. (1998) Atmosphere as an aesthetic concept, *Daidalos*, **68**, pp. 112–15.

Böhme, G. (2005) Atmosphere as the subject matter of architecture. In Ursprung, P. (ed.) *Herzog & de Meuron: Natural History*, Zurich: Lars Muller Publishers, pp. 398–406.

Böhme, G. (2013) The art of the stage set as a paradigm for an aesthetics of atmospheres, *Ambiances: International Journal of Sensory Environment, Architecture and Urban Space*. Retrieved from http://ambiances.revues.org/315.

Bridge, G. (2008) City senses: on the radical possibilities of pragmatism in geography, *Geoforum*, **39** (2008), pp. 1570–84.

Buchanan, C. (1964) *Traffic in Towns*, Harmondsworth: Penguin.

Bukdahl, E. M. (2011) *The Re-enchantment of Nature and Urban Space: Michael Singer. Projects in Art, Design and Environmental Regeneration*, Aalborg: Utzon Centre.

Bunschoten, R., Hoshino, T. and Binet, H. (2001) *Urban Flotsam: Stirring the City*, Rotterdam: 010 Publishers.

Burns, C. and Kahn, A. (2005) Why site matters. In Burns, C. and Kahn, A. (eds) *Site Matters*. New York: Routledge. pp. vii–xxix.

Büscher, M. and Urry, J. (2009) Mobile methods and the empirical, *European Journal of Social Theory*, **12**(1), pp. 99–116.

Büscher, M., Urry, J. and Witchger, K. (2011a) Introduction: mobile methods. In Büscher, M., Urry, J. and Witchger, K. (eds) *Mobile Methods*. London: Routledge. pp. 1–19.

Büscher, M., Urry, J. and Witchger, K. (eds) (2011b) *Mobile Methods*, London: Routledge.

Campbell, F. A. K. (2008) Refusing able(ness): a preliminary conversation about ableness, *M/C Journal*, **11**. Retrieved from http://journal.media-culture.org.au/index/, mcjournal/article/viewArticle/46.

Carmona, M., Tiesdell, S., Heath, T. and Oc, T. (2010) *Public Places. Urban Spaces: The Dimensions of Urban Design*, 2nd edn, Oxford: Architectural Press.

Chase, J., Crawford, M. and Kaliski, J. (eds) (1999) *Everyday Urbanism*, New York: The Monacelli Press.

Clark, B. (2013) Generating publics through design activity. In Gunn, W., Otto, T. and Smith, R. C. (eds) *Design Anthropology: Theory and Practice*, London: Bloomsbury, pp. 199–215.

Classen, C. (2005) The deodorized city: battling urban stench in the nineteenth century. In Zardini, M. (ed.) *Sense of the City: An Alternate Approach to Urbanism*, Montreal: Canadian Centre for Architecture, pp. 292–321.

Coaffe, J. and Headlam, N. (2008) Pragmatic localism uncovered: the search for locally contingent solutions to national reform agendas, *Geoforum*, **39** (2008), pp. 1585–99.

Corner, J. (ed.) (1999a) *Recovering Landscape*, New York: Princeton Architectural Press.

Corner, J. (1999b) Introduction: recovering landscape as a critical cultural practice. In Corner, J. (ed.) *Recovering Landscape*, New York: Princeton Architectural Press, pp. 1–28.

Corner, J. (1999c) The agency of mapping: speculation, critique and invention. In Cosgrove, D. (ed.) *Mappings*, London: Reaktion Books Ltd., pp. 213–52.

Crang, M. and Graham, S. (2007) Sentient cities: ambient intelligence and the politics of urban space, *Information, Communication & Society*, **10**(6), 2007, pp. 789–817.

Cresswell, T. (2004) *Place: A Short Introduction*, Oxford: Blackwell.

Cresswell, T. (2006) *On the Move: Mobility in the Modern Western World*, London: Routledge.

Cresswell, T. (2010) Towards a politics of mobility. In *Environment and Planning D: Society and Space*, **28**, pp. 17–31.

Cresswell, T. and Merriman, P. (2011) (eds) *Geographies of Mobilities: Practices, Spaces, Subjects*, Farnham: Ashgate, pp. 189–203.

Cullen, G. (1961/1996) *The Concise Townscape*, Oxford: Architectural Press.

Cutchin, M. P. (2008) John Dewey's metaphysical ground-map and its implications for geographical inquiry, *Geoforum*, **39**, pp. 1555–69.

D'Hooghe, A. (2010) The objectification of infrastructure: the cultural project of suburban infrastructure design. In Stoll, K. and Lloyd, S. (eds) *Infrastructure as Architecture: Designing Composite Networks*, Berlin: Jovis Verlag, pp. 78–87.

Dahl, H. (2008) *Den Usynlige Verden*, København: Gyldendal.

Danish Road Directorate (2011) Byernes trafikarealer: Hæfte 9. Anlæg for parkering og standsning i byer. Vejdirektoratet.

Danish Road Directorate (2012) Håndbog i trafikplanlægning i byer. Vejdirektoratet

Davis, M. (1990) *City of Quartz: Excavating the Future of Los Angeles*, New York: Vintage Books.

Degen, M. (2008) *Sensing Cities*, New York: Routledge.

Degen, M. and Rose, G. (2012) The sensory experiencing of urban design: the role of walking and perceptual memory, *Urban Studies*, **49**(15), pp. 3271–87.

Degen, M., Rose, G. and Basdas, B. (2010) Bodies and everyday practices in designed urban environments, *Science Studies*, **23**(2) (2010) pp. 60–76.

Deleuze, G. and Guattari, F. (1987/2003) *A Thousand Plateaus: Capitalism and Schizophrenia*, London: Continuum.

Dennis, K. and Urry, J. (2009) *After the Car*, Cambridge: Polity.

Descombes, G. (1999) Shifting sites: the Swiss way, Geneva. In Corner, J. (ed.) *Recovering Landscape*. New York: Princeton Architectural Press, pp. 79–86.

Dewey, J. (1916) *Democracy and Education*, New York: Free Press.

Dewey, J. (1931) The development of American pragmatism. In Thayer, H. S. (ed.) (1982) *Pragmatism: The Classic Writings*, Indianapolis: Hackett Publishing Company, pp. 23–40.

Dewey, J. (1986) Logic: the theory of inquiry. In Boydston, A. (ed.) *John Dewey: The Later Works, 1925–1953*, Carbondale: Sourthern Illinois University Press.

Dodge, M., Kitchin, R. and Perkins, C. (eds) (2011) *The Map Reader: Theories of Mapping Practice and Cartographic Representation*, Chichester: Wiley-Blackwell.

Dolmage, J. (2015) Disabling studies, disability studied and disability studies. Retrieved from http://disablingstudies.wordpress.com/

Doucet, I. and Cupers, K. (2009) Agency in architecture: reframing criticality in theory and practice, *Footprint*, **4**, pp. 1–6.

Dunham-Jones, E. and Williamson, J. (2011) *Retrofitting Suburbia: Urban Design Solutions for Redesigning Suburbs*, New Jersey: John Wiley & Sons.

Dunne, A. and Raby, F. (2013) *Speculative Everything: Design, Fiction, and Social Dreaming*, Cambridge, MA: The MIT Press.

Dunne, A. and Raby, F. (2015) Critical design FAQ, blog post. Retrieved from www.dunneandraby.co.uk/content/bydandr/13/0

Dyrssen, C. (2011) Navigating in heterogeneity: architectural thinking and art-based research. In Biggs, M. and Karlsson, H. (eds) *The Routledge Companion to Research in the Arts*, New York: Routledge, pp. 223–39.

Easterling, K. (2014) *Extrastatecraft: The Power of Infrastructure Space*, London: Verso.

Edensor, T. (2003) M6-Junction 19–16. Defamiliarizing the mundane roadscape, *Space and Culture*, **6**(2), pp. 151–68.

Edensor, T. (2015) Producing atmospheres at the match: fan cultures, commercialisation and mood management in English football, *Emotion, Space and Society*, **15**, pp. 82–9.

Edwards, B. (2010) *Sustainability and the Design of Transport Interchanges*, London: Routledge.

Elliott, A. and Urry, J. (2010) *Mobile Lives*, London: Routledge.

Ellis, C. (2002) The new urbanism: critiques and rebuttals, *Journal of Urban Design*, **7**(3), 2002.

Erell, E., Pearlmutter, D. and Williamson, T. (2011) *Urban Microclimate: Designing Spaces between Buildings*, London: Earthscan.

Erlhoff, M., Heidkamp, P. and Utikal, I. (eds) (2008) *Designing Public: Perspectives for the Public*, Basel: Birkhäuser.

Fallan, K. (2008) Architecture in action: traveling with actor-network theory in the land of architectural research, *Architectural Theory Review*, **13**(1), pp. 80–96.

Farías, I. (2010a) Introduction. In Farías, I. and Bender, T. (eds) (2010) *Urban Assemblages: How Actor-Network Theory Changes Urban Studies*, New York: Routledge, pp. 1–24.

Farías, I. (2010b) Interview with Nigel Thrift. In Farías, I. and Bender, T. (eds) (2010) *Urban Assemblages: How Actor-Network Theory Changes Urban Studies*, New York: Routledge, pp. 109–20.

Farías, I. (2010c) Interview with Stephen Graham. In Farías, I. and Bender, T. (eds) *Urban Assemblages. How Actor-Network Theory Changes Urban Studies*. New York: Routledge. pp. 197–206.

Farías, I. (2010d) Interview with Rob Shields. In Farías, I. and Bender, T. (eds) (2010) *Urban Assemblages: How Actor-Network Theory Changes Urban Studies*, New York: Routledge, pp. 291–302.

Farías, I. and Bender, T. (eds) (2010) *Urban Assemblages: How Actor-Network Theory Changes Urban Studies*, New York: Routledge.

Fincham, B., McGuinness, M. and Murray, L. (eds) (2010) *Mobile Methodologies*, Basingstoke: Palgrave Macmillan, pp. 1–10.

Fisker, C. (2011) *End of the road? Loss of (auto)mobility among seniors and their altered mobilities and networks – a case study of a car-centered Canadian city and a Danish city*, PhD Thesis, Aalborg University.

Fleming, S. (2012) *Cycle Space: Architecture and Urban Design in the Age of the Bicycle*, Rotterdam: Nai 010 Publishers.

Flyvbjerg, B. (1998) *Rationality and Power: Democracy in Practice*, Chicago: University of Chicago Press.

Fraser, N. (1990) Re-thinking the public sphere: a contribution to the critique of actually existing democracy, *Social Text*, **25/26**, pp. 56–80.

Friedmann, J. (2002) *The Prospect of Cities*, Minneapolis: University of Minnesota Press.

Gad, C. and Jensen, C. B. (2007) Post-ANT. In Jensen, C. B., Lauritsen, P. and Olesen, F. (eds) *Introduktion til STS*, København: Hans Reitzels Forlag, pp. 93–118.

Gatt, C. and Ingold, T. (2013) From description to correspondence: anthropology in real time. In Gunn, W., Otto, T. and Smith, R. C. (eds) *Design Anthropology: Theory and Practice*, London: Bloomsbury, pp. 139–58.

Gehl, J. (1971/96) *Livet mellem husene*, København: Arkitektens Forlag.

Gehl, J. (2010) *Cities for People*, Washington DC: Island Press.

Gibson, J. J. (1977) The theory of affordances. In Shaw, R. E. and Bransford, J. (eds) *Perceiving, Acting, and Knowing*, Hillsdale, NJ: Lawrence Erlbaum Associates.

Gibson, J. J. (1986/2015) *The Ecological Approach to Visual Perception*, New York: Psychology Press.

Gimmler, A. (2005) Amerikansk Pragmatisme: Hverdagslivets kreativitet. In Jacobsen, M. H. and Kristiansen, S. (eds) *Hverdagslivet – sociologier om det upåagtede*, København: Hans Reitzels Forlag, pp. 72–108.

Gimmler, A. (2008) Nicht-epistemologische Erfahrung, Artefakte und Praktiken: Vorüberlegungen zu einer pragmatischen Sozialtheorie. In Hertzel, A., Kertscher, J. and Tölli. M. (eds) (2008) *Pragmatismus: Philosophie der Zukunft?*, Göttingen: Velbrück Wissenschaft, pp. 141–57.

Gimmler, A. (2012) Pragmatisme og 'practice turn', *Distinktion*, (64), 2012, pp. 43–58.

Goffman, E. (1959) *The Presentation of Self in Everyday Life*, New York: Doubleday.

Graham, S. and Marvin, S. (2001) *Splintering Urbanism: Networked Infrastructures, Technological Mobilities and the Urban Condition*, London: Routledge.

Griffero, T. (2014/2010) *Atmospheres: Aesthetics of Emotional Spaces*, Farnham: Ashgate.

Guy, S. (2013) Pragmatic ecologies. In Harrison, A. L. (ed.) (2013) *Architectural Theories of the Environment: Posthuman Territory*, London: Routledge, pp. 138–50.

Habermas, J. (1961/91) *The Structural Transformation of the Public Sphere: An Inquiry into a Category of Bourgeois Society*, Cambridge, Mass.: The MIT Press.

Hagson, A. (2000) *Stads- och trafikplaneringens paradigm*, Göteborg: Chalmers Tekniska Högskola.

Hajer, M. and Reijndorp, A. (2001) *In Search of New Public Domain,* Rotterdam: NAI Publishers.

Hannam, K., Sheller, M. and Urry, J. (2006) Editorial: mobilities, immobilities and moorings, *Mobilities*, **1**(1), pp. 1–22.

Harder, H. (2003) A 'Network' and a 'Dictum', Conference paper for the AESO ACP Third join Congresse, Leuven 2003.

Harman, G. (2011) On the undermining of objects: Grant, Bruno, and radical philosophy. In Bryant, L., Srnick, N. and Harman, G. (eds) *The Speculative Turn: Continental Materialism and Realism*, Melbourne: re-press.org.

Harris, S. and Berke, D. (eds) (1997) *Architecture of the Everyday*, New York: Princeton University Press.

Harvard Graduate Design School (n.d.) "On Asphalt" project webpage, Retrieved from www.onasphalt.com (accessed June 2013; web domain has since shifted content).

Harvey, D. (1966) *Justice, Nature and the Geography of Difference*, Oxford: Blackwell.

Hasse, J. (2012) *Atmosphären der Stadt: Aufgespürte Räume*, Berlin: Jovis Verlag.

Healey, P. (1997) *Collaborative Planning: Shaping Places in Fragmented Societies*, London: Macmillan.

Healey, P. (2009) The pragmatic tradition in planning thought, *Journal of Planning Education and Research*, **28**, pp. 277–92.

Heft, H. (2010) Affordances and the perception of landscape: an inquiry into environmental perception and aesthetics. In Thompson, C. W., Aspinall, P. and Bell, S. (eds) *Innovative Approaches to Researching Landscape and Health*, London: Routledge, pp. 9–32.

Hepple, L. W. (2008) Geography and the pragmatic tradition: the threefold engagement, *Geoforum*, **39**, pp. 1530–41.

Hemmer, L. (2013) Transforming the Park Avenue tunnel with light and sound: voice tunnel, YouTube video published 9 July 2013. Retrieved from www.youtube.com/watch?v=jmRnLUVt4kE.

Houben, F. and Calabrese, L. M. (eds) (2003) *Mobility: A Room with a View*, Rotterdam: NAi Publishers.

Howes, D. (2005) Architecture of the senses. In Zardini, M. (ed.) *Sense of the City: An Alternate Approach to Urbanism*, Montreal: Canadian Centre for Architecture, pp. 322–31.

Høyer, S. A. B. (1999) Things take time and time take things: the Danish landscape. In Corner, J. (ed.) *Recovering Landscape*, New York: Princeton Architectural Press, pp. 69–78.

Ingersoll, R. (2006) *Sprawltown*, New York: Princeton Architectural Press.

Ingold, T. (2000) *The Perception of the Environment: Essays On Livelihood, Dwelling And Skill*, London: Routledge.

Ingold, T. (2007) *Lines: A Brief History*, London: Routledge.

Ingold, T. (2011) *Being Alive: Essays on Movement, Knowledge and Description*, London: Routledge.

Ingold, T. (2012) The atmosphere, *Chiasmi International* **14**, pp. 75–87. DOI: 10.5840/chiasmi20121410

Ingold, T. (2013) *Making: Anthropology, Archaeology, Art and Architecture*, New York: Routledge.

Ingold, T. (2014) Designing environments for life. In Hastrup, K. (ed.) *Anthropology and Nature*, New York: Routledge, pp. 233–46.

Ingold, T. (2015) *The Life of Lines*, New York: Routledge.

Jacobs, A. and Appleyard, D. (1987) Toward an urban design manifesto, *Journal of the American Planning Association*, **53**(1), pp. 112–20.

Jacobs, A. B. (1993) Conclusion: great streets and city planning. In Larice, M. and MacDonald, E. (eds) (2007) *The Urban Design Reader*, New York: Routledge, pp. 387–90.

Jacobs, J. (1961) *The Death and Life of Great American Cities*, New York: Random House.

Jacobs, J. M. and Merriman, P. (2011) Practicing architectures, *Social and Cultural Geography*, **12**(3), pp. 211–22.

Jain, J. (2009) The making of mundane bus journey. In Vannini, P. (ed.) *The Culture of Alternative Mobilities: Routes Less Traveled*, Farnham: Ashgate, pp. 91–110.

James, W. (1884) What is an emotion? In Richardson, R. (ed.) (2010) *The Heart of William James*, Cambridge MA: Harvard University Press, pp. 1–19.

James, W. (1899) Philosophical conceptions and practical results. In Richardson, R. (ed.) (2010) *The Heart of William James*, Cambridge MA: Harvard University Press, pp. 183–202.

Jensen, O. B. (2004) There is nothing so practical as a good theory, *Planning Theory and Practice*, **5**(2), 2004, pp. 254–6.

Jensen, O. B. (2006) 'Facework', flow and the city: Simmel, Goffman and mobility in the contemporary city, *Mobilities*, **1**(2), pp. 143–65.

Jensen, O. B. (2007) City of layers: Bangkok's sky train and how it works in socially segregating mobility patterns, *Swiss Journal of Sociology*, **33**(3), pp. 387–405.

Jensen, O. B. (2009) Flows of meaning, cultures of movement – urban mobility as meaningful everyday life practice, *Mobilities*, **4**, pp. 139–58.

Jensen, O. B. (2010a) Negotiation in motion: unpacking a geography of mobility, *Space and Culture*, **13**, pp. 389–402.

Jensen, O. B. (2010b) Erving Goffman and everyday life mobility. In Jacobsen, M. (ed.) *The Contemporary Goffman*, New York: Routledge, pp. 333–51.

Jensen, O. B. (2013) *Staging Mobilities*, London: Routledge.

Jensen, O. B. (2014) *Designing Mobilities*, Aalborg: Aalborg University Press.

Jensen, O. B. (2015) (ed.) *Mobilities – Critical Concepts in Built Environment*, (4 vol.), London: Routledge.

Jensen, O. B. (2016) Non-representational theory. In Schiermer, B. (ed.) (2016) *Kultursociologi og kulturteori – en grundbog*, København: Hans Reitzel (In Press).

Jensen, O. B. and Lanng, D. B. (2016) Mobilities design – towards an experimental field of research and practice. In Griffiths, S. and von Lünen, A. (eds) *Spatial Cultures*, Farnham: Ashgate.

Jensen, O. B. and Freudendal-Pedersen, M. (2012) Utopias of Mobilities. In Jacobsen, M. H. and Tester, K. (eds) (2012) *Utopia: Social Theory and the Future*, Farnham: Ashgate, pp. 197–217.

Jensen, O. B. and Morelli, N. (2011) Critical points of contact: exploring networked relations in urban mobility and service design, *Kortlægning og Arealforvaltning*, **46**(1), pp. 36–49.

Jensen, O. B. and Richardson, T. (2004) *Making European Space: Mobility, Power and Territorial Identity*, London: Routledge.

Jensen, O. B., Lanng, D. B. and Wind, S. (2016) Artefacts, affordances and the design of mobilities. In Spinney, J., Reimer, S. and Pinch, P. (eds) *Mobilising Design, Designing Mobilities: Intersections, Affordances, Relations*. London: Routledge.

Jensen, O. B., Sheller, M. and Wind, S. (2014) Together and apart: ambiences and negotiation in families' everyday life and mobility, *Mobilities*, 2014, DOI: 10.1080/17450101.2013.868158.

Johnson, B. (2007) Japan's melody roads play music as you drive, Guardian UK. Retrieved from www.guardian.co.uk/world/2007/nov/13/japan.gadgets

Jones, O. (2008) Stepping from the wreckage: geography, pragmatism and anti-representational theory, *Geoforum*, **39** (2008), pp. 1600–12.

Kaufmann, V., Bergman, M. M. and Joye, D. (2004) Motility: mobility as capital, *International Journal of Urban and Regional Research*, **28**(4), pp. 745–56.

Keeling, D. (2008) Transport geography: new regional mobilities, *Progress in Human Geography*, **32**(2), pp. 275–283.

Kelbaugh, D. (2007) Toward an integrated paradigm: further thoughts on the three urbanisms, *Places*, **19**(2), pp. 12–20.

Kilpinen, E. (2008) *Pragmatism as a Philosophy of Action*, paper presented at the First Nordic Pragmatism Conference, Helsinki, June 2008.

Kimbell, L. (2011) Rethinking design thinking: part i, *Design and Culture*, **3**(3), pp. 285–306.

Kimbell, L. (2012) Rethinking design thinking: part ii, *Design and Culture*, **4**(2), pp. 129–48.

Koolhaas, R. (1995) The generic city. In Koolhaas, R. and Mau, B. (1995) *S, M, L, XL*, New York: The Monacelli Press, pp. 1239–64.

Kraftl, P. and Adey, P. (2008) Architecture/affect/inhabitation: geographies of being-in buildings, *Annals of the Association of American Geographers*, **98**(1), pp. 213–31.

Krauel, J. (2009) *Urban Spaces: Environments for the Future*, Barcelona: Links Books.

Krieger, A. (2009) Introduction: an urban frame of mind. In Krieger, A. and Saunders, W. S. (eds) *Urban Design*, Minneapolis: University of Minnesota Press, pp. vii–xix.

Lang, J. (2005) *Urban Design: A Typology of Procedures and Products*, Oxford: Architectural Press.

Lanng, D. B. (2014) How does it feel to travel through a tunnel? Designing a mundane transit space in Denmark, *Ambiances, Experimentation – Conception – Participation.* Retrieved from http://ambiances.revues.org/454

Lanng, D. B. (2015) *Gesturing Entangled Journeys: Mobilities Design in Aalborg East, Denmark*, PhD thesis, Aalborg University.

Lanng, D. B. (forthcoming) A 'more-than-representational' mapping study: lived mobilities and mundane architectures, *Nordic Journal of Architectural Research.*

Lanng, D.B. and Jensen, O. B. (2016) Linking wayfinding and wayfaring. In Hunter, R. H., Anderson, L. A. and Belza, B. L. (eds) *Community Wayfinding: Pathways to Understanding*, New York: Springer, pp. 247–60.

Lanng, D. B., Harder, H. and Jensen, O. B. (2012) Towards urban mobility designs: en route in the functional city. In *Selected Proceedings from the Annual Transport Conference at Aalborg University*, 2012.

Larsen, J. and Meged, J.W. (2012) At fotografere og filme byen – visuelle etnografier. In Andersen, J., Freudendahl-Pedersen, M., Koefoed, L. and Larsen, J. (eds) *Byen i bevægelse. Mobilitet – Politik – Performativitet.* Frederiksberg: Roskilde Universitets Forlag, pp. 302–17.

Latham, A. and McCormack, D. (2009) Thinking with images in non-representational cities: vignettes from Berlin, *Area*, **41**(3), pp. 252–62.

Latour B. (2003) The promises of constructivism. In Ihde, D. and Selinger, E. (eds) *Chasing Techno-science: Matrix for Materiality*, Indiana University Press, pp. 27–46.

Latour, B. (2004) Why has critique run out of steam? From matters of fact to matters of concern, *Critical Inquiry*, **30**(2), pp. 225–48.

Latour, B. (2005a) *Reassembling the Social: An Introduction to Actor-Network-Theory.* New York: Oxford University Press.

Latour, B. (2005b) From realpolitik to dingpolitik – or how to make things public. In Latour, B. and Weibel, P. (eds) (2005) *Making Things Public: Atmospheres of Democracy*, Cambridge MA: MIT Press, pp. 14–41.

Latour, B. (2008) A cautious Prometheus? A few steps toward a philosophy of design (with special attention to Peter Sloterdijk), keynote lecture for the 'Networks of Design' meeting of the Design History Society, Falmouth, Cornwall, 3 September 2008.

Latour, B. and Yaneva, A. (2008) Give me a gun and I will make all buildings move: an ANT's view of architecture. In Geiser, R. (ed.) *Explorations in Architecture: Teaching, Design, Research*, Basel: Birkhäuser, pp. 80–9.

Latour, B. and Weibel, P. (2005) *Making Things Public: Atmospheres of Democracy*, Cambridge, MA: MIT Press.

Law, J. (2002) Objects and spaces, *Theory, Culture and Society*, **19**(5/6), pp. 91–105.

Law, J. (2004) And if the global were small and noncoherent? Method, complexity, and the baroque, *Environment and Planning D, Society and Space*, **22**(1), pp. 13–26.

Lawson, B. (2004) *What Designers Know*, London: Architectural Press.

Lee, J. L. and Ingold, T. (2006) Fieldwork on foot: perceiving, routing, socializing. In Coleman, S. and Collins, P. (eds) *Locating the Field: Space, Place and Context in Anthropology*, Oxford: Berg, pp. 67–86.

Lefebvre, H. (1996) *Writings on Cities*, Oxford: Blackwell.

Lippard, L. (1997) *The Lure of the Local: Senses of Place in a Multicentred Society*, New York: The New Press.

Lorimer, H. (2005) Cultural geography: the busyness of being 'more-than-representational', *Progress in Human Geography*, **29**(1), pp. 83–94.

Loukaitou-Sideris, A. (2012) Addressing the challenges of urban landscapes: normative goals for urban design, *Journal of Urban Design*, **17**(4), pp. 467–84.

Lund, A. (2013) Stille nu, *Landskab*, (4), 2013, p. 105.

Lund, H. (2003) Testing the claims of new urbanism: local access, pedestrian travel and neighboring behaviors, *Journal of the American Planning Association*, **69**(4), 2003, pp. 414–29.

Lury, C. and Wakeford, N. (eds) (2012) *Inventive Methods: The Happening of the Social*, London: Routledge, pp. 1–24.

Lynch, K. (1981) *Good City Form*, Cambridge MA: MIT Press.

Lynes, R. (1965) Mobility and design, *Connection*, **2**(38), Cambridge: Harvard University, pp. 9–12.

MacPherson, H. (2010) Non-representational approaches to body-landscape relation, *Geography Compass*, **4**(1), pp. 1–13.

Madanipour, A. (2003) *Public and Private Spaces of the City*, London: Routledge.

Madanipour, A. (2006) Roles and challenges of urban design, *Journal of Urban Design*, **11**(2), pp. 173–93.

Marling, G. (2003) *Urban Songlines*, Aalborg: Aalborg Universitetsforlag.

Marot, S. (1999) The reclaiming of sites. In Corner, J. (ed.) *Recovering Landscape*, New York: Princeton Architectural Press, pp. 45–58.

Massey, D. (2005) *For Space*. London: Sage.

McGuirk, J. (2015) Why design? Retrieved from www.domusweb.it/en/interviews/2013/01/09/why-design-.html

Melles, G. (2008a) New pragmatism and the vocabulary and metaphors of scholarly design research, *Design Issues*, **24**(4), pp. 88–101.

Melles, G. (2008b) An enlarged pragmatist inquiry paradigm for methodological pluralism in academic design research, *Artifact*, **2**(1), pp. 3–11.

Merriman, P. (2004) Driving places: Marc Augé, non-places and the geographies of England's M1 motorway, *Theory, Culture and Society*, **21**, pp. 145–67.

Mid-America Regional Council (n.d.) Parking lots to parks: concepts in sustainable parking-lot planning and design. Kansas City and Green Parking Council.

Middleton, J. (2010) Sense and the city: exploring the embodied geographies of urban walking, *Social and Cultural Geography*, **11**(6), pp. 575–96.

Misak, C. (2013) *The American Pragmatists*, Oxford: Oxford University Press.

Molotch, H. (2005) *Where Stuff Comes From: How Toasters, Toilets, Cars, Computers and Many Other Things Come to Be as They Are*, New York: Routledge.

Mossop, E. (2006) Landscapes of infrastructure. In Waldheim, C. (ed.) *The Landscape Urbanism Reader*, New York: Princeton Architectural Press, pp. 163–77.

Moudon, A. V. (1992) A catholic approach to organizing what urban designers should know. In Cuthbert, A. R. (ed.) (2003) *Designing Cities: Critical Readings in Urban Design*, Oxford: Blackwell, pp. 362–82.

Mumford, E. (2000) *The CIAM Discourse on Urbanism, 1928–1960*. Cambridge MA: The MIT Press.

Murray, L. (2010) Contextualising and mobilising research. In Fincham, B., McGuinness, M. and Murray, L. (eds) *Mobile Methodologies*, Palgrave Macmillan, pp. 13–24.

Norman, D. (2013) *The Design of Everyday Things*, New York: Basic Books.

Oliver, J., Savičić, G. and Vasiliev, D. (2011) The critical engineering manifesto, Berlin 2011. Critical Engineering Working Group (2011). Retrieved from https://criticalengineering.org/en

Paans, O. and Pasel, R. (2014) *Situational Urbanism: Directing Post-war Urbanity. An Adaptive Methodology for Urban Transformation*, Berlin: Jovis.

Pallasmaa, J. (2005/1996) *The Eyes of the Skin: Architecture and the Senses*. Chichester: Wiley.

Pallasmaa, J. (2011) *Space, Place and Atmosphere: Peripheral Perception and Emotion in Architectural Experience*, lecture given 5 October 2012 at ESARQ, Spain.

Peirce, C. S. (1994) *Semiotik og Pragmatisme*, Copenhagen: Gyldendal.

Peter Bredsdorffs Tegnestue A/S (1973) *Arbejdsrapport nr. 3, Generalplanlægning for Aalborg Kommune, Oktober 1973*. Aalborg: Aalborg Municipality.

Pink, S. (2008a) An urban tour: the sensory sociality of ethnographic place-making, *Ethnography*, **9**, pp. 175–96.

Pink, S. (2008b) Mobilising visual ethnography: making routes, making places and making images, *Visual Research in Social Science: The Reader*, **9**(3), pp. 1–17.

Pink, S. and Mackley, K. L. (2012) Video and a sense of the invisible: approaching domestic energy consumption through the sensory home. In *Sociological Research Online*. Retrieved from www.socresonline.org.uk/17/1/3.html

Pink, S. and Mackley, K. L. (2014) Moving, Making and atmosphere: routines of home and sites of mundane improvisation, *Mobilities*, DOI: 10.1080/17450101.2014.957066.

PlaNYC/NYC Environmental Protection (2010) NYC green infrastructure plan: a sustainable strategy for clean waterways, The City of New York, Office of the Mayor.

PlaNYC/NYC Environmental Protection (2012) NYC green infrastructure. 2012 annual report, The City of New York, Office of the Mayor.

Rauterberg, H. (2012) *Talking Architecture: Interviews with Architects*, London: Prestel.

Ravn, C. (2015) Smarte kombiløsninger: Tænk parkering som et byrum med muligheder. Retrieved from https://realdania.dk/nyheder/seneste-nyt/realdania%20by%20og%20byg/realdania%20by/2015/smarte-kombiloesninger-taenk-parkering-som-et-byrum-med-muligheder.

Realdania By (2014) *Parkering og Bykvalitet: Eksempelsamling*. København: Realdania.

Relph, E. (1976) *Place and Placelessness*, London: Pion.

Richardson, R. (ed.) (2010) *The Heart of William James*, Cambridge MA: Harvard University Press.

Richardson, T. and Jensen, O. B. (2008) How mobility systems produce inequality: making mobile subject types on the Bangkok sky train, *Built Environment*, **34**(2), pp. 218–31.

Rittel, H. W. and Webber, M. M. (1973) Dilemmas in a general theory of planning, *Policy Sciences*, **4**, pp. 155–69.

Rodríguez, D. A., Asad, J. K. and Evenson, K. R. (2006) Can new urbanism encourage physical activity?: Comparing a new urbanist neighborhood with conventional suburbs, *Journal of the American Planning Association*, **72**(1), pp. 43–54.

Rohbrandt, K. (1948) *Skitseforslag til dispositionsplan for Aalborg-området 1948*. Aalborg: Aalborg Kommune.

Sandercock, L. (2003) *Cosmopolis II: Mongrel Cities for the 21st Century*, London: Continuum.

Scheldeman, G. (2011) Beyond A to B. In Ingold, T. (ed.) *Redrawing Anthropology: Materials, Movements, Lines*, Farnham: Ashgate. pp. 129–41.

Schwarzer, M. (2004) *ZoomScape: Architecture in Motion and Media*, New York: Princeton University Press.

Sennett, R. (1994) *Flesh and Stone: The Body and the City in Western Civilization*, London: Faber & Faber.

Shane, D. G. (2005) *Recombinant Urbanism: Conceptual Modelling in Architecture, Urban Design, and City Theory*, Chichester: Wiley

Shaw, J. and Hesse, M. (2010) Transport, geography and the 'new' mobilities, *Transactions Institute of British Geographers*, New Series, **35**(3), pp. 305–12.

Shawchuck, K. (2014) Impaired. In Adey, P., Bissell, D., Hannam, K., Merriman, P. and Sheller, M. (eds) (2014) *The Routledge Handbook of Mobilities*, London: Routledge, pp. 409–20.

Sheller, M. (2004) Automotive emotions: feeling the car, *Theory, Culture and Society*, pp. 221–42.

Sheller, M. (2011) Mobility, *Sociopedia.isa*, pp. 1–12. Retrieved from www.sagepub.net/isa/resources/pdf/mobility.pdf

Sheller, M. and Urry, J. (2006) The new mobilities paradigm, *Environment and Planning A*, **38**, pp. 207–26.

Shoup, D. C. (2005) *The High Cost of Free Parking*, Chicago: University of Chicago Press for American Planning Association.

Shove, E., Pantzar, M. and Watson, M. (2012) *The Dynamics of Social Practice: Everyday Life and How It Changes*, London: Sage.

Shove, E., Watson, M., Hand, M. and Ingram, J. (2007) *The Design of Everyday Life*, Oxford: Berg.

Shusterman, R. (2008) *Body Consciousness: A Philosophy of Mindfulness and Someaesthetics*, Cambridge: Cambridge University Press.

Simmel, G. (1998) *Hvordan er samfundet muligt? Udvalgte sociologiske skrifter*, København: Samlerens Bogklub

Simonsen, J., Bærenholdt, J. O., Büscher, M. and Scheuer, J. D. (eds) (2010) *Design Research: Synergies from Interdisciplinary Perspectives*, London: Routledge.

SLA (no date) North West Park. Retrieved from: http://sla.dk/en/projects/kvarterparknv/

Soja, E. (2000) *Postmetropolis: Critical Studies of Cities and Regions*, Oxford: Blackwell.

Sorkin, M. (2009) The end(s) of urban design. In Krieger, A. and Saunders, W. S. (eds) *Urban Design*, Minneapolis: University of Minnesota Press. pp. 155–82.

Spinney, J. (2009) Cycling the city: movement, meaning and method, *Geography Compass*, 3(2), pp. 817–35.

Spinney, J. (2011) A chance to catch a breath: using mobile video ethnography in cycling research, *Mobilities*, **6**(2), pp. 161–82.

Steinø, N. (2005) Urban design som proces. In Botin, L. and Pihl, O. (eds) *Pandoras boks: Metodeantologi*, Aalborg: Aalborg Universitetsforlag, pp. 80–103.

Stoll, K. and Lloyd, S. (2010) Performance as form. In Stoll, K. and Lloyd, S. (eds) *Infrastructure as Architecture: Designing Composite Networks*, Berlin: Jovis Verlag, pp. 4–7.

Tait, M. and Jensen, O. B. (2007) Travelling ideas, power and place: the cases of urban villages and business improvement districts, *International Planning Studies*, **12**(2), pp. 107–27.

Talisse, R. B. and Aikin, S. F. (eds) (2011) *The Pragmatism Reader: From Peirce through the Present*, New York: Princeton University Press.

Thayer, H. S. (ed.) (1982) *Pragmatism: The Classic Writings*, Indianapolis: Hackett Publishing Company.

Thibaud, J. (2001) Frames of visibility in public places, *Places*, **14**(1), pp. 42–7.

Thibaud, J. (2011) The sensory fabric of urban ambiances, *Senses and Society*, **6**(2), pp. 203–15.

Thomsen, S.U. (2002) *Det værste og det bedste*. København: Forlaget Vindrose.

Thompson, E. (2005) Noise and noise abatement in the modern city. In Zardini, M. (ed.) *Sense of the City: An Alternate Approach to Urbanism*, Montreal: Canadian Centre for Architecture, pp. 190–1.

Thrift, N. (2004) Driving in the city, *Theory, Culture and Society*, **21**(4/5), pp. 41–59.

Thrift, N. (2008) *Non-representational Theory: Space. Politics. Affect*, London: Routledge.

Tietjen, A. (2011) *Towards an Urbanism of Entanglement – Site Explorations in Polarised Danish Urban Landscapes*. Aarhus: Arkitektskolen Forlag.

Till, J. (2009) *Architecture Depends*, Cambridge: The MIT Press.

Toronto City Planning (2013) Design guidelines for 'greening' surface parking lots. Retrieved from www1.toronto.ca/city_of_toronto/city_planning/urban_design/files/pdf/greening_p-lot_guidelines_jan2013.pdf

Trancik, R. (1986) *Finding Lost Space: Theories of Urban Design*, New York: Van Nostrand.

United States Environmental Protection Agency (2008) Green parking lot resource guide. Retrieved from www.epa.gov/nscep

Urry, J. (2000) *Sociology Beyond Societies: Mobilities for the Twenty-First Century*, London: Routledge.

Urry, J. (2004) The 'system' of automobility, *Theory, Culture and Society*, **21**(4/5), pp. 25–39.

Urry, J. (2007) *Mobilities*, Oxford: Polity Press.

Vannini, P. (2010) Mobile cultures: from the sociology of transportation to the study of mobilities, *Sociology Compass*, **4**(2), pp. 111–21.

Vannini, P. (2012) *Ferry Tales: Mobility, Place and Time on Canada's West Coast*, London: Routledge.

Vannini, P. (ed.) (2015) *Non-representational Methodologies: Re-envisioning Research*, London: Routledge.

Votolato, G. (2007) *Transport Design: A Travel History*, London: Reaktion Books.

Waldheim, C. (2006) Landscape as urbanism. In Waldheim (ed.) *The Landscape Urbanism Reader*, New York: Princeton Architectural Press, pp. 35–54.

Walker, S. (2011) *The Spirit of Design: Objects, Environment and Meaning*, London: Earthscan.

Wall, A. (1999) Programming the urban surface. In Corner, J. (ed.) *Recovering Landscape*, New York: Princeton Architectural Press, pp. 233–49.

Walzer, M. (1986) Pleasures and costs of urbanity. In Kasinitz, P. (ed.) (1995) *Metropolis: Center and Symbol of Our Times*, New York: New York University Press, pp. 320–30.

Weiss, M. and Manfredi, M. (2015) *Public Natures: Evolutionary Infrastructures*, New York: Princeton Architectural Press.

Whitelegg, J. (1997) *Critical Mass: Transport, Environment and Society in the Twenty-first Century*, London: Pluto Press.

Whyte, W. H. (1988) *City: Rediscovering the Centre*, Philadelphia: University of Pennsylvania Press.

Wind, S. and Lanng, D. B. (2014) Designing affective atmospheres on the move. Paper presented at the Cosmobilities Conference 2014, Copenhagen, Danmark.

Winner, L. (1980) Do Artifacts Have Politics?, *Daedalus*, **109**(1), pp. 121–36.

Wood, N. and Smith, S. J. (2008) Editorial: pragmatism and geography, *Geoforum*, **39**, pp. 1527–9.

Yaneva, A. (2005) A building is a 'multiverse'. In Latour, B. and Weibel, P. (eds) *Making Things Public: Atmospheres of Democracy*, Cambridge: The MIT Press, pp. 530–5.

Yaneva, A. (2009a) Border crossings: making the social hold: towards an actor-network theory of design, *Design and Culture*, **1**(3), pp. 273–88.

Yaneva, A. (2009b) *Made by the Office for Metropolitan Architecture: An Ethnography of Design*. Rotterdam: 010 Publishers.

Yaneva, A. (2012) *Mapping Controversies in Architecture*. Aldershot: Ashgate.

Zardini, M. (ed.) (2005) *Sense of the City: An Alternate Approach to Urbanism*, Montreal: Canadian Centre for Architecture.

Zumthor, P. (2006) *Atmospheres: Architectural Environments – Surrounding Objects*. Basel: Birkhäuser.

Web Sites

www.csla-aapc.ca/awards-atlas/edwards-gardens-sustainable-parking-lot-retrofit

www.greenparkingcouncil.org (accessed 02/08/15)

www.oala.ca/edwards-gardens-sustainable-parking-lot-retrofit/

www.onasphalt.com (accessed 02/06/13)

www.parkingday.org (accessed 13/08/15)

www.rvanderson.com/index.php/news-events/item/351-edwards-gardens-sustainable-parking-lot-demonstrates-low-impact-development-techniques

www.topotek1.de Spielparkplatz, Flämingstrasse, Berlin (accessed 10/08/15)

www2.epa.gov/water-research/experimental-permeable-pavement-parking-lot-and-rain-garden-stormwater-management (accessed 13/08/15)

Index

Page numbers in **bold** denote figures.